# HARDSHIP POST

With terrorism on the rise and his marriage
on the ropes, an American moves to
Pakistan to work for the Aga Khan

# Robert J. Taylor

outskirtspress

DENVER, COLORADO

Hardship Post
With terrorism on the rise and his marriage on the ropes,
an American moves to Pakistan to work for the Aga Khan

Outskirts Press, Inc.
http://www.outskirtspress.com

ISBN: 978-1-4787-0692-2

Outskirts Press and the "OP" logo are trademarks belonging to Outskirts Press, Inc.

PRINTED IN THE UNITED STATES OF AMERICA

*To Susan, and the many roads traveled.*

# Table of Contents

# 1

# IN VAIL, DREAMING OF KARACHI

"I have a good job and a shaky marriage and I don't want to move to Pakistan," I said, a telephone in one hand and a can of Coors in the other.

I was in Vail, Colorado, in a condo I'd rented with a few hospital management colleagues from Minneapolis. I was talking to Merlin, an old friend, gazing out at the fairytale village and the darkening mountain beyond. It was January 20, 1981, and my roommates were watching a replay of Ronald Reagan's inauguration speech from earlier in the day. I considered hanging up and joining them but I wasn't enamored with Reagan. Merlin already had my attention, as if he were his magician namesake about to conjure up a Bengal tiger from the ether.

"And they kidnap people over there," I added. I'd heard the news a few minutes before Merlin's call. The television anchor said the Iranian hostages had been released; fifty-two Americans captured in the siege of the American Embassy in Tehran. They'd been held 444 days. Negotiating their freedom was the last hurrah of Jimmy Carter's presidency.

"That was Iran," said Merlin.

"That's small comfort," I said. "Pakistan and Iran *are* neighbors. And wasn't it just a year ago they burned down the American Embassy in Islamabad? A couple of people were killed."

Merlin Olson was a fellow graduate of the University of Minnesota Program in Hospital Administration and we had worked together on a number of alumni projects. He was clever and quick, and I liked him. He was often sarcastic but was now unusually solicitous, putting me on guard.

"Give me one good reason why I should come for an interview," I said. I loved my job at Hennepin County Medical Center. The doctors were terrific, I liked my boss, and I got along with the county commissioners. Minneapolis was a great town. *Why would I want to leave?*

"Bob, these guys work for the Aga Khan," Merlin said. "He's like religious royalty, rich as sin, and he's building a big, modern hospital in Karachi. They want to do this right. They want someone like you who knows American hospitals. I'm not asking you to leave the country. I just want you to come to Houston. I want to show these guys we can line up qualified candidates."

"Yeah, right," I said. "I'm having a good time in Vail. I fly home Saturday, and Sunday's the Super Bowl." Ever the optimist, I almost believed the usual pre-game hype that the Super Bowl would be a real contest. I was less sure about the hype from Merlin. "I have to be back to work on Monday and I don't want to fly to Texas."

"Come on, come to Houston." There was silence on the line. "It's not even out of your way."

I could almost see his smirk. "You're looking at a different map than I am."

"Come for me."

"Merlin, you're shameless. I'll call you back tomorrow. I want to hear the rest of Reagan's speech," I lied, and hung up.

I leaned back in my chair, took a sip of beer, and gazed out at the twinkling lights of town, the expected full moon still hiding behind the ski mountain. I watched the headlights of a snow cat climbing the steep face of a ski run, grooming the hard-packed snow. *This could so screw things up*.

The excuses I'd rattled off to Merlin were all true but only one was of real consequence; after eighteen years of marriage and two wonderful children, Sue had asked for a separation. She was bored with our marriage, bored with me. We'd fallen into a quagmire of normalcy.

I felt like a ball in a Ping-Pong match, with no control over the game but getting slammed back and forth, from despair to optimism and back. We'd gone to a marriage counselor and had gut-wrenching conversations. Then we'd gotten together to celebrate a pleasant Christmas holiday. We hadn't talked of divorce, but it lurked out there menacingly. Nothing was certain, but I wasn't about to abandon hope, or my family, by moving to the other side of the world.

I looked at my beer can, surprised to find it now empty and crumpled tightly in my fist. I studied it like it would reveal the secrets of the universe. *They have beer in Pakistan, don't they?*

I flew into Houston early Saturday afternoon.

The meeting was set up in a conference room at Merlin's downtown office. He gave me a briefing. "They already know who you are. Just be your charming self. I'll take you to my club for dinner after this is done. It's the best place in town."

"Good. You owe me."

He turned toward the door. "I'll be back in a minute."

I stood staring at his back. I wondered if my interrogators would be like emissaries of the royal family or the pope. Would they be stuffy and formal, arrogant, intimidating? Would they be dressed in uniforms, gold braid at the shoulders? Or turbaned in long robes and wearing silver slippers with pointed toes? I was dressed in a wool plaid shirt and blue jeans, the best I could assemble from my ski wardrobe. *If I sit with my back to the window, maybe they won't notice.* I took a deep breath and exhaled slowly.

Merlin returned with two quite human-looking gentlemen and made introductions. I guessed they were both about a decade older than my forty years. Aziz Currimbhoy was slender and wore a dark suit, white shirt and tie. With a receding hairline and dark-rimmed glasses, he looked like an accountant. He had a soft handshake and a vaguely British accent laced with the clipped undertones of the Indian Subcontinent. Cheves Smythe, a lanky American doctor, had short gray hair that looked like he combed it with his fingers. He wore a wry smile, a bowtie, and a rumpled suit, and shook my hand with a firm grip. He had a melodious drawl, something southern, but I wasn't sure it was Texan. I couldn't tell whether he was a good-ole-boy or a Brahmin aristocrat.

As Merlin excused himself, the two men took off their suit jackets and draped them across the back of their chairs. A nice gesture, but I was still wary.

"Let me tell you about the Project," said Aziz, taking charge of the interview. Merlin had said he was the secretary of the Project's board of directors.

Cheves leaned back in his chair, his long fingers laced under his chin, perfectly at ease in his back-up role.

"The Aga Khan is the forty-ninth Imam of the Ismaili Muslim community," Aziz said. "His Highness has several million followers worldwide. He has offices in Switzerland and France." He explained that in addition to his religious duties and business interests, the Aga Khan sponsored over two hundred clinics and hospitals in five countries. "The 721-bed hospital we're building in Karachi will be the flagship of the Aga Khan Health System." Aziz's face glowed and he sat up straighter in his chair. "The hospital will be of the highest international standards architecturally and operationally."

Aziz threw out information quickly with terms and references that left me puzzled but intrigued. I wasn't sure how he would take an interruption, but my curiosity was growing. When he paused, I probed.

He explained that the Ismailis are a progressive Shia sect that traces its heritage to a daughter of Mohammed. The hereditary title "Aga Khan" was granted by the Shah of Persia in the eighteen-thirties.

Cheves added. "You might remember a photo, in the mid-nineteen-fifties, of His Highness's grandfather, a portly man sitting on a scale, being presented his weight in platinum by his followers. Unfortunately, it was sort of a King Farouk image—a fat, rich potentate. Most people didn't know that his weight was the goal for a fundraising campaign to support his health care clinics."

I was mentally trying to calculate the value of two hundred and fifty pounds of platinum, but quickly gave up the effort.

"He served as Aga Khan for over seventy years until his death in 1957," Cheves concluded.

"His Highness was given his royal title by the Queen of England," Aziz said. "His predecessors were peace keepers during the Muslim uprisings in India."

Aziz explained that the grandfather, in his will, flaunted tradition and bypassed his firstborn son, Ali Khan, an international diplomat. Instead, he designated his grandson as his successor, Prince Karim al-Husseini, to serve as Aga Khan IV. The grandfather said he wanted to be succeeded by a young man who was brought up in the new age and who would bring a new outlook to the office. "Prince Karim was only twenty, and a student at Harvard, when he assumed leadership," Aziz said. "He is every bit the businessman that his grandfather was, and philanthropist."

A few things started to fit into place. I remembered Ali Khan, the Aga Khan's father; but as a playboy rather than a diplomat. Maybe that was why he was bypassed. He divorced his first wife and married Rita Hayworth, a red-haired movie actress who was my image of the ideal woman until she was eclipsed by Brigitte Bardot in my hormone-sodden teenage years. Ali Khan died in an automobile accident when I was in college.

"We've just started construction of the Aga Khan Hospital," Aziz said. "It was designed by a world-class architect from Boston and will be the finest hospital on the subcontinent. Your job will be to commission the hospital, to hire the staff and develop the organization so we're ready to open as soon as the buildings are finished, about two years from now, *Insha'lah*. The nursing school is already built and we've admitted the first class of students."

Cheves described their plans for a medical college and their intent to become a university. I learned he was currently serving as the medical advisor to the Project and was expected to become dean of the medical college.

We talked for over three hours. By the end of the day I felt like I'd been served a huge bowl of mulligatawny soup[1]—tantalizing and intriguing, but too much to digest and bound to keep me up at night.

I didn't have much appetite when I met Merlyn for dinner. "They think you walk on water," he said.

"Please, Merlin, I'm too tired for more hype."

"You listened attentively. You were respectful. You asked good questions. They've seen your CV."

"You don't have any other candidates?"

"No. I mean yes. They talked to a number of others. They liked you."

I wasn't sure how to take his answer. He must have lined up candidates well in advance but called me only a few days before.

"I thought of inviting you a couple of weeks ago," he said, reading the look on my face. "But I know you and Sue are having some troubles and I didn't want to complicate your life. Then I reconsidered and figured you could make up your own mind."

I suspected I was being bamboozled, but Merlin was smooth. I let it pass.

"I think they're going to invite you and Sue to visit Karachi to see the construction site. Then they'll want you to visit Paris to meet the Aga Khan and some of his bigwigs. They'll let me know in a week or so, after they check with the folks in Karachi."

"But Merlin, I came here as a favor. I'm not a serious candidate. I can't accept an invitation like that."

"Sleep on it, talk to Sue. I'll call you as soon as I hear."

My Sunday evening flight to Minneapolis boarded shortly after the kickoff for Super Bowl XV—a match-up between the Oakland Raiders and the Philadelphia Eagles. When we leveled off at cruising altitude the pilot came on the intercom. "We know how disappointed you are to miss the Super Bowl, but we'll keep you posted on the score."

"He's got that right," I mumbled to my seatmate. I *was* disappointed, but I rationalized that I couldn't concentrate on the game anyway. My head was spongy with questions. *What will Sue say? What about the kids? What's it like to work for a Muslim?*

My jumbled thoughts were interrupted by the pilot. "It's the end of the first quarter and the score is fourteen to nothing," he said, then clicked off.

"Wait," said my seatmate. A swell of amused rumblings swept among the passengers. A flight attendant opened the cockpit door and poked her head in.

A moment later the pilot came back on. "I apologize. I didn't tell you who's ahead." There was a long Jack Benny pause. "Fourteen," he said, and clicked off.

Laughter bubbled throughout the cabin, followed by ripples of muttering as we waited through another well-timed silence. Finally, there was an audible click, and just enough hesitation for someone to say pleadingly, "Please."

To a now rapt audience the pilot announced, "Oakland's ahead." There was a mix of cheers and groans.

After his comic routine, the pilot fell into a pattern of updating us whenever the score changed and after every quarter. Oakland won, 27 to 10, over the slightly favored Eagles; the first wildcard underdog team to win the Super Bowl and a personal victory for Jim Plunkett, Oakland's Latino backup quarterback, who had been all but written off a few months before.

There's hope for the down-trodden, I thought. But not seeing the action on TV, it seemed like a lopsided end to another over-hyped contest.

I was fascinated but befuddled by yesterday's conversation. What an audaciously ambitious project. The "finest hospital on the sub-continent" sounded like Super Bowl propaganda. What kind of game would I get myself into if I moved to Karachi? What kind of arena was that, and what were the rules?

Before I landed in Minneapolis I knew I would have a hard time focusing on my job.

# 2

## AMBIVALENCE

I went back to work in the frigid grip of a Minnesota winter and tried to immerse myself in the familiar if ever demanding pleasures of administering an urban teaching hospital. I telephoned Sue and told her of my stop in Texas.

"It's an intriguing opportunity," I said, "but I don't think much will come of it."

"Let me know when you learn more," she said.

I hadn't pitched the job with much enthusiasm and her reaction was muted, neither yes nor no. I hung up not knowing where I stood, on job or marriage.

After a few days the opportunity seemed ethereal. I decided there were two likely scenarios. Merlin was too good a friend not to phone. More likely, he would say it was all a mistake, to which I would reply, with some relief, "Thanks for your consideration." Or, as unlikely as it now seemed, he might call with an invitation. I was prepared to say, "Thanks, but no, I'm not a serious candidate." I was content with the maturity of my decision.

It was another week before Merlin called. "They want you and Sue to come to Pakistan, and then to Paris." Before I could pull up my rehearsed response, he added, "Talk to Sue before you say yes or no."

He was right. It was too important a decision to make on my own.

"What do you mean you can't accept their invitation?" Sue said. "Karachi sounds exotic. And then Paris? For crying out loud."

"But," I sputtered. "I'm not sure I can accept the job if they do offer it."

"That's the point of the trip, to find out if they like you and you like the job. Don't prejudge."

"But what about housing and school for the kids? It's a poor country. I'm not sure it's safe."

"Maybe yes, maybe no. That's another good reason to go, to check it out."

"What about us?" My tongue was dry. "I'm not going over there alone."

"I want to go. A week in Karachi and a week in Paris sound too good to pass up."

My knees went weak. I wasn't sure how either of us would react to Karachi. But Paris? Paris was fraught with promise.

In 1964, two years into our marriage and right after I finished graduate school, Sue and I had visited Paris for the first time. We traveled throughout Europe for three months in a Fiat 600, a car the size of a kitchen table but with less horse power, and a copy of Arthur Frommer's *Europe on Five Dollars a Day*. We stayed ten days in a little two star hotel near Luxembourg Gardens. Parking our car and walking the city, hand in hand, we were awed by the impressionist exhibit at the Jeu de Palme. On the rue de Bonaparte, we ate escargot from little crocks washed down with cheap red wine drawn from a huge glass carboy—savoring the residue of garlic butter on each other's lips. At a sidewalk café on the Boulevard St. Germaine, we ate French baguettes with unsalted butter and orange marmalade and drank heavily sugared coffee diluted with hot milk. We poked around for hours in the Latin Quarter. We snapped our fingers in applause in a back-alley jazz club, the air thick with pungent smoke from French Gauloises cigarettes that we called galoshes.

We splurged for dinner at a restaurant that rated three stars in the *Michelin Guide*; staring into each other's eyes and swooning over caviar on slivers of truffle, roast duck in orange sauce, and an endive salad with slices of fresh pear and a crumbled blue cheese. Our waiter stretched one bottle of champagne from appetizer to dessert.

We had loved Paris. Maybe a revisit would relight our marriage.

"When do we go?" Sue asked.

"They haven't said," I croaked, a hard lump in my throat. "I'll talk to Merlin and let you know."

"They can't get all their ducks lined up until early April," said Merlin.

"Just as well," I said. "It will give us a chance to do some homework."

Sue and I met at the library.

My geography was weak. I got the continents right, but even in the States I had trouble fitting the pieces together. Is Louisiana east or west of Mississippi? And the subcontinent—is that Asia? Or is Pakistan part of the Middle East?

At least I could read a map. "I know Pakistan shares a border with India," I whispered to Sue, an atlas open on the library's oak table. "But look here." I traced my finger along the mountainous lands that traverse Pakistan's Northwest Frontier Provinces. "What do you make of this?" I said, pointing to a spot labeled 'Tribal Area' along the border with Afghanistan.

A spent a moment studying Afghanistan and all the Stans of the Soviet Union that lay beyond. The rugged and unknown lands stretching thousands of miles to the north and west, over impassable mountains and desolate deserts, from Karachi to Moscow, took my breath away.

"I knew Pakistan and Iran were close," Sue said as she drew her finger along Pakistan's western edge. "It looks like they share several hundred miles of border."

I pointed to another mountainous area to the northeast where Pakistan touched the expanse of China.

We studied Pakistan's southern coastline on the Arabian Sea, the same latitude as the Florida Keys, with Karachi a few miles farther south than Miami. The country was much larger than either of us imagined, reaching north a thousand miles, to the same latitude as the mouth of the Chesapeake Bay in Virginia.

An almanac said the Islamic Republic of Pakistan had a population, in 1980, of about eighty-three million people, predominantly Muslim, about seventy-five percent Sunni and twenty percent Shia, whatever that meant, and a few Sufi, Parsi, Hindus and Christians. It was the eighth largest country in the world, like stuffing a third of the population of the United States into California, Nevada, and Arizona.[2]

Sue talked to the librarian and dredged up old news reports from the region. We were reminded how much turmoil was going on over there. There had been disturbing stories in the news, but they were in distant lands and we had read them before with detachment. Now they seemed more significant.

The overthrow of the Shah of Iran, in early 1979, and later that year, the siege of the U. S. Embassy in Tehran and the capture of the American hostages, had caught everyone's notice. President Carter's failed attempt to rescue the hostages left me with vivid images of a wrecked helicopter abandoned in the blowing desert sand. In the middle of all that drama, in late 1979, the Soviet Union invaded Afghanistan.

The most disturbing news was the burning of the American Embassy in Pakistan, on November 20, 1979, less than three weeks after the capture of the hostages in Tehran. A crowd of students had gathered in the streets of Islamabad, loudly but peacefully protesting U.S. policies in Cambodia, when they got a radio report out of Iran saying, erroneously, that the United States had bombed Islam's holy site at Mecca. Incensed, the students stormed the U.S. Embassy and burned it to the ground. Most Americans on duty survived by hiding in a reinforced area of the building but a Marine security guard and another American were killed.[3]

"The reports suggest it was spontaneous rather than planned," I said to Sue, as if that made a difference.

"Maybe they can tell us more about it when we're in Karachi," she offered.

Sue also found a few articles on Pakistan in back issues of *National Geographic* with photos of stark and beautiful landscapes, garishly decorated trucks, and women covered from head to toe. There were also accounts of age-old tribal and religious conflicts and stories of Pakistan's remote, untamed, and ungoverned regions in the north—those "tribal areas" we'd seen on the map.

We checked out a few books for later reading, including a copy of *Freedom at Midnight*, Collins and Lapierre's account of the last days of the British Raj, the partition of India in 1947 and the creation of Pakistan.[4]

In the following weeks, Sue and I read and talked, telephoning each other to compare notes and impressions. We both noticed a regular stream of newspaper articles and reports from the region. "Has there always been this much news coverage?" I asked.

"I'm sure seeing more," Sue said. "It makes me wonder what else I'm missing. I'm trying to catch up. I have a few things you should read."

She's really into this, I thought. "I'll stop by and pick them up," I said, my heart doing a tap dance in my chest.

"Did you see the news about the hijacking?" I said to Sue over the telephone.

"Yes. It's pretty disturbing."

It was early March, when our attention to all things Pakistani was at its peak. A Pakistan International Airline flight, on its way from Karachi to Peshawar with 144 people on board, had been hijacked and diverted to Kabul, Afghanistan. The hijackers demanded the release of ninety-two political prisoners from Pakistani jails. When Pakistan's president, Zia-ul-Haq, refused, they murdered a Pakistani diplomat. Twenty-nine of the passengers were released in Kabul. A week later the airplane took off headed for sanctuary in Libya but ended up in Damascus, Syria. The incident lasted thirteen days before the hijackers surrendered and the rest of the passengers were released.[5]

During the two weeks the hijacking was in the news, Sue and I talked everyday, sharing our concerns. When it was over, I asked, "Do you think we should go?"

"It was a terrible incident but the whole trip is too exiting to pass up," Sue said. "Call Merlin. See what he thinks."

I did.

"It's a big world," he said. "Things happen, but hijackings are pretty rare. I don't think there's any real danger."

He's as ignorant as we are, I thought. Still, I was beginning to think that Pakistan was enticingly foreign and Paris was rich with promise. Sue's enthusiasm gave me courage, as well as palpitations. Even if nothing comes of it, we *have* to go, I thought.

# 3

# KARACHI

We arrived in Karachi in the middle of the night. As we stepped down the ramp from our air-conditioned airplane we were assaulted by the heat radiating off the tarmac. Yellow lights on high stanchions cast diaphanous shrouds in the thick humid air. Travel weary and suddenly over-dressed, our skin damp with a sticky amalgam of dew and perspiration, we stood in a crowded open-air bus for the ride to the un-air-conditioned, dimly lit, and cavernous terminal—ominously dank and smelling of mildew.

We waited in a long line to have our papers processed, apprehensive of the crowd of strangers pressed up against the glass doors beyond customs. As we cleared passport control, I saw a sign with "MR AND MRS ROBERT" printed in bold letters, held by a man wearing a tan safari suit.

"I hope that's us," I said.

"*A'Salam A'Lakum*," the man said, extending his hand to me. "How is your good self?"

"Fine, thank you," I said, "but tired."

He nodded to Sue but didn't extend his hand. "Welcome to Pakistan, Let us collect your luggage, *Insha'lah*, and then I will assist you in clearing customs." He turned and walked away as we hurried to keep up.

We pointed out our bags and he hefted them onto a trolley. With us in tow, he pushed the cart, one wheel wobbling and screeching, past a long line of other passengers waiting to clear customs. He nodded to the agent as we walked through without slowing. Outside the terminal we followed him closely, threading our way among a throng of clutching men shouting, "Taxi, Sahib," and, "Good price."

We were quickly ensconced in the plush back seat of a black, and blessedly air-conditioned, sedan. Our greeter gave instructions to the driver, then turned in his seat. "After your long airdash, I am sure you are keen to retire," he said. "We will go to the guest house straightaway. Everything is arranged for tomorrow, isn't it." It was a statement, not a question.

As we pulled from the curb with a lurch, Sue gasped and grabbed my hand. Then her grip relaxed. "Sorry. I forgot they drive on the wrong side of the road over here."

I gave her hand a squeeze. "Welcome to Pakistan."

On the drive into the city the scene passed quickly, our driver apparently on a mission of some urgency. Sue and I were both agape, our eyes darting back and forth from windshield to side windows. The car's headlights cut through the haze. The trees lining the boulevard, their trunks painted white, flickered past. Frequently, the rear end of an unlighted truck or motorbike loomed out of the dim ahead, then flashed by to disappear in our wake. Out the side windows we peered into impenetrable black with intermittent scenes of softly lit buildings set back from the road, like a slideshow of old sepia-toned photographs. The faint aroma of burning charcoal crept into the car.

The ride was mesmerizing but we were both exhausted. We had been traveling for better than twenty-four hours. We were asleep within half an hour of arriving at the guest house.

In the clear morning light and the fog of a jet-lag stupor we visited the site of the emerging Aga Khan University; eighty-four acres of scrub land, dusty and devoid of trees. The property was surrounded by a high wall and a deep moat of dry drainage ditches.

There were a few buildings already erected on the campus. The most prominent was the school of nursing, located near the far back wall—a low sprawling building, its façade finished in mellow salmon stucco with deep-set windows. A second building, near the entry gate, was the project office; a simple, one-story temporary structure reminiscent of the Quonset huts used after World War Two as student housing on college campuses all across America. Between the office and the school, the construction site looked as if it had been used for bombing practice with dozens of craters pock-marking the open field. On closer inspection, the craters had metal rebar sticking up like tufts of porcupine quills—foundations for the hospital and medical school waiting the poring of concrete.

I stood with Sue among the craters, awed by the barren expanse, so empty and full of dreams.

Over the next few days, Sue and I toured the school of nursing, met the handful of project-people already on site, and were briefed on the Project's hopes and plans—all fascinating but more faces and details than our still fogged minds could fully absorb. We asked about personal concerns: work for Sue, school for the kids, and housing.

Sue had been working for a consulting firm as a conference planner, assisting the University of Minnesota's Underground Space Center organize meetings on the development of underground structures, from homes to commercial buildings. She was also in the middle of co-authoring a book on building and financing earth-sheltered homes. We were assured that work could be found for her once we arrived in Karachi. If they had said no, it would have been a deal-breaker. Neither of us could imagine her without challenging work no matter how interesting the environment.

We were dropped off for half a day at the Karachi American School and were impressed by its buildings and lush green campus. "I had no idea," I said, as we sat in the shade of a sprawling acacia, sipping sodas and admiring the school's country club swimming pool. We were talking to the school's superintendent, Tony Horton.

"It's like a private school," Sue said. "I think Jennifer and David would like it."

"We *are* a private school," Tony said. "We're sponsored by the State Department, but ninety-five percent of our budget comes from student tuition. There are American schools all over the world. There's a school up in Islamabad, the International School, and another in

New Delhi. We have exchanges with the other schools—sporting and cultural events a few times every year. We follow an American curriculum and have American teachers."

I asked him about the burning of the American Embassy in Islamabad the year before. "I heard the school closed. What happened?"

"It was a terrible incident," Tony said, "but not like the Embassy in Iran where they planned the takeover and took hostages. Crowds here can be volatile, even a small incident can lead to violence. The demonstration in Islamabad took a bad turn. The crowd was incited by a radio report out of Iran. It was bogus. They accused America of attacking a mosque at Medina."

Sue was nodding her head, blank-faced.

"The International School in Islamabad closed," he continued. "They paid off their teachers and sent them home, back to the States. It was a mistake. They lost a lot of their faculty and still haven't recovered."

"And you closed too, right?" I asked.

"Yes. There was also a mob here in Karachi," Tony said.

"Whoa," I said. Sue looked as surprised as I was. "We hadn't heard."

Tony took a long sip of his soft drink. "It was the same day as the burning in Islamabad. The crowd was headed toward our American Consulate but was broken up by the police. The Consulate closed for several months, but I don't think they thought it was too serious."

"Why not?" Sue asked.

"Well, the Consulate decided to send home all non-essential staff. Consulate officers went through the list of personnel. They came to the name of a woman, a senior security officer. One guy said, 'She's a woman, so she should go.' But another said, 'Yeah, but she's a good tennis player.'" Tony chuckled. "They kept her here."

Tony sat forward in his chair. "I also thought the danger was overblown. We sent our faculty to Thailand for a month, at the school's expense, and we were back in business in six weeks—with more students than ever."

*This guy's unflappable*, I thought.

Sue was silent.

After visiting the school we were driven to a couple of residential neighborhoods: Karachi Development Authority, or KDA, an older neighborhood near the school and the hospital; and the Defence Housing Society, a newer neighborhood but farther away. It was hard to tell one neighborhood from the other. Along every residential street the houses were hidden behind high concrete walls.

We toured a few houses we might rent and found one unfinished place we especially liked in Defence. The house was larger than our home in Minneapolis. The master suite was generous and there were enough bedrooms for both children to have their own, plus an extra room for guests. Every bedroom had a bathroom with a tub or shower.

In one of the bathrooms I noticed the shadow of soiled feet on the toilet seat. The landlord saw my surprise. "Modern commodes in every bathroom," he said. "Asian toilet only for servants." He was referring to the small rooms at the back of the house for the household staff and the *chokidar*, the security guard. Their Asian toilet was a hole in the floor with foot pads on each side. I pictured a workman who was accustomed to the Asian style, not knowing how to use the modern commode in our bathroom, standing on the seat, squatting low as he did his business.

The kitchen was humble but adequate, with the promise of Italian appliances. The dining room was spacious enough to seat a dozen or more. The living room opened onto a wide veranda, elegantly tiled in onyx, which swept across the front of the house, shaded by an overhanging ledge.

"Wow," said Sue. "A big house, servants; I expected something more modest."

"Me too," I said. "It's not the Peace Corps. More like shadows of the British Raj, but with air conditioning. I'll have to buy a pith helmet."

That evening, Orville Landis, the project engineer and the only American expatriate we had met so far, invited us to his home for a drink and dinner. His place was similar in size and features to the rental properties we'd visited. I mentioned the house we'd found.

Orville looked dubious. "Have you looked at any of the houses here in KDA? It's a well-established neighborhood. Most of the houses here have the kinks worked out."

"Sue and I talked about it. We want to be in a Pakistani neighborhood, among the locals. I think Defence suits us better. Besides, the house is new. It needs to be finished, but we have plenty of time."

I sounded like the owner of the house we'd liked, a retired commander in the Pakistani Army. "All the house needs is a little work to finish things up," he had said. "It will be a fine home for your lovely wife and family." His fingers played an imaginary piccolo as he counted off the house's special features. "And it will have central air-conditioning," he concluded. "Very, very modern, isn't it."

It sounded good to me. Sure, the air-conditioning was not yet installed. Not all the bathroom fixtures were in place. A couple of windows were leaning against a column out on the veranda, ready to be set into the wall. The enclosed yard was still a construction site, cluttered with leftover rebar and stacks of bathroom tile. A yellow plastic bag danced on eddies in the hot afternoon sun. But it was easy to see the house's possibilities. If I took the job, we wouldn't be moving in for at least four months—I had to resign my current job, give a couple of month's notice, then a couple of weeks to pack, and a family vacation on the way over. There was plenty of time for the landlord to "finish things up."

Orville nodded his head as I effused. "You know," he said, "every neighborhood in Karachi is Pakistani. Even here in KDA, the expatriates are spread around." He asked a few more polite questions, but I was too wrapped up in my own righteousness to hear the concern in his voice.

The next day, after a full schedule of interviews, Sue and I were invited to dinner by a prominent Pakistani surgeon, the uncle of a colleague of mine from Minneapolis. Again, their home was similar to the house we might rent, with a spacious living room generously furnished with an enormous sofa and a number of equally massive chairs. Before dinner, Sue and I sat on the sofa, opposite our host and his family.

We were talking about health care and I was repeating what I had been hearing about the Aga Khan Hospital. As our host began to respond, a lizard scurried out from between Sue's feet, dashed across the floor and up the wall behind our host, where it paused, looking over its shoulder at us with its beady eyes.

"Oh." said Sue. "Your pet lizard escaped."

Being from Minnesota, neither of us had seen much of lizards, except an occasional salamander we discovered under a log when we were kids, or at the Shrine Circus where chameleons were hawked as pets.

Our host smiled faintly but ignored the lizard, a gecko it turns out, and continued talking about how pleased he was to know that a good quality hospital would finally be available in Karachi.

Sue and I spent our last day in Karachi touring the city. The books and articles we'd read didn't begin to capture the city's vibrancy, chaos, and contrasts.

Once a sleepy fishing village, Karachi's prominence grew under the British Raj as a trading center because of its protected harbor on the Indian Ocean and its ready access inland via the Indus River. After partition, whatever reputation the city had as a charming seaport was overwhelmed by a crush of immigrants fleeing India.

We only saw a corner of the city's vast and rapidly expanding urban sprawl; seven million people drawn from all corners of the country seeking work, jammed together in overcrowded neighborhoods near the industrial centers. Everything was in motion, a fascinating swirl of unhurried and frenetic.

The streets were teeming with men walking at a leisurely pace, like they had no place to go and were in no hurry to get there. Some had full beards and turbaned heads and were dressed in *shalwar kameez*, a knee-length shirt over baggy pantaloons. Others were bare headed and dressed in western style white shirts and dark slacks. We saw men in sandaled feet strolling hand-in-hand. Others hunkered on their haunches in the shadows smoking cigarettes.

We saw few women on the streets, but more than we expected. Most were on motorbikes, riding side-saddle behind their husbands, their bodies camouflaged beneath the female version of the loose fitting *shalwar kameez*, their hair covered with a shawl or *dupatta*. A handful of women were invisible altogether, hiding in plain sight as they walked in the markets, draped from head to toe in pastel blue burqas.

Pariah hawk-kites circled overhead, dark against the bright sky, their watchful eyes looking for any opportunity to swoop down and snatch some unprotected savory morsel from the hands of the unwary.

In contrast to those on foot, the roadways were frenzied with the dash and noise of traffic—gaily painted trucks and overloaded buses. Small black taxis, mostly old beat-up Datsuns, limped through the streets like wounded animals on worn-out shocks, their discordant horns whistling and blaring, as they forced their way through traffic. Over-burdened motorbikes and three-wheeled motor-rickshaws sputtered and putted as they weaved through narrow gaps among larger vehicles. Gangly camels strode along the margin, a contrast of centuries, pulling wood wagons loaded with motorbikes or auto tires destined for market. At intersections, beggars darted and hobbled among the cars, tapping on the side windows with upturned palms. Noxious clouds of exhaust billowed in the air. A pall of dust muted the color of leaf and flower.

"It's so different from the school," Sue said. "And the lovely homes and gardens we've seen. A lot of the city's beauty is hidden behind those high walls."

We were taken to Bohri bazaar, a colorful and claustrophobic warren of crowded narrow alleyways snaking among hundreds of stalls peeking out from under high canvas awnings. As we got out of the car, a woman dressed in a soiled *shalwar kameez* approached me, pulled on my sleeve, and held out her cupped hand. Out of the corner of my eye I could see another woman and a couple of small boys hurrying my way. I was startled and unsure what to do. I wasn't carrying any rupees and I didn't know how to say "I'm sorry." I pulled the woman's hand free, grabbed Sue's arm, and rushed to catch up to our guide.

The bazaar smelled of incense, perfume, sweat and mildew. It was a hodgepodge of color and noise and bustling bodies—both male and female—and it took a while to divine the order in the chaos. There were long rows of cotton merchants, narrow booths stacked high with bolts of cloth, richly hued samples draped decorously. There were aisles and intersections devoted to kitchen utensils, red and yellow plastic furniture, thread, bicycle parts, sporting goods, and pots and bowls made of shining copper and brass. We would not have found our way out without an escort.

We also visited Empress Market, a major food bazaar; again, tight rows of booths and stalls. There was fresh produce, some recognizable: lettuce, tomatoes, green peppers; and some not. Spice *wallahs* sat among burlap sacks filled to overflowing with conical piles of vibrant red paprika, powdered yellow turmeric, and whole black peppercorns, their pungent aromas blending in a wafting bouquet of aromatic curry. There were wicker trays mounded with fresh figs, glossy black dates, amber-colored raisins, roasted peanuts, fresh almonds, and salted pistachios. We passed a corner of the meat market where live chickens hung by trussed legs. The faint aroma of blood and spoiled meat seeped from the market's dark recesses. We were steered away from a more intimate tour by our protective guide.

The bazaars were pulsating and alive, mysterious and confusing, and we poked about too long. We were over-heated and dehydrated and eagerly drank the tap water that was offered to us when we got back to the guest house.

Later that evening, ignoring the bubbling in my stomach as we packed our bags, I asked Sue, "What do you think?"

"It's exotic, all right, but far more livable than I expected. The city's so alive. The school is outstanding, there's good housing, and the people have been really nice. How about you?"

I agreed with everything Sue said and was buoyed by her enthusiasm. Still, I was circumspect. "What did you think of Tony's story about the Embassy burning?"

"He didn't seem too upset. I guess we shouldn't put too much weight on it."

"Fair enough," I said. "Overall, I think the interviews went well and it looks like a great project and a great job. But don't get your hopes up just yet. We have to see what the higher-ups say in Paris."

# 4

# APRIL IN PARIS

We commandeered the heads for most of the ten-hour flight to Paris. The half-hour we spent clearing customs at Charles de Gaulle was a test of will. Try saying, "Nothing to declare," with your teeth and cheeks clinched and not look suspicious.

Blessedly, we were able to check into our hotel early. We were at Le Meurice, a refined old hotel on the rue de Rivoli in the heart of Paris, an easy walk from Place de la Concorde, the Louvre, and the Tuileries Gardens. It should have been the perfect scene for a romantic reconciliation. But now, seventeen years after our first visit, in April even, when we weren't traveling on the cheap and someone else was paying our tab at an expensive hotel, we were sick and confined to our room.

That afternoon, after a nap, Sue was mostly recovered but I still felt weak and fuzzy headed and fearful of wandering too far from a lavatory. I did not feel up to treading the streets of Paris let alone sitting through more interviews or, more critically, meeting the Aga Khan. It would be poor etiquette to say, "Hold that thought, Your Highness. May I use your toilette?"

Sue found some Pepto Bismol in a local market and I dosed up. I was still feeling woozy that evening when we were invited to dinner to meet Shamsh Kassim-Lakha, the university project's chief executive officer, and maybe my future boss.

I teetered the two blocks from our hotel to the restaurant. Shamsh met us at the door. He was dressed in a tailored dark suit, distinguished looking, gracious, and sensitive to my illness. I must have looked green. Throughout dinner he was informative and inquisitive, obviously well educated and smart. I was surprised to learn he had gotten his degree in business administration from the University of Minnesota, at about the same time I was there. I felt dim-witted and out-classed and I don't remember much of the conversation. I picked at my food and didn't put together an intelligent sentence the whole evening.

The next day I was feeling physically better but not too optimistic. Over a light breakfast of French bread and coffee, I said to Sue, "I didn't do so well last night."

"You were pretty flat, alright," she said. "But Shamsh seemed like a nice man. I'll bet he gave you the benefit of the doubt."

"Maybe," I said, but I didn't believe it.

Mid-morning, we were picked up at the hotel by a chauffeured limousine and driven out to Aiglemont (Eagle Mountain), the Aga Khan's residential and corporate estate near Chantilly, just north of Paris. We drove in the gate along a narrow road winding through a thinly wooded forest, the ground dappled by light filtering through budding branches. "How French," Sue said, "like a painting by Monet or Renoir."

To one side we caught a glimpse of white fencing, the stables for the Aga Khan's thoroughbred horses, a tradition going back several generations. The grounds looked tranquil, welcoming. The soft greens of early spring were soothing. It seemed an unhurried place and an enchanted venue.

"If I get the job," I said, "I'd be coming here two or three times a year for meetings."

"If you do," Sue said, putting her hand on my arm, "we could get a hotel in Paris. I can tour the city while you work. We'd have our evenings together." She squeezed my arm and smiled.

I threw my head back and closed my eyes. "God, I hope this works out," I whispered.

We were dropped off at the Secretariat, a low, modern office building; straight lines of stone and glass. The interior reception area was spare and understated, decorated with simple, comfortable furniture of contemporary design.

After a brief wait we were greeted by one of the Aga Khan's most trusted advisors, a westerner and a non-Ismaili I'd been told to ask for by the folks back in Karachi. He put us at ease, chatting with us in the reception area. He had seen my resume and had been briefed on both of us.

After twenty minutes or so, the Aga Khan swept out through the door of his office, the air of a man of consequence, his face alight with a cordial smile.

He was tanned and fit and had a firm handshake. He'd been a skier in the 1964 Winter Olympics at Innsbruck and looked like he could still carve an agile turn. My first thought was, *He's older than his pictures.* The only photographs I'd seen were taken when he was in his twenties. He's forty-two or forty-three, I reminded myself. He's only a couple of years older than I am, *at the peak of his powers.*

We stood in the reception lounge as he asked if we had children. Our conversation was pleasant but short. I may have asked him about his skiing, but I have no recollection. We never discussed the hospital nor covered anything of substance.

On the drive back to Paris, I said to Sue, "I don't know if this is going to happen. That was awfully brief. He's obviously relying on others to judge my worth, or he's already written me off."

Sue and I slept on the airplane most of the way back to Minneapolis, too dumbstruck, doubtful, and drained to be lucid.

I asked the taxi to wait while I walked Sue to the door of our house—we were still living separately.

Our fifteen-year-old daughter, Jennifer, greeted us. "I can tell by your faces that we're going."

I gave her a hug. "Maybe, but they haven't asked me yet. Nothing's for sure." I turned to Sue, "I'll talk to Merlin. I'll call you when I know what's going on."

"Let's keep our fingers crossed," she said, and gave me a hug.

As the taxi drove me to my apartment I felt that *nothing* was certain. I was drawn to the project. It was ambitious but they did seem to have the will and the means to pull it off. But I didn't think I had performed very well. Sue seemed ready to make the move. I wasn't sure how she'd feel if we didn't get a chance to go.

I didn't sleep well that night. I dreamt I was in a railroad switching yard, a lumbering locomotive bearing down on me, my feet leaden and fixed between the tracks. By morning I was in a pessimistic funk.

# 5

# GAMBLE EVERYTHING FOR LOVE

It was a long, restless week before Merlin called.

"They want you," he said.

"Really?" I had been expecting the worst.

"They're offering a three-year contract, rather than the two we talked about." He said more, probably about salary, and timing, and such, but my mind was already awhirl.

I managed, "I'll let you know," and said goodbye.

I called Sue. "They want me. I'll stop by if it's all right."

"I'll make coffee," she said.

When I arrived at the house, I asked, "So, what do you think?"

"It will be a great job for you and a real adventure for us. And maybe we'll get to France once in awhile. Of course we should go."

"It's a big job. I don't know if I can do it." I was thinking, *I don't know if anybody has ever done a job like this.*

"Of course you can. *They* think you can too. They asked you."

"If this doesn't work out I can always get another job, I guess." I was being more cavalier than I felt. A few years earlier I had taken a year off, a sabbatical of sorts. I got a grant to do research on human dynamics in hospital mergers and to develop materials for a class on change management. It was all an excuse to move to Colorado for a year, a fantasy Sue and I had shared since we skied together as teenagers—a bit like the dream of working and playing in Paris two or three times a year. To take the sabbatical, I quit my job. When I announced my intent, I got a bit of notoriety among my colleagues. Some thought I was a crazy-assed dope to leave a good job and I'd never work again. A few thought I was making a daring career move. A couple of guys said that earlier in their careers they had dreamed of doing something similar, and regretted not doing anything about it.

We had a good year in Colorado. Sue was happy skiing and exploring the back country, always eager to pack up the kids and drag our tent trailer on some less-traveled dirt road. "Oh, we've never been that way before," she said, more times than I could count. At the end of the year we both hoped I'd find a job somewhere new, and we were thrilled when I was invited to San Francisco for an interview. When it didn't work out, we were both disappointed.

Later, when I was offered the job at Hennepin County, it was too good to pass up. On the long U-Haul drive back to Minneapolis, as we crossed the Colorado border into Nebraska, Sue wept, "I don't want to leave Colorado." I think she was also saying, "I don't want to go back to Minneapolis." Three years later we were separated.

*I hope this is different,* I thought. "Okay, but what about us?" I stammered.

"You weren't so hot in Paris," she said with a chuckle. "But it sure was interesting and we did have an amazing time exploring Karachi."

"It was great," I said, realizing I had been holding my breath. "You for it?"

"I've always wanted to live overseas, but you've been reluctant."

"Yeah, I know. I thought you meant France, or Italy, or Germany, or maybe Lichtenstein. I couldn't figure out how to make it happen. But Pakistan?"

"I think being somewhere else will give us a chance to start over. I've been thinking about it, about us, and I'd like to try again. We always got along but lately there hasn't been much life in our marriage. Maybe Pakistan will provide the spark we need."

My eyes watered and I couldn't have talked even if I'd known what to say.

Sue filled the silence. "After we're done here, I'll help you pack your things."

Sue and I talked for a couple of hours, thinking out loud. It was hard to get my head around the idea of moving to Pakistan—the concept was so enormous, the likelihood so remote, the considerations overwhelming. As we talked, Sue jotted down in a notebook everything that needed doing: resign our jobs, prepare the kids, talk to our parents, rent the house, pack, and on and on. It was a long list, but each item seemed less formidable now that our intent was clear, a task to be dealt with and then checked off.

As we worked on the list, my heart was a-flight. I was excited about the job and as smitten with Sue as I'd ever been.

Sue and I had attended the same schools in Minneapolis, starting in grade school. She was a year behind me and I hadn't noticed her until we were in high school. I was working as a soda jerk at a neighborhood drugstore. One day she came in dressed in a pink shirtwaist, her dark hair and petit figure aglow, a backlit vision as she stood inside the smoke-glass door. "Where's the pharmacy?" she asked. I was speechless but managed to point to the back of the store. After she left I got her name off the prescription bottle, "Susan Shapiro." A few days later I noticed that she walked home with a friend of mine, a guy I walked to school with every morning. On the days I didn't have to work after school, I made a point to walk home with my friend—and with Sue.

We started dating and continued off and on through high school. As I started at the University of Minnesota and Sue went off to Mills College in California, our relationship languished until one summer when we met again back in Minneapolis. It was a sunny Sunday afternoon and we were each canoeing with our dates on one of the city lakes. Sue and I spotted each other and I paddled my boat alongside hers. We must have annoyed our dates by our too long and too animated conversation. That fall Sue transferred to the University of Minnesota and we were married a year later, the day after I graduated.

With those memories on my mind, I did the first thing on our to-do list. I called Merlin and took the job.

That evening I moved back to the house—excited and nervous—a boy on a first date and on the brink of a new life. I wasn't sure if Sue really wanted to get back together or was just caught up in the whole adventure—and I didn't care.

Fifteen-year-old Jennifer and ten-year-old David had their concerns, particularly leaving school friends. Sue and I talked with them about the Karachi American School, and the house, and showed them photographs. They seemed okay with the idea, if not enthusiastic. Maybe they were resigned to their parents' pattern of odd behavior—that year we'd spent in Vail, for example, and they attended school in Minturn, just down-valley. A year in the Colorado Mountains had worked well for them, and then we had moved back to Minneapolis. Maybe they figured that's what we would do again. I know they were more concerned than they let on, but the fact we were going to be a family again trumped all.

My mother was encouraging. She was the daughter of Swedish immigrants and the personification of American mythology. Raised in a log cabin on a homestead in the north woods, she walked through the snow to a one room school. She was always open to whatever came her way. "Oh, I'm so happy you and Sue are back together," she said. "What an exciting adventure." It was clear, of her six children, she loved me best.

My two older sisters and three younger brothers thought moving to Pakistan was a hoot. They were glad to see Sue and me together again and our family off on another hair-brained adventure.

I wasn't so sure how my father would react. He was seventy-eight and had been fighting heart disease and diabetes for several years. Still, he seemed to be holding his own. "What do you think?" I asked him.

Dad was taciturn, but fair-minded and supportive, and I knew he was one of my best fans. His career had been in health management and it was the easy friendships and respect he had among his colleagues that had drawn me to the same field. "If I had an opportunity like this," he said, "I'd already be on the airplane." I hugged him, as tears welled up in my eyes.

Sue's older brother, her only sibling and a high school teacher, was excited. "I am glad you're back together," he said, as he gave each of us a hug. "Now I'll have a place to visit over summer break."

Over the years, Sue's folks had been unfailing champions of our marriage and generous with their love. Nevertheless, they could be controlling, attaching expectations with each act of generosity, and Sue and I had been cautious with them, careful to protect our prerogatives. They had been unhappy with Sue when she asked for a separation and she felt they were too critical and not as supportive of her and the children as she would have liked. Ironically, now that Sue and I were getting back together, we were leaving the country, leaving them.

Sue's mother, Adelle, like my mother, was from rural stock, raised in a Norwegian town in central Wisconsin. She had moved to Minneapolis while still a teenager where she met her first husband, Curly, Sue's father. When Sue was three, Curly died of complications from Rheumatic fever. Adelle eventually married Curly's younger brother, Nate, who raised Sue as his own. Adelle was feisty and tough and cooked a killer leg of lamb. She could also get moody if she was unhappy. When Sue told her our news, Adelle got quiet. She must have felt we were abandoning her.

Nate had been a successful insurance broker, gregarious, and the center of attention at every social gathering. Lately, he had been plagued by bladder and kidney problems. His illness had slowed him down. He wasn't his usual generous self when he said, "Well, we'll sell the cabin if you won't be here to use it."

"Oh, please don't do that," Sue pleaded. "The place is too important to you." They'd had a cabin for years, a lake place in northern Minnesota where they spent countless weekends. Even with the constraints of age and illness, the cabin was still the center of their summer lives. Adelle could sit on the dock for hours, patiently waiting for a red and white bobber to glide or dip. Nate could spend half a day buying and preparing a rolled roast, then tending it patiently over an open-flame barbeque. Sue and I and the kids loved the place, but we could manage to visit only a few times each summer. Selling it would hurt them far more than us.

"I'll write often," Sue said. "And we'll be back at least once a year. We'll stay with you here or at the cabin when we're home."

After meeting with her folks, Sue said, "I feel bad about leaving and I know they're hurt, but we really need some space. We need to be away from Minneapolis and out-from-under family for a while if we're going to mend our relationship. I wish they weren't so negative and could understand and take it better." Her voice cracked. "I think they're hurting too much to say they'll miss us."

Most of the other things on our list were easier. I quit my job, saying goodbye to a wondrous cadre of colleagues. One of the county commissioners surprised me when he said he had attended a workshop on Islam at Harvard. In the four years I worked with him, he had never mentioned it. He was envious, wished me well, and offered his advice. "To work in Pakistan you'll need to stay patient and flexible. You'll need an *Insha'lah*, God willing, attitude and a sense of humor."

A colleague at the hospital was concerned about a recent flap in Libya. President Reagan had thrown out all of Libya's delegates after learning Muammar Gadhafi was plotting to assassinate United States diplomats in Rome and Paris. "Isn't Libya near you?" he asked.

"No, no," I said. "We'll be in Asia. Libya's in the Middle East." When I got home I checked the atlas just to make sure. I was right. They were about three thousand miles apart—farther than the distance from New York to Los Angeles.

A friend, a military service veteran who had been stationed overseas, was concerned about my marriage. "You know," he said, "living in a foreign country can go either way. Once the thrill is over, the strain can draw you closer or tear you apart."

I knew it was a gamble, but there was no winning if we stayed at home.

Now that Sue and I were back together, I vowed to fight the insidious corrosion of normalcy. On June third, Sue's fortieth birthday, she awoke to find three long-stemmed Sonya roses taped to her vanity mirror. At breakfast, there was a vase of two dozen on the kitchen table. I had another dozen delivered to her at work. The count was up to thirty-nine. I was holding one back for later.

That evening we joined Sue's parents for dinner at a fancy downtown restaurant where our waiter, to my surprise, presented each of the ladies with a single Sonya rose. Sue stared at me with a "How'd you pull this off" look in her eye.

I tried to look pleased with myself.

When we got home and Sue discovered a forty-first rose on her pillow, she looked puzzled. "One more for our adventure ahead," I said, having thought about it for the last few hours, and gave her a kiss.

"You outdid yourself," she said, and came up with a wonderful way of saying thank you.

We sorted our possessions into piles: to store away until our return, to ship, to schlep with us as carry-on luggage. One of the biggest piles was stuff to give away or throw out. "Casting off burdens of the past," I said.

"Oh, shut up, and pass me the tape," said Sue, as she sealed a box destined for Goodwill.

We packed and shipped what we thought we would eventually need in Karachi, mostly clothes, a few favorite family photographs and knickknacks to help us feel at home. We were told not to send furniture; we could get what we needed in Karachi, at the Project's expense. The day before the packers came, David's bike was stolen and it was too late to buy another. "We'll get you a new bike when we get there," I promised.

Several friends gave us bottles of Pepto Bismol, which we packed with our carry-on luggage so it would be ready at hand—we had learned something from our first visit. Other friends gave us four tubs of peanut butter, which we packed in our shipment—another lesson waiting to be learned. We rented our house furnished, with trepidation, to a group of young men. We arranged to have a trusted friend handle local mail and bills. We said a round of cheerful and tearful goodbyes to more friends than I knew we had.

By late July we were ready to leave. We were traveling heavy, our bags packed with what we would need in Karachi until our shipment arrived.

We flew to Paris and spent a week showing the kids the highlights. Jennifer, dark haired and svelte, had her portrait drawn by a Bohemian street artist up on Montmartre; and David, his blond hair glinting in the sun, sailed a toy boat in a fountain in the Tuileries.

We flew on to Frankfurt, rented a car, and drove the Romantic Highway, exploring castle towns and hiking in the Black Forest. At a small town trout fest we ate fish caught from mountain streams, sang German drinking songs, and linked arms with locals while we rocked back and forth to the pulsing rhythm of an accordion and the foot-taping beat of a tuba. Sue and Jennifer danced with the town mayor and every man at our table.

Then we flew to Karachi.

# 6

# SOMEPLACE ELSE

At the Karachi airport, we watched, bug-eyed, as a flock of women covered from head to foot in black burqas, their faces hidden behind silver beaked masks, hovered and pecked for their luggage among the unclaimed bags like marauding ravens. They had come in on a flight from Dubai.

"We are someplace else," said Jennifer.

"Yah got that right," I said in my best Minnesota lilt.

Again, we were met at the airport and swept through customs and into a van and shuttled onward, this time to the Holiday Inn where we planned to spend a couple of weeks, until our shipment arrived and our house was ready.

We checked the kids into an adjacent room and spent our first few days recovering from what had been weeks of frantic activity, luxuriating by the pool, reading and re-reading the copy of the *International Herald Tribune* we picked up on our inbound flight. We napped frequently, and sampled the cuisine of the hotel's restaurant and coffee shop. We hired a car and driver and ventured out to take the kids to register at the American School and tour the campus. They were delighted with the pool and grounds and seemed eager to start, the first day of class less than a week away.

While we were staying in a western hotel, we weren't sheltered from the elsewhere realities of our new world. One morning, a few days after we arrived, as the four of us were finishing breakfast in the coffee shop, I was approached by a young man, another guest at the hotel whom I'd seen in the lobby a few times. He had caught my eye and we had exchanged nods. "May I speak to you in private?" he asked. I stepped away from the table to join him. He introduced himself, said he was from Iraq, and gave me a brief summary of his family lineage and his business credentials. "Would you be so kind, sir, to accept this small gift?" he said, holding out in both hands a small package of figs wrapped in cellophane, his head bowed. When I took the figs, he smiled and asked, "May I have your permission to propose to your daughter?"

If I'd been playing poker I would have lost the pot. *Jennifer is only fifteen.* I tried to maintain my composure and match his earnest tone. "Thank you for asking, but no, she is not available."

He looked disappointed, but thanked me for my consideration. Bowing slightly, he backed away.

I told the others. Sue was amused, David smirked, but Jennifer was peeved. "I wonder," she said, "if he's the same creep who knocked at our door at two in the morning? He said he was from room service but I didn't open the door."

"Good girl," Sue said. She had cautioned Jennifer to dress modestly, but we hadn't thought to warn her about opening her door to strangers.

When Sue and I returned to our room, I set the package of figs on the dresser.

The next morning Sue picked up the figs, intending on a snack. "Oh gross," she said, wrinkling her nose. There were little white worms crawling around inside the package.

She looked at me and winced. "Don't say it," she implored, but it was too late.

"Beware of strangers bearing gifts," I said. I'd waited my whole life to quote that cliché.

The headline in *Dawn*, the local newspaper, read, "Independence Day—Unprecedented Fervor Pervades." It was Friday morning, August 14, 1981, a few days after our arrival, and I was lingering over breakfast in the hotel cafeteria, having a second cup of double-dose black instant coffee. Sue and Jennifer were writing letters to family back in Minnesota. David was sleeping-in, not feeling well, maybe coming down with something. The house musician, a round-faced man with an unceasing smile, was playing an electric organ in the lobby, giving every melody a disco beat.

*Dawn* was one of Pakistan's English language newspapers. While Urdu was the official language of the country, educated Pakistanis were usually fluent in English, a legacy of decades of British domination. But the paper's rendition of both local and international news was sifted thin and unsatisfying by government censors, and the hotel didn't have a television. What joy when a copy of the *International Herald Tribune* or *Time Magazine* showed up in the lobby, a castoff from some airline passenger, like ourselves, or crew member who over-nighted at the hotel. Within a couple of days it was in tatters, devoured by the hotel's foreign guests.

Most often *Dawn* sufficed. According to this morning's edition, it was the thirty-fourth anniversary of Pakistan's creation during the 1947 partition of India. President Muhammad Zia-ul-Haq was calling for all traffic to stop at nine o'clock so everyone throughout the country could spontaneously join together, in one voice, to sing the national anthem, "to keep alive the spirit of the Pakistan Movement."

I hadn't thought of Pakistan as a movement, but from what I'd read, Zia had a point. After the Second World War, in anticipation of a British withdrawal from the Indian Subcontinent after two hundred and fifty years of occupation, the president of the Muslim League, Muhammad Ali Jinnah, united the historically disparate Muslim forces behind the idea of a separate Muslim state.[6] The British hastily drew boundaries for the new country, in some cases dividing towns and even family farms. With the British on the sidelines, the partitioning of India resulted in one of the largest and bloodiest cross-migrations in human history as millions of Muslims and Hindus fled their homes to find refuge in a safe haven.

At first there were two Pakistans, East and West, a bifurcated Muslim country carved out of the flanks of predominately Hindu

India and separated by eleven hundred miles. East Pakistan became Bangladesh in 1971.

When we arrived, Pakistan was still fighting to become a unified nation, trying to create a sense of national unity among far-flung regions with differing languages and traditions. Even within regions, tribal loyalty was way more important than allegiance to any governmental authority.

A few minutes before Zia's designated hour for spontaneous fervor, I stood outside the hotel's front entrance with a small gathering of other guests. The Pakistan flag, a white star and crescent on a green background, was hanging from the hotel's flagpole, limp in the breezeless air. Up and down the street miniature flags hung from signposts. Buildings were draped with strings of colored lights. Many of the vehicles on the street were painted in gay colors, or decorated in green and white bunting.

I watched the passing traffic as first a car festooned with bunting came to a halt, and then several motorbikes, and then, on command, every car, motor-rickshaw, motorbike, bus, truck, push cart, and camel-drawn wagon. People climbed out or off of their vehicles and at nine o'clock, prompted by music from a nearby sound truck, began to sing in Urdu:[7]

> *Blessed be the sacred land*
> *Happy be the bounteous realm*
> *Symbol of high resolve*
> *Land of Pakistan!*
> *Blessed be thou, citadel of faith*

A hotel guest standing next to me said, to no one in particular, "Today is a good day to stay put here at the hotel."

"It's not that anybody's targeting you," said another hotel guest, echoing what we'd been told earlier by Tony Horton, the school superintendent. "But crowds can be volatile."

*Do they put that warning in their travel brochure?* I thought. "Visit exotic Karachi, land of history and splendor, but beware of crowds?"

After the anthem, a small parade passed by on the street in front of the hotel, a cacophony of celebrants. Decorated trucks and flag-covered cars were followed by a marching band of short musicians in tall hats playing drums and discordant horns loudly and with great enthusiasm. Following the band, a disarray of men dressed in *shalwar kameez* stomped their sandaled feet to the beat of the drums, their arms raised in the air as they chanted and danced about.

"Unprecedented fervor pervades," I mumbled, and retreated back into the hotel lobby.

On Monday morning, finally recovered from jet-lag and feeling human again, I hired a car and driver and visited the project office. I wasn't scheduled to start work for a couple of weeks, giving myself time to ease into our new environment, but I thought it good form to stop by and pay my respects.

The office was quiet, nearly abandoned. I introduced myself to a man standing in the lobby. He was a dignified and well attired Ismaili with a slender face and a Canadian accent. I was glad I had worn a tie and jacket. "Where is everybody?" I asked.

"It's the end of Ramazan," he said. "Everybody's stretching the holiday by a few days. Your boss, Shamsh, will be back at the end of the week. You're right on time, though. I'm on my way over to the School of Nursing to talk to the students. Join me."

Ten minutes later I was in front of fifty young women, a bubbling sea of covered heads and eager faces haloed by dark hair shimmering in the overhead lights. My host introduced me to the director of the school, Winnie Warkentin, and to the assembled students and faculty as one of the officials from the hospital.

Winnie asked me to say a word or two about the plans for the hospital. *Well, so much for starting slow,* I thought, as I parroted a few key phrases I'd heard from others.

After the meeting, and my promise to Winnie to return soon for a get-to-know-you session, my host walked me back to the office building. The sun was directly overhead as we followed a path across the sand, my shadow covering only my dusty shoes. The hazy shape of a bird glided across our path. I glanced up at a kite-hawk circling above our heads, expectant, all but invisible against the glaring sun.[8]

The office building was a charmless structure made of concrete block, with a humped tin roof and dozens of humming air-conditioners poking out of its walls. "Let me show you your office," my host said, leading me through the front door.

We walked to the back of the building where he introduced me to a young woman dressed in *shalwar kameez*. Her hair was tied back in a bun, uncovered, her *chadar*, dupatta headscarf, draped around her neck. "Bob, this is Nazia Azizuddin, your secretary. Nazia, why don't you show him around and you two can get acquainted. After you're done, please take him over to meet Mohajir," he said, then excused himself.

Nazia had round rosy cheeks and a big smile, and excellent English. "Welcome, Mister Robert, we've been expecting you," she said. "We thought you might stop by yesterday."

"Yesterday? Yesterday was Sunday."

"Yes, our work week starts on Saturday. We work through Wednesday. Some people also work Thursday morning. But Friday is *Juma*, when we have prayers." She handed me a desk calendar. "Here, this will help." The days of the week were listed across the calendar's top, but with Friday on the left and Thursday on the right.

I had never seen a calendar like it.

She showed me my office, its walls painted a chalky white, already furnished with a simple wood desk, a desk-chair upholstered in black vinyl, a credenza set against the back wall, and two side-chairs for guests. A square window looked out across several feet of sand where the view ended abruptly at a high concrete wall, the southern perimeter of the property. An air-conditioner, set into the wall near the ceiling, buzzed softly. *I need to make this space my own.*

As I sat down opposite Nazia at her desk, a slight young man wearing a light colored *shalwar kameez* and a wide smile arrived and looked expectantly at Nazia. "This is Mohammad Ali," she said.

I stood and extended my hand. I considered making a joke about his namesake but thought better of it. "*A'Salam A'Lakum*," I said. "I'm pleased to meet you."

Mohammed Ali looked perplexed. He dropped his gaze but managed to offer his limp hand. I sensed I'd crossed some social boundary. I gave his hand a tentative shake before releasing my grip. He looked relieved as he took a step back and asked, "Chai-coffee, Sahib?"

"Yes, coffee please."

Mohammad Ali waggled his head, turned, and hurried away.

On the wall above Nazia's desk was a framed photograph of the Aga Khan. "You're Ismaili, I gather." Nazia nodded. "You said Friday is *Juma*. Can you tell me about what you do on *Juma*?"

Before Nazia could answer, Mohammad Ali returned balancing a tray on one hand. He bowed his head and thrust his free hand forward, his fingers locked together as if he were going to deliver an ineffectual karate chop, and politely parted the air between Nazia and me. He set the tray down on her desk, stood back and smiled. There were two empty cups with saucers, a glass filled with spoons, a bowl stacked high with sugar cubes, a thermos bottle of hot water, several tea bags, a can of instant coffee, and a jar of powdered creamer. Nazia asked how I liked my coffee—an extra measure of instant coffee, no sugar, no cream—and proceeded to assemble my cup as Mohammad Ali watched attentively.

After he departed, Nazia said, "He doesn't speak much English, but he will remember what you like." She glanced up at the photo of His Highness. "You asked about *Juma*. Many Muslims go to a mosque on *Juma*. We go to the Jamat Khana. We go there often, not just Juma. It is a prayer hall and social center all in one."

"And women are welcome?"

She looked amused. "Oh yes, why not?"

Later Nazia showed me several vacant offices nearby. "These are reserved for your associates," she said. "And here is a conference room." The setup was simple but serviceable.

Nazia was a delight, assertive and quick and of good humor, and I was pleased with the office arrangement.

After my tour, Nazia took me to another building, a small structure I'd missed on my first visit. "Administration," she said. She introduced me to a middle-aged man with a square face, a thin mustache, and the upright posture of retired military. He was dressed in a tan safari suit—a short sleeve tunic with flap pockets and epaulets on the shoulders over matching trousers.

He looked cool and comfortable while I was feeling hot and constricted in my sport coat and tie. *I've got to get me one of those outfits*, I thought.

"Mohajir will take care of anything you need: your house rental, your car and driver, your shipment when it comes," Nazia said, then excused herself.

"*A'Salam A'Lakum*," said Mohajir as he smiled and extended his hand. His grip was firm. "Welcome, Mister Robert."

He was the fourth or fifth person who'd called me Mister Robert. *I guess I'm Mister Robert.*

"Your car is ready and I have a driver you can give a try. See if he is to your satisfaction. I will send the hotel car back to the Holiday Inn."

"Thank you," I said, surprised and pleased.

"Now, let us talk about the house you are keen to rent," he continued. "The house is not yet finished and we have not yet signed a rental agreement. You must go see for yourself and tell us what you want us to do. Your driver knows how to find the house."

*Oh, shit,* I thought. *This will go over big.* I'd told Sue and the kids we'd be in the hotel only a week or two.

When I got back to the Holiday Inn, I introduced Sue and the kids to our new driver, Sohir, a dainty man of indeterminate age with thinning black hair, gray showing at the roots, and passable English. Sohir was eager to show us our new car; a small, white, Toyota four-door with stick shift. He opened the back door. "Memsahib," he said, bowing slightly as he held his hand out toward the car. Sue and the kids climbed in. It was tight for three, but doable, and I could sit in front when we all traveled together. Sohir opened the trunk. "See, the boot is big," he said proudly.

Then I told Sue and the kids the bad news. "The house isn't ready yet. We'll need to spend a couple of weeks here at the hotel, until I start work."

"Can we at least see the place?" asked Sue, as Jennifer and David nodded their heads vigorously.

"I've already called the landlord," I said. "He's eager to show us the house. We can go tomorrow, right after breakfast."

# 7

# LIMBO

On the drive out to the house, I rode in the front seat with Sohir. There was no seat belt, no steering wheel to hold on to, and my nose was only inches from the windshield. I expected to have a camel or motor-rickshaw in my lap at any moment.

The traffic was heavy and chaotic; cars and trucks and buses and motorbikes competed for position, some so close I hunched my shoulders to keep the sides of our new car from being scratched. At a traffic light, vehicles of every sort lined up in an unbroken line from curb to curb, facing off against another row at the other side of the intersection. When the light changed, the two lines charged each other like horse cavalry in the heat of battle. I had both hands on the dash board and both feet pushing down on the floorboards. Somehow Sohir maneuvered our way through as cars and motorbikes came at us, dodging and weaving, missing us and each other by inches.

The Defence Housing Society was a confusing maze of meandering streets. Some houses were numbered based on when they were built rather than in sequence down the block. All the homes were walled off from the street and their neighbors, hidden behind eight foot parapets capped with shards of broken glass that sparkled in crystal and green in the bright sunlight. Occasionally, I caught a glimpse of a house and yard through a wrought iron gate.

When we arrived at the house, Jennifer and David went off on their own, checking the bedrooms, picking out their spaces. The house looked more complete then when we'd seen it in April, but nowhere near habitable. The windows were installed and bathroom fixtures were in place, but little else. The yellow plastic bag, or its progeny, was still doing its lazy ballet out in the now barren yard.

"Why the delay?" I asked the landlord. "We said we wanted the place and you said it could be finished quickly."

"The A/C unit is caught up in customs," he said. "We require an advance of eight thousand dollars, American. Your employer has not agreed. As soon as I get the payment we can be ready in two weeks, *Insha'lah*, three at the most."

"I'll need to talk to the hospital," I said, not knowing who to blame. "I'll get back to you right away."

I was annoyed and disappointed with the delay but Sue and the kids were enthusiastic about the house. "My room's perfect. I have a walk-in closet and my own bathroom," Jennifer said.

"Me too," echoed David.

When we got back to the hotel, Sue said, "Let's go look at furniture. We know the layout. We can make the big purchases now and have it delivered before we move in."

Again, I went to Orville Landis—still the only expat we knew. We hoped to meet others when school started, but that was still a few days away. "Do you have a suggestion where we can buy furniture?" I asked.

"You can't." Orville said, trying hard to not look perplexed by my naiveté. "What's available in the market will be too big for what you want. It won't be a style you like. You'll need to have your furniture made."

"I wish I'd known," I said. "I was told not to bring furniture." I thought back to the furnishings in the home of the Pakistani doctor we'd visited back in April, the one with the pet gecko. "You may be right about things being too big, but I know Sue wants to see what's available."

After a few words between Sohir and Orville's driver, Sue and I were driven to the section of town where the furniture *wallahs* sold their goods. Unlike supermarkets where merchandise of all sorts is brought together under one roof, Karachi *wallahs* congregated by specialty, a holdover from the old guild system. All the motorbike repair shops lined up on one street, all the electronics shops on another. On our way to the furniture *wallahs* we passed a street of auto repair shops. Cars sat atop precarious columns of concrete blocks, surrounded by a scattering of wheels and parts carefully arrayed on the grease-stained ground. One shop specializing in fender repairs had the apt sign "Dentist" hung above its garage door.

The furniture shops were set back along a wide street. Chairs, sofas, and tables were on display outside on the sandy fringe between the storefronts and the roadway. There were chairs nearly as wide as loveseats and deep enough to swallow a Punjabi Potentate, with ornately carved wood trim and plush upholstery in bold reds and greens. Sofas were equally over-sized. Dining tables were made in dark shisham, a local rosewood, and enormous, with skirts and legs carved in a baroque style. Everything we saw was overpowering in design and scale.

After more than an hour looking, we drove back to the Holiday Inn. I was chagrined but Sue was undaunted. "I'll contact one of those furniture makers Orville recommended," she said.

The furniture maker met us at the hotel, a short round fellow with hennaed hair and a smile that showed two gold-capped teeth. He handed us a small stack of magazines—a couple of copies of *Good Housekeeping*, one *Architecture Digest*, and a few others—all well-worn and a couple of years old or older. "You are looking through these," he said. "You see what you fancy; we are making it for you, no problem. It will take three weeks, *Insha'lah*."

We perused the furniture magazines and resigned ourselves to living in the Holiday Inn for a little while longer.

# 8 | HARDSHIP POST

In 1981, the Karachi Holiday Inn was new, a recently constructed franchise owned by a couple of Ismaili businessmen. It wasn't elegant, but nicely appointed, with a full restaurant on the second floor and a casual cafeteria off the first floor lobby. It had an outdoor terrace and swimming pool out back, discreetly shielded to keep locals from gawking at scantily clad foreigners. The building made a good presentation from the street, except for one blemish. To the owners' consternation, there was a small mosque in the front driveway, a makeshift assembly of broken concrete block and plywood, a temporary concession made for the construction workers that now could not be torn down because it was a holy place.

In all, the Holiday Inn was the best hotel in town, outclassing the older, time-honored but shopworn, Intercontinental. As testament to the world's optimism about Pakistan's economic future, the Sheraton and Hilton chains had new hotels under construction, but both were a year or more away from completion.

The Holiday Inn was managed by Chris Windfur, a handsome and charming German, somewhere in his thirties. Chris had a beautiful French wife, Pascale, and a robust eight-month-old son they called Bambi. In the late afternoon we often saw Pascale and the baby out by the pool, which had become our favorite place to relax.

Sue and I and the kids settled into adjoining rooms, but before the end of the first week our stomachs were decidedly unsettled. All four of us were debilitatingly ill. We dosed ourselves with the Pepto Bismol we'd brought along in our suitcase. We sipped orange Fanta, ate soda crackers, and tethered ourselves to our two-room universe.

"It's the plague," I said, only half joking. "I feel worse than I did in Paris."

"Maybe it's amebic dysentery," offered Jennifer.

We'd all been given shots for typhoid and yellow fever, and we were taking pills for malaria. But the list of other possibilities, including amebic dysentery, was unnerving. I called Orville.

"It's probably just the Karachi Crud," Orville said, "Bhutto's Revenge." He was referring to Zulfikar Ali Bhutto, Pakistan's former Prime Minister, who had been deposed and hanged the year before by Zia-ul-Haq, the current president.[9] "Everyone gets it when they first get here no matter how careful they are. Locals call it 'loose motions.' If you aren't better in a couple of days, see a doctor. Your daughter could be right, but I doubt it."

"Don't eat food unless it's cooked," Orville continued. "No fresh vegetables or cold salads, even in your hotel. Don't drink un-bottled water. Never take ice with your drink."

This time I was listening to him more carefully.

He wasn't done. "The only place that's safe is your own home and the home of another expatriate or well-to-do local. Even at home, don't shower with your mouth open. Don't even brush your teeth with tap water."

It pained me to see Sue and the kids so sick. But we all stoically bore our Pepto Bismol burden, sipped liquids, ate lightly, and in a couple of days the motions passed and we did improve. Feeling better, I hoped we were now all immune to the Karachi Crud.

Yeah, right.

Jennifer and David got healthy just in time to start school. At seven-thirty in the morning, Sohir, who had eight children of his own, drove the kids from the hotel to campus, which immediately became the center of their new world. They seemed to be off to a good start, quickly into a pattern of staying on campus until near dinner-time—studying, swimming, or just hanging out. I kept my fingers crossed that it would work for them.

Sue and I were still cloistered in the Holiday Inn. From our hotel room window, we looked enviously at the park across the street. It was a treed oasis in the spare landscape of the city. One morning, the kids gone, we took the opportunity to explore.

We strolled for half an hour along a concrete pathway that meandered through the park, consciously not holding hands, sensitive to the advice we'd received to not show affection in public. Ironically, we'd seen several male couples holding hands on the street and in the bazaars; we didn't know what to make of that dichotomy. Sue had been told that when she was out in public she needed to keep her arms and legs covered. To comply, she was wearing loose fitting slacks and a long-sleeved cotton blouse.

We walked past a couple of waterless fountains and among acacia trees and beds of heat-stressed red flowers for which we had no name. The few patches of grass in the park were brown and untended. The smell of exhaust fumes from passing traffic overwhelmed any aroma of earth or vegetation. The heat of the day was beginning to build as we stopped to admire Frere Hall, a congregational edifice dating back to the British Raj. It looked like an Anglican cathedral, its spire stripped of its cross.

On the side of the park opposite our hotel, we were drawn to a row of palatial houses—much larger than the one we intended to rent. We stopped in front of a particularly grand house and peered in through the metal bars of its imposing gate.

The house was set well back from the street, a gothic building of cut stone and blunted turrets. Two donkeys, one black and one white, grazed on the lawn. A flock of peafowl scratched the ground in the shade of a tree; the peacock perched on a low branch flaunted his ostentatious tail. Off to the side we could see the corner of a tennis court.

"Wow," Sue said. "I wonder who lives here?"

A disembodied voice, like the Wizard of Oz behind the curtain, boomed in response, "The American Counsel General."

We both startled. We looked around and spotted a small speaker and microphone imbedded in the gate post.

Recovering quickly, Sue leaned toward the microphone. "Hi," she said, no Dorothy quaver in her voice. "We're the Taylors. We're from America."

"One moment please," rumbled the voice.

A minute later a woman emerged from the house and walked toward the gate. The two donkeys looked up curiously but were quickly bored and returned to their lazy grazing. The woman wore a simple dress and a white apron that she was using to wipe her hands. *The maid, or the Good Witch of the North?*

As she approached, a Marine in full uniform stepped out of the gate house. His laughing eyes belied his stern expression. He winked at us, then bowed slightly as he opened the gate far enough for the woman to step through.

"Hi," she said. "I'm Anne Post, the Counsel General's wife. Come in for a moment. I've just baked cookies."

We followed her through the gate and up the long driveway and in a side door to the kitchen—the aromas of roasted coffee and fresh baked cookies were mouthwatering. We sat down at a small table and she served Toll House cookies, warm from the oven, and real American coffee, not instant. *Definitely the Good Witch.*

Anne asked what brought us to Karachi and did we have children? Then she offered a few comments about the local scene. "This used to be the home of the American Ambassador until the capital was moved up to Islamabad. People back in Washington consider this a hardship post. It *is* a closed society, there are few restaurants and no bars, and it can be dangerous. It's all true." She glanced around the room. "But look at this place. Life here is good. When you move to your own home, it will be good for you too. We live well, we have servants. We have what we need and get along fine with what we don't have. And our Consulate staff gets bonuses for living here." She smiled. "We're not inclined to tell the people in Washington that they're wrong."

A man in high leather boots and riding gear strode into the kitchen. "Hi, I'm Dick Post," he said. "Sorry I can't stay to talk. I'm off to polo practice." He gave his wife a peck on the top of her head. "Be back after lunch," and he was gone.

"Would you like to go to a polo match?" Anne asked.

Sue glanced at me, a "can this be real" look on her face.

"We'd love to," I said. "When?"

"Later this week. Come by and we'll drive over together."

The Karachi Polo Grounds were built during the height of the British Raj, a wide expanse of grass—green and lush from regular watering—in the heart of the city not far from our hotel.

The scene was dominated by a *shamiana*; a cotton tent with bold geometric appliquéd patterns of yellow, orange, blue and red providing shade over a spread of oriental rugs and huge upholstered chairs lined up facing the field of play. Behind the chairs was a neat line of linen-draped tables with plates of snacks and refreshments. The small crowd was dominated by clean shaven Arab men, gold watches on their wrists and gold pens stuck in the breast pockets of their long white robes, their heads covered in *kufiyat* patterned scarves held down with circles of black braid. Sue and Anne were the only women there. Anne said the event was sponsored by the Saudis in honor of Saudi Arabia Day.

I surveyed the snacks—sweet pastries and salted nuts, a combination favored by locals—and decided I could eat around anything that might pose a threat to our health. Sue and I nibbled judiciously and sipped chai: boiled tea with sugar and milk, served in clear glass cups.

The polo ponies were small sleek beasts, their coats glistening with sweat. They pounded the ground, dashing this way and that, their ears flitting and nostrils flaring as their hooves scattering divots from the turf. The crowd was inattentive but the riders were grim-faced with determination and, as far as I could tell, well-skilled. They moved so fast. I was amazed they could stay in the saddle let alone hit that small ball with their long-handled mallets.

"Polo originated in this part of the world, you know," said Anne. "Up north they use a goat carcass and there aren't any rules."

"I've seen movies of that," I said. "This too, but never for real."

I tried to memorize the scene: the intense blue sky, the colorful patchwork tent, stark white robes floating just above the ground, and amber tea in clear cups; the thud of hoof-beats, the whack of mallet hitting ball, and the smell of horses and grass.

"How did we get here?" Sue whispered.

"It's a dream," I said. "Click your heels and you'll wake up in Minnesota."

# 9

# RULES OF THE ROAD

Sue had a twisted smile. "Sohir took me shopping today," she said over dinner.

"How'd it go?"

"He knows where everything is. At the bazaar, he dropped me off and waited for me. He took my packages. It was all very convenient. But it's going to take some getting used to, for both of us."

"How so?"

"I think I frustrated him. When we left the hotel, he held open the car door so I could sit in the back seat. But at our first stop I was out of the car before he could come around to assist me. At the next stop, he sprang out of his seat and raced around to my door. It was a valiant try, but I was too quick for him. I was out of the car and had closed the door before he could get there. Poor guy, he looked bewildered."

"It's like in the States," I said. "It's damn difficult to act like a gentleman with all this women's liberation stuff and the push to pass the Equal Rights Amendment. I've given up trying to hold a door for you or any other woman under the age of fifty. I'd get stepped on." I paused to see if I'd get any reaction.

"Yeah, I know. But it's against my nature to sit in the back like a Memsahib, waiting demurely until Sohir opens my door to allow my graceful exit. It seems so arrogant and privileged. I should wait, let him to do his job, but it rankles my Midwestern sensibilities."

"I feel a little awkward having a driver too," I said. "But there's no way I could find my way around town without Sohir, at least not yet. These streets are too tangled and indecipherable, and the traffic's too dangerous. You saw that article in the paper, 'bus plunges into wadi, eighteen killed,' and there was another one last week. People here are getting wiped out all the time."

The streets of Karachi were always on the edge of mayhem. An article in *Dawn* said Karachi was the second most deadly city in the world for traffic accidents, right behind Sydney, Australia.[10] Lots of places had more accidents per capita, but our chosen city had the honor of the most deaths per accident. I thought testosterone played a leading part in the carnage.

Karachi's streets were like a race track. Cars and taxis were in constant competition. At every intersection they fendered for position, lining up six abreast. Inexplicably, they turned off their engines to save fuel as they waited impatiently. In anticipation of a green light, they started their engines in unison, then raced away, their horns twittering insistently, braking only for the next light. Lane designations were meaningless.

Sohir was no different than other drivers. His unrelenting aggressiveness led to habits I found distressing: jackrabbit starts, a mad dash at top speed to the next intersection, and sneering disdain for pedestrians. I studied him closely, trying to divine the rules that underlined the chaos. The fundamental law seemed to be: biggest, fastest, first. In city traffic, if our car was only a few inches ahead of another, Sohir seized the right of way. If another car was a few inches ahead of us, it could pull into our lane, make a turn in front of us, or all but force us off the road. Sohir wasn't about to let that happen. To hell with the cars behind us; they needed to look out for themselves. Sohir only gave way to a larger vehicle traveling fast.

While I couldn't control others, I was trying to retrain Sohir. "Your main job is our safety, especially Jennifer and David," I said. On several occasions I placed a hand on his shoulder to remind him to slow down. I think he felt diminished in the eyes of other drivers and I'm sure he misbehaved when Sue or I wasn't with him. I was afraid David egged him on when I wasn't there.

"We need to learn the mechanics of driving on the wrong side," I said, in spite of my fears. "We need to try."

"If we could drive we could visit a different restaurant on occasion, someplace nearby," Sue said, as she pushed her food around on her plate with her fork. "Somehow, we need to be able to break loose from this hotel."

We agreed that the next weekend, when Karachi's intimidating traffic was less frantic, would be a good time to test our driving skills.

Thursday, instead of taking the car to his home, as he did most evenings, Sohir left the car at the hotel.

Out in the hotel parking lot Sue and I stood looking at the Toyota. It seemed smaller than usual, more fragile. "You go first," Sue said.

I stepped forward and unlocked the car door and got inside. "Hmm," I said. I got out and held the door open for Sue. "You'll want to sit here." Sue looked dubious but got in anyway. I walked around to the other side. This time there was a steering wheel. "This is better," I said, as I adjusted the seat and mirrors.

Before starting the car, I practiced shifting. It was awkward at first, but I thought I was getting the hang of it. "It's just like the MG, but with the left hand," I said, referring to a little red sports car we owned when we were a young couple. We sold it when Sue couldn't fit her pregnant belly behind the steering wheel.

I turned the key in the ignition and the car lurched. Sue's hand went to the door handle, but she stayed in the car.

"Okay, clutch in," I said, and turned the key again, this time with success. I shifted into first gear but kept the clutch in for a few moments as I studied the parking lot, the way out toward the street. *Remember, exit to the left.*

I drove to the curb and stopped, conscious of the need to look right, into the teeth of passing traffic. With no vehicles in sight I pulled left into the closest lane. "Piece of cake," I said and continued to the intersection. A glut of cars waited impatiently for the light to change. *What happened to lighter traffic on weekends?* "I'll take another left, just for practice," I told Sue, already eager to be done with the main road and not yet ready to brave the cross-traffic maneuver needed for a right hand turn.

As I approached the intersection, I steered well to the left and stopped a few feet behind the car ahead. Sue had both hands pressed against the dashboard. A taxi drove up close on my right, invading my space. I was about to move a little to my left when another car shot into the narrow gap between me and the curb. Then, to my far right, beyond the line of now three or four cars, a motorbike, loaded with a family of four, broke from the line and passed between us and the cars ahead, perpendicular to the flow. The driver balanced the over-loaded bike on his toes as he wobbled the gauntlet of bumpers and fenders then ducked into a slot between two cars. He continued his toe-dancing weave until he reached the intersection and immediately accelerated into the passing traffic.

I was watching the motorbike's journey, with awe and apprehension, when the light changed. Instantly, the car on my right jumped in front of me to turn left, followed by another car ready to do the same. Cars behind began to honk. I reached for the gear shift with my right hand, grabbing air. *No, the other side.* I regained control and crept forward.

By watching Sohir I had learned the necessity of the "insistent creep," even if I hadn't yet practiced it. I had to assert myself. I inched the car forward in a slow left-bending arc, hoping others would avoid me, if I couldn't avoid them. I made the corner with no scratches and continued on to the next intersection, where another left turn seemed the most prudent choice.

"We need to find a back street where traffic isn't so crazy," I said.

"Great idea," said Sue, her voice cracking, the first words she'd uttered since we left the safety of the parking lot.

I drove into a quiet area where the streets were mostly residential. I circled a couple of blocks a few times, making several right hand turns as well as left, stopping and starting frequently for practice. Sue did the same after first practicing her shifting routine. We saw only a few other cars.

After an hour we were both feeling rather confident. "Enough for today?" I asked.

Sue nodded.

"Why don't you drive us back to the hotel," I said.

Sue turned the corner toward the Holiday Inn, driving up a long straight stretch of road. A block or so ahead a Bedford truck was approaching at speed, its radiator grill haloed in a shining chrome frame. As the truck rushed toward us, Sue instinctively turned the car into the right lane. "Why doesn't he pull over?" she said.

I was thinking the same as the truck continued on its path, not slowing.

Sue turned more to the right. The truck bore down on us, its glistening grill grinning ghoulishly.

If we were going to get killed in Karachi traffic, it was likely to be by a careening truck or bus. An article in *Dawn* said that ten truck and bus drivers had been selected at random and tested for drugs. When seven tested positive, authorities thought there had been some error and decided to select another sample. In the second study, nine out of ten tested positive.

Trucks were ornately attractive but lethal. Their wood cargo boxes were cut and assembled by hand, mounted on imported Bedford cabs and frames, then painted by local artisans with fanciful landscapes, flowers, poetry, jet airplanes, and birds of prey. Their cabs were capped with high, brightly painted, wood tiaras. Their windshields, grills, and headlights were framed in shining metal, painstakingly bent, hammered and snipped by skilled craftsmen into filigreed patterns and shapes. Once on the streets, though, trucks rushed unstoppable, loaded with beef carcasses hanging from racks or stacked high with teetering sacks of rice or flour.

Compared to trucks, city buses were ramshackle and dull, but just as lethal. Worn down to rambling hulks by overuse, buses plied the streets festooned with riders clinging precariously to handholds and each other.

From a brief foray out of the city, traffic in outlying areas seemed to be even more dangerous than in Karachi. Suburbs were served by "yellow devils" —vans and small buses designed to carry ten or twelve passengers that were often overloaded with eighteen or twenty as they rushed and weaved to beat their competitors to the next stop. We saw several buses, their roofs turbaned with passengers hunkering among burlap-wrapped bundles. Those lucky enough to get a seat inside peered with resigned faces through clouded side windows as they rocked and lurched from village to village. Rural roads were narrow, often not wide enough for trucks to meet without driving onto the shoulder. We knew that trucks, buses and cars often traveled at night with their lights off.

Sue and I had been upset seeing the wrecked and burned-out steel skeletons that lined the roadways like dinosaur carcasses—charred testimony to the ability of an amphetamine cocktail to wreak havoc with all the effectiveness of alcohol—especially when mixed with an undiluted dose of testosterone.

Sue and I were wide-eyed as the truck bore down on us like an avenging demon, its sing-song horn warbling menacingly. We could see the driver. He was leaning over the wheel, no detectable expression of concern on his face.

My consciousness finally overcame my instincts and I shouted, "Turn left! Left!" and put out my hand to grab the wheel. But Sue had already turned it hard back to the left, accelerating into the left lane just as the truck swept past our rear fender.

Sue pulled over to the curb and stopped. We were both breathing hard. "I can't believe I did that," she said.

"Uh, huh," I muttered. "Sorry, I wasn't any help."

We drove to the hotel without further comment.

That night I had a nightmare of that sneering, silver-toothed truck grill swooping down on us. Even years later, I still have flashbacks when I drive past the rusted husk of a wreck lying next to the road.

When I ponder the perversities of the human psyche and the abuses of power, I think there ought to be a maxim: be careful whom you allow to drive a big truck.

# 10

# CABIN FEVER

Sue glanced over her shoulder and grimaced at the organist play-ing in the hotel lobby. "Does every song have to have a disco beat?" she said.

Our rooms were getting smaller, the cafeteria menu less imagina-tive, and the pool out back more claustrophobic.

We practiced our driving but didn't yet feel confident to venture too far from the hotel. Even as our driving skills improved, we knew we couldn't find our way around town. We had a city map but it was more notional than specific. I was told that government authorities didn't want to publish a detailed map. They were paranoid that India would use it to plan bombing raids.

We looked around for entertainment close to home. Was there someplace we could get a drink in a dry country? Somewhere to dance?

Chris Windfur, the hotel manager, said, "You can get a drink here, but only in your room. You just need to fill out this form."

He handed me a tan colored document the size of a newspaper. The form required that I prove I was a foreigner and declare that I was addicted to alcohol. With the necessary papers on file, I could ask room service for a Murree beer or one of the few hard liquors—gin, vodka, or scotch—made in Pakistan, a carryover from the British oc-cupation but now tightly controlled by the government. Murree beer, served very cold, was tolerable—after Chris showed me the trick of pouring off the glycerin that floated on top. The gin and vodka were best served with quinine water, if you could find it, and a strong dose of lime. The scotch was best served to somebody you didn't like much.

Ordering liquor to our room was expensive and not very satisfying, so I went back to Chris.

"With that form I gave you, you can also buy imported liquor from a local dealer," he said. He put me in contact with a liquor *wallah*.

The man picked me up at the hotel and drove me to a go-down, a warehouse near the harbor. He led me though a dimly lit hallway past several rooms with garage doors secured with fist-sized padlocks. He stopped at one door and pulled out a Medusa-headed keybunch. To my amazement the first key he tried worked and the padlock opened with a heavy thunk. The metal door screeched and clattered as it rolled upward, revealing a small unlighted room. It was hot and smelled of urine and mildew.

"I have a torch," he said, as he turned a flashlight into the room. It looked empty until he trained the light on two sagging cardboard boxes moldering in the corner.

I saw a cockroach scurry out of the flashlight's glare.

"Here you are," he said. "All name brands. Your choice."

One box held several dusty bottles of wine, their labels water stained and streaked with black. I guessed they had been there for months, or longer, and were probably spoiled by the heat. The other box held several bottles of liquor, all as dusty and discolored as the wine and no two alike. There was a bottle of Jim Beam, another of Jack Daniels, a bottle of Smirnoff, and a few others.

I pulled out the bottle of Jim Beam. It felt gritty and had someone's name scrawled on the label. "How much?" I asked, as I held it up to the light of his torch.

"Only fifty American dollars," he said.

"That's more than I can spend."

"For my American friend, a special price."

"I think twenty dollars is fair," I offered. "That's twice its normal price."

"Oh, but sir, in Pakistan this is very rare. Very hard to come by, isn't it. I cannot take less than forty-five dollars. "

Being special friends, we finally settled at forty dollars.

When I got back to the hotel I washed the bottle and took a shower. Later, I asked Chris. "Where does this stuff come from?"

"It's confiscated at the airport or from smugglers."

"Thanks for the tip, but that's more than I've ever spent on one bottle of booze. I probably won't be doing that again soon."

"You need to make a friend with commissary privileges," he said, "someone who works for your government."

"I'll keep that in mind."

"You also asked about dancing. Thursday night, right here at the Holiday Inn, we're having a disco party just for our foreign guests and friends. No liquor, but music and dancing."

"We'll check it out."

"Anne Post left a message at the desk," Sue said. "She invited me to come to a meeting of the American Women's Club next week."

"Great," I said. "Sounds like a chance to meet some people."

"She also said there will be an American movie showing this evening at the American Consulate, not far from here. She said we need to bring our passports."

The Consulate was a short drive from our hotel, well within my sphere of confidence. When the four of us arrived at the Consulate, we were directed to the parking lot around back. Street lights glowed softly in the still humid air, their bare bulbs reflecting orange and yellow on the hoods and fenders of six or seven parked cars. Within seconds, my arms were covered with a sheen of dew and I could feel my shirt beginning to cling to my back.

A dozen adults and half a dozen children were in the middle of the parking lot setting up folding chairs in haphazard rows on the macadam. One fellow was busy threading a reel of thirty-five millimeter film into a movie projector. A black extension cord snaked off into the shadows.

Everyone looked our way as we approached. "You're new in town, aren't you." a man said, holding out his hand. "Welcome to Karachi."

Sue and I made the rounds, introducing ourselves, as Jennifer and David picked out children they recognized from school.

"Where's the screen?" I asked, looking around.

"Up there, on that building," the man said, pointing to a blank vertical wall that climbed two stories above the surface of the parking lot. "Take a chair from that rack over there, and find yourself a spot. There's soda pop and popcorn over on the table."

When the movie began, we turned our attention to the wall where a stage coach, its driver frantically whipping a team of four horses, was trying to outrun a pursuing band of Indians across a western American desert. The wall's beige paint gave the desert rocks and hills a realistic patina. The sounds of hoof beats and gunshots echoed off the canyon of surrounding buildings.

"The films are brought in for the Marines," explained our new friend. "Before they send them back to the States, we get our turn." He shrugged his shoulders and pointed to the flickering image. "Some are better than others. But it's fun, a chance to get together, and nobody here has television."

Sue and I spent the rest of the week taking care of details: setting up a local bank account, registering with the American Consulate and the local police, and writing our folks. I checked on the status of our shipment (it would be several weeks yet); I followed up with Mohajir about approving the advance for the A/C unit (it's with the accountant); and Sue and I studied magazines for furniture we might like (Danish Modern, Queen Anne, Oriental?). We spent weekday afternoons at the hotel pool.

By the weekend Sue and I were nursing another case of the loose motions, although much less severe, taking everything at a slow pace. The kids seemed fine.

Thursday evening the hotel's grand meeting hall was decorated with red and yellow crepe paper garlands. Several round tables were set out around the dance floor, covered with checkered tablecloths sprinkled with silver and gold stars. A rotating mirrored ball hung from the ceiling; glints of light circled the dimly lit room. In one corner a pulsating light flashed in a rhythm sure to produce nausea or set off a Grand Mal seizure. Disco music blared from speakers as a small crowd of foreign visitors stood about sipping bottled sodas through paper straws. There were very few women and nobody was dancing.

If Sue and I had felt better we might have stayed, but we were accosted by the frantic music and a bit depressed by the whole scene.

We went to bed early.

"We can't miss tonight's dinner," Sue said. I thought she was being facetious. We were all healthy but bored with hotel food. I understood her enthusiasm when she pointed out a sign in the lobby, "A Night in America, join us in the dining room." It said they'd be serving hamburgers, pizza, apple and cherry pie.

We had seen similar signs for other special theme dinners: "A Night in Romantic Italy," and "A Night in Exotic Asia." We all looked forward to theme night, a break in the monotony. We had memorized the hotel menu and none of us had eaten "American" food since we'd left Minnesota. Several hotel staff pointed out the sign. "Be sure to come," said one. "It is right up your alley, isn't it," said another.

"They're so nice," Sue said. "I think they planned this just for us."

In the dinning room, a boldly painted bald eagle carved from blocks of Styrofoam perched atop a long buffet table draped with red, white, and blue bunting. The eagle's white head was a little small, and its round eyes and yellow beak dove-like, but its outstretched wings and generously taloned yellow feet were imposing. On the wall, an American flag hung next to a photograph of Ronald Reagan.

A line of copper chafing dishes stretched along the buffet table: hot dogs, baked beans, hamburger patties, slices of pizza, and "chips," the British term for French fries. There were platters of hotdog and hamburger buns, bowls of pickles, and containers of ketchup and mustard. We eagerly filled our plates.

While it all looked like American food, the hot dogs had an unfamiliar flavor, more like European sausage than ballpark wieners. My hamburger was a little chewy and left a waxy coating on the roof of my mouth—I suspected it was water buffalo rather than beef. The bun was as hard as a day-old bagel. The Italian pizza and French fries were authentic American, if that's not an oxymoron.

Sue and I thought the hotel had made a worthy effort, given the scarcity of imported ingredients. In any case, we were not going to complain given all the work that had gone into the preparation. Jennifer and David wrinkled their noses.

For dessert, I was eager to try a piece of cherry pie. I didn't see it on the dessert table; only the usual: rice pudding with a microscopically thin sheet of silver adorning the top, flan, and an array of fruits. I asked the waiter.

"It comes from the kitchen, sir, served warm with ice cream."

I ordered the cherry pie, Sue the apple pie. The kids made do with the dessert table. Sue's apple pie arrived, a European style tart with a thick bottom crust topped with sliced apple crescents layered in neat concentric circles, all covered with a translucent sugar glaze. A scoop of vanilla ice cream adorned the plate. It was attractive and tasty but nothing like the proverbial American apple pie.

My cherry pie looked more like an American pie: a crust on top, a crust on the bottom, a scoop of ice cream on the side. *We could bake this at home*, I thought, *if we had a home*. Optimistic, I cut off a fork full, lifted it to my mouth, and took a bite. My eyes got big as I choked back a laugh, in serious danger of spraying bits of pie across the table. Tears were running down my face when I turned the pie toward Sue and the kids. David snorted his pudding. The pie was made with Maraschino cherries.

# 11

# COLLEAGUES

It was the grandest and most pretentious job title I've ever had: "Director General of Commissioning and Operations for the Aga Khan Hospital." It was difficult to fit onto a business card.

The morning I officially started work, two weeks after arriving in Karachi, I was greeted by Nazia's rosy face and warm smile. I already felt welcome. "I have found you an in-box," she said, her eyes twinkling. "And I have put a few things in it for your attention."

The in-box sat on the corner of my desk, piled several inches high with papers. I eyed it skeptically. *That thing could control my life.*

I had just settled into my desk chair when Mohammad Ali appeared at my doorway with a coffee tray, his eyes asking for permission to enter. "Salam," I said, and motioned with my hand, inviting him in. He assembled a cup of coffee just as he had been shown by Nazia two weeks earlier. *"Shukria*, thank you" I said, as he bowed slightly and backed out of the room.

My first task, besides the in-box, was to make my office my own, a mindless challenge but good for my soul. I leaned back in my chair, my coffee cup cradled in both hands, to study my new space. A flit of movement on the wall opposite my desk caught my eye. I had an office mate, a gecko that had neither a tail nor hind legs. It moved its abbreviated torso across the wall with a staccato side shuffle, hand to hand, like a cat burglar hanging by his fingers from a windowsill. It was a maneuver only a gecko could pull off, its finely feathered fingers binding with the wall at the molecular level. I'd already learned a thing or two about lizards.

"Nazia," I called. "Come see this."

Nazia looked at the gecko and put her hand to her mouth to stifle a gasp. She went and got a dust pan which she put under the gecko, then thumped the wall with her fist. The gecko dropped into the pan and she turned to leave.

"Wait," I said. "Where are you going with that?"

"It does not suit you, Mister Robert. I will take it to the School of Nursing."

I didn't think to ask her, "Why there?"

With the lizard gone, I had Mohajir hang a chalkboard on the wall opposite my desk chair. I put Nazia's calendar next to a writing pad on my desk, and a pen and pencil set I'd received as a going-away gift from colleagues back in Minneapolis.

On the back wall, above the credenza, I hung a Les Blacklock photo I'd clipped from an outdated calendar, a red canoe pulled up on the rocky shore of a lake in northern Minnesota. On the side wall I hung a photo of snowy mountain peaks reflecting in a lake near Vail, Colorado. The photos were fantasy images to balance the austerity of the view out my office window. I hoped that Sue and I could live near the water someday, maybe in the mountains, after this adventure in Pakistan.

On the credenza I arranged several family photos, including one of Sue when she was in her twenties, her head turned, her eyes sparkling and her smile radiant, the curve of her neck just so.

Mid-morning I met with my new boss, Shamsh Kassim-Lakha. "You look better than the last time I saw you," he said with a smile. "You had a fire-in-the-belly at the time, but I wasn't sure it was the kind needed to do the job."

It sounded like he wasn't sure I was up to it. *That's two of us.* "Thanks for giving me a chance," I said. "I'm eager to get started."

"His Highness wants a forecast of when the hospital beds will open," Shamsh said. "He also wants a projection of operating costs. That's your main job, that and recruiting key staff."

"That should keep me busy for a few days," I said, knowing it would be a daunting task.

Shamsh smiled. "In your free time, I also want your input on a master plan for the use of the whole eighty-four acre project site, including your thoughts on where the campus mosque should be located."

Having seen the problems of the temporary mosque at the Holiday Inn, I agreed its location was a priority but was also fraught with pit-falls. I vowed to finesse the issue by asking insightful and probing questions of every prominent Muslim I met. "Where do *you* think the mosque should be located?" seemed like a good tactic.

Before I took on anything more ambitious than my in-box, though, I thought I ought to meet some people and get oriented. I started with the School of Nursing.

When I was a young assistant administrator at a Minneapolis hospital, my boss, the hospital's CEO and a meticulous fellow, had a strained relationship with the director of our school of nursing. One afternoon when he was visiting the school he poked his head into her office. He looked around at the papers and books she had piled on every horizontal surface. He shook his head and clucked, "Cluttered desk, cluttered mind."

A week later the school director was wandering around the hospital and stopped by the CEO's office. She poked her head in and looked at him behind his spotlessly clean desk and credenza, shook her head slowly and said, "Empty desk." She paused for a moment as if to finish the thought, then turned and walked out.

I loved her for that, and had been fond of nursing school directors ever since.

Winnie Warkentin, a Canadian, and the Director of the Aga Khan School of Nursing, was no exception. By the time I started work, Winnie had been on the job over two years, had hired and trained the faculty, and launched the school. She was clear eyed behind saucer sized glasses, strong and determined, the kind of person you want on your side, or more accurately, whose side you want to be on. The first class of students was already well settled on campus, and applications for the second class were being processed.

I was sitting in Winnie's office, following up on my promise to return for a visit. We were drinking coffee. Plastic bags of imported cookies and locally made chili chips sat on her desk. I eyed the Oreos. She nibbled a few chili chips.

"The Nursing School is a bold experiment," she said. "The status of nurses here in Pakistan is atrocious. It mirrors the status of women. You don't see a lot of nurses, their training is lousy, and they don't get any respect." She leaned forward and pushed the chili chips in my direction. "Try some."

The chips looked like shoestring potatoes but were seasoned with a tangy red pepper. I took a couple and popped them in my mouth. "Wow," I said.

"Don't rub your eyes," Winnie warned, before she continued. "We're not just another nursing school. As the Aga Khan said at the dedication in February, our primary mission is to raise the standards and standing of the nursing profession itself." She explained that the school had gotten consulting assistance from McMaster University in Hamilton, Ontario, with supportive funding from the Canadian International Development Agency. "For one thing, we teach differently."

"How so?"

"You remember when you first stopped by the school? You made a few comments and then invited questions?"

"Yes."

"Well, in most Pakistani schools, teachers don't do that; they lecture. Here we treat our students like adults and encourage them to look you in the eye and ask questions. At first they don't know what to make of it, but they learn."

"I didn't think much about it."

"When you did that, I knew right away we'd get along."

"Recruiting students is a hard sell," she continued. "His Highness is breaking new ground here, by promoting advanced education for women. He thinks women are the great teachers in the family and they need to be educated themselves. But in many families daughters aren't highly valued." She leaned across her desk and took another handful of the spicy chips. The Oreo bag sat neglected. "Too often, girls are valued for the dowry they can draw. For most of the young women who come here, it's their first time away from home. It's also the first time they have a living space of their own. That's a little scary for the girls and gives their families anxiety attacks. It can be pretty hard to adjust and we need to help them, and protect them."

By now I was into the chili chips too, smacking my lips and relishing the burn.

"The dedication of the School was a big deal," said Winnie. "President Zia was here, and the Aga Khan, and a host of dignitaries from overseas. As you've seen, the first class of students is already on campus, fifty of them. They will graduate in time to help you staff the new hospital."

"Good timing," I said. "I'm sure they'll be a great help."

"Yes, but I think a lot of our graduates will never work. They'll graduate, get married, and we'll never see them again. Well, maybe in ten or fifteen years. But we know that, and it's okay. They'll still be educated women, educated mothers."

"Do you think we can recruit nurses here in Pakistan?"

"Not easily. You might find a few, or attract some back to the profession. But the ones who were trained at other schools here won't be great. You'll have to do a lot of on-the-job-training. You'll have to recruit from overseas: Canada, Great Britain, the Philippines, even the States, maybe Malaysia or Singapore, too. You might find some Pakistanis who have trained or worked abroad and want to come home, or are married to some enlightened guy who's living here. You've got your work cut out for you."

I left Winnie's office with my brain churning and my lips afire.

A few days later I was in my office, working through my in-box, when I heard a chirp, like a small bird. I looked up from my desk to see the abbreviated gecko was back, shinnying along the wall near the ceiling. I was in awe. That thing must have dragged its way over a hundred yards of dangerous terrain, like a soldier walking on his elbows ducking hostile gun fire, somehow avoiding snakes and kites and other perils. "Nazia," I called. "See here. Our colleague has returned."

"I will take care of it straight away," she said, and turned to fetch the dust pan.

"No," I said. "This is her home too. She fought for it. She stays." Actually, I had no idea what the gecko's sex was—I didn't know *that* much about lizards—but it had graduated from the school of nursing.

Nazia smiled. "Just so," she said.

I settled into my office, with a cup of coffee served by the ever-smiling Mohammad Ali, and reviewed our staffing needs.

The University Secretariat already had a team in place. My boss, Shamsh, was the Project's CEO and Chairman of the Owner's Representative Board, ORB for short, and Aziz Currimbhoy, served as its Secretary. The Secretariat also had a staff of young, eager, and able Ismailis, several of whom had fled to Canada from their homes in Uganda, escaping Idi Amin's purge back in 1972.[11] They now served in personnel management, accounting, and public relations. There were non-Ismailis as well; Mohajir and his staff in Administration, for example.

Winnie Warkentin and the nursing school faculty and staff were firmly in place; and Orville Landis and his crew in Buildings and Grounds were onboard. There was also a well staffed Construction Division with a cadre of architects, purchasing agents, construction managers, engineers, supervisors and laborers.

Cheves Smythe, the doctor I'd met in Houston, was well entrenched and highly respected as the head of the hospital's professional services and slated to be dean of the medical college. It turned out he *was* a good-ole-boy, not a Texan but from Carolina, *and* an aristocrat, with a college degree from Yale and a medical degree from Harvard. He had a sharp wit and crackling intelligence. Cheves had spent time with Sue and me before we left the States, giving his candid and sage assessment of Ismailis, the Project, and the Aga Khan. "Remember," he said, "it's *their* project. We're hired help."

The Project's Director General for Finance was a diminutive, pinch-faced Brit who wore a tie to the office and an ascot at home. He imported wheels of Stilton cheese and single malt scotch from

London and reminisced about fox hunting. He smoked incessantly and, at work, kept a bottle of beer beneath his desk, pressed between his ankles. Shortly after I started work, he took me aside. "The rupee is on the slide in relation to the dollar," he said. "I've been asked to talk to you about adjusting your salary."

We didn't know each other yet, and he was obviously a little uncomfortable approaching me. "You're planning to increase my pay, how nice," I said.

He looked befuddled and sputtered, "No, no." Then he picked up on my smile and relaxed.

"That's not going to happen," I said. "But you already know that."

"Yes," he said, "but it is a problem."

I'd been thinking about it too. "How about paying part of my monthly salary in rupees? Enough to cover local costs like food and household help."

"I was thinking along those same lines," he said. We agreed to use a similar approach for other expatriates who would be hired later.

I started a list of people we'd need to hire for the Hospital Directorate. At present we had a staff of three: Nazia, Mohammad Ali, and me, plus Cheves who would double as medical director. To set up and run a 721-bed hospital and its outpatient services, we would need a few more. I thought I should start with a director of nursing; an associate administrator; directors of medical records, food service and housekeeping; and several other management staff who could help plan how the hospital services would function, and would hire, train, and mentor the mostly local staff we would need when construction was finished. It was my job to find these key people and bring them to Karachi.

I went to the office of Zaher Lalani, one of the young Canadian Ismailis, a former ink engineer, and a smart and upbeat fellow who was acting head of personnel. "I'm here to talk about recruitment," I said.

"Close the door," he suggested, "so we can have some quiet."

We were just getting started when there was a knock on the door and the head of public relations walked in. He closed the door, apologized for interrupting, and began to discuss arrangements for visiting dignitaries.

Zaher was about to respond when there was another knock on the door and in walked Shamsh. "Sorry to disturb you," he said, and started to talk to Zaher about another issue. When Shamsh was satisfied, he left.

The PR fellow then finished his business and he left, closing the door behind him.

I turned back to Zaher. "I forgot why I came," I said.

He studied my face as I raised my eyebrows and pursed my lips. "Get used to it. It's how we work here," he said, looking amused. "Recruitment, we were talking recruitment. We need to visit Canada and the States. I have some contacts in Toronto. Any ideas for the U.S?"

"I know my way around Minneapolis. It's a good hospital town and I know there are some folks there who might be interested. I can write some letters."

Zaher and I agreed that a trip in January or February would allow enough time to line up candidates. I took our plan to Shamsh. "Good. Set it up," he said.

# 12

# SOCIAL LIFE

"The Hortons have invited us to a party at their house," Sue said, excited. "It's a chance to meet other new parents and members of the school faculty."

"Welcome to Karachi," Tony and Nana said in unison when we arrived.

They had pitched a *shamiana* that canopied over their enclosed yard. Oriental rugs covered the grass. A bar was set up in one corner of the tent tended by a young Pakistani fellow dressed in white. A brass rice pan, six inches deep and as big around as a wash tub, overflowed with ice and imported beer. *They do have beer in Pakistan.*

A long table was covered with plates and bowls of food, some familiar and some not, all arrayed on a tablecloth patterned in deep maroons and purples. John Williams' classic guitar played from a speaker hanging from the concrete colored trunk of one of the majestic royal palms that edged the yard.

Tony had an athletic build, a strong handshake, and a warm smile.

Nana was wiry and effervescent. "Jennifer and David seem to be making a good adjustment," she said.

"Yes, Jennifer's already made several friends," Sue said. "There's even a boy she's mentioned more than once."

"I've seen them hanging out," Tony said. He's a good kid. He's a fine student and an excellent athlete."

I guessed there was little that happened on campus that Tony and Nana didn't know about.

"David's hooked up with a couple of Korean boys," I said. "They've asked him to join the Boy Scouts. I guess their dad's the Scout Master."

"That's the Kirsch boys," said Nana. "They're adopted twins from Wisconsin. Both their parents are on the faculty." Nana put her hand on Sue's arm. "I love your earrings. Southwest Indian, aren't they?"

"Yes," said Sue as Nana led her away.

"Been out to French Beach yet?" Tony asked me.

"No. Where's French Beach?"

"Just west of the city, on the Indian Ocean beyond Hawkes Bay. You can rent a beach hut and swim and windsurf."

"Windsurf? I've never done that. Lots of water-skiing, though, and snow skiing—and a bit of sailing."

"Then it should be easy. I have one in the garage, a windsurfer. Want to take a look?"

"Absolutely."

"First, let's get you a drink." Tony led me to the bar. "We have most things, just ask. We have access to the American commissary."

"I was told I need to find a friend like you," I said as Tony smiled. "Any Bourbon?" I added, ready to be disappointed.

"Jim Beam okay sir?" said the bartender.

"Perfect. Make it neat."

"The ice is safe here," said Tony.

"How'd you know I wanted ice?"

"Americans usually want to fill their glass with ice. The Brits want a cube or two, if any."

The bartender tonged a lowball glass full with ice and poured a too-generous measure of liquor before I could say, "Whoa."

On the way to the garage, Tony gave me a quick tour of their house. I was struck by their eclectic collection of furniture and art; each piece with its story of a memorable episode in their adventurous lives. I stopped to admire a well-executed drawing of camels and turbaned herdsmen. "Where's this from?" I asked.

"Right here in Karachi," Tony said. "It was done by Gulgee, a local artist; maybe the most famous in Pakistan. He lives over by the school."

"I hope I get a chance to meet him."

In the garage, I admired the windsurfer's graceful lines. I picked up one end of the board and was surprised by its lightness. I examined its mast and colorful sails.

"It's for sale," Tony said. "You can carry it on top of your car and it comes with lessons."

When we rejoined the party, Sue was bubbling about all the great ideas she'd gotten from Nana. "She knows everything," she said. "She knows where to buy linens, the best place for carpets, the best places to eat. I really like her."

"I like Tony too," I said. "I bought a windsurfer."

Sue's raised her eyebrows. "How much?"

I looked at my near empty glass. "Probably too much."

"No. Not how much have you had to drink. How much did the windsurfer cost?"

"Good question either way."

"Is there a place to use it?"

"Yes, French Beach. Tony's invited us out to their beach hut. He said he'd teach us."

Sue shook her head. "A windsurfer? A beach hut? I thought this was a hardship post."

A few days after the Horton affair, my boss, Shamsh, and his wife, Kadijha, threw a party at their home in our honor. The invitation said "7:30 P.M.," and being from Minnesota, that's when we arrived. We were greeted at the door by a middle-aged man dressed in a white shirt and dark pants. He looked a bit surprised, but graciously welcomed us in and ushered us to the empty living room. "Please wait here. I will inform Memsahib," he said. He gave a short bow before retreating.

Sue and I sat looking at each other for ten minutes. "Did we get the date wrong?" I said. "Or the time?"

Sue was shaking her head when Kadijha came into the room and sat down. "Shamsh is getting dressed," she said.

"Are we early?" asked Sue, getting right to the point.

Kadijha seemed a little hesitant to answer. "Well, guests usually arrive about eight-thirty or nine," she said.

Which they did. By nine o'clock the house was filled. There were members of the Owners Representative Board, executive officers, and a couple of doctors—all Pakistani—and a handful of expatriates: Winnie Warkentin, Orville Landis and his wife, Cheves Smythe, and those from Canada and Uganda.

To my surprise, hard liquor was served, although it was mostly expats who took advantage of the opportunity to have a cocktail. We talked about the Project, politics, and Pakistan/American relations. Our host told a couple of jokes.

The conversation continued for nearly two hours, with no sign of dinner. I was beginning to wonder if we were supposed to have eaten before we arrived, but rich aromas were wafting into the living room, making my mouth water and giving me hope. It was near eleven when the man who greeted us at the door announced, "Dinner is served." The guests reacted as if he'd been accompanied by trumpets.

We were directed to a dining room with a long table festooned from edge to edge with brimming bowls and platters. Pungent aromas of curry and spice filled the air. Guests began filling their plates. Sue and I held back.

"Please," said Shamsh, sweeping his outstretched hand toward the table as the crowd parted.

There were potato-stuffed pastries. "Those are *samosa*," someone offered. There were unknown meats smothered in wickedly dark sauces, chicken *biriyani* and lamb *swarma*. A platter was piled with skewered chicken with a menacingly red glaze, chicken *tikka*. Another plate was stacked with layers of bread, some flat, *chapatti*, and some puffy, *nan*. Saucers of nuts and raisins, and bowls of cool yogurt raita and tangy chutney, were strategically placed around the table.

Sue and I were unfamiliar with Pakistani food, except mild Indian curries served back in Minnesota in an anemic Mid-Western style. Even the local fare at the Holiday Inn was censored for the mostly foreign clientele. With eager trepidation, we filled our plates with a little of everything in the hope that something would suit our tastes.

Determined not to embarrass ourselves or our hosts, we cautiously sampled each dish. Everything was generously spiced, and the flavors were rich and intoxicating. Our lips burned. It was the start of a life-long love affair.

The guests stood around with their plates in hand, engrossed in their food. There wasn't much room for conversation, but there was room for dessert. As soon as someone put down their dinner plate they went to the dessert table and filled a fresh plate with spoonfuls of rice pudding, chocolate mousse, or flan—or all three.

Immediately after dessert, guests discarded their plates and were gone. No lingering over an after-dinner coffee or a cordial. Just talk, eat, thank you, and goodbye.

It was after midnight when we got back to the hotel.

A few evenings later we were at the home of a well-to-do Pakistani family. This time we showed up at a quarter to nine. We were the last to arrive and the party was in full swing. I asked Tony Horton for advice.

"It is confusing. If your host is an expat or someone who deals with expats a lot, come on time, or half an hour late," he said. "If it's an upper-crust local, come an hour late, usually."

I was reminded of the advice I got that year we lived in laid-back Colorado, "Show up when it feels right."

The house was aswarm with people: school board members, the Hortons and other school administrators, and parents we had not seen at the first party. Based on the diversity of their dress, they weren't all from America.

Our host, a member of the KAS board, said, "About a third of our students are Pakistani, mostly children of people who have lived abroad. Another third are American. The others come from more than twenty countries."

As we turned from our host and were headed to the bar, Sue and I were approached by a stunning Pakistani woman. She wore a cross between a western cocktail dress and a *shalwar kameez*. Her bodice was generously filled. Long silken folds of iridescent purple and blue fell from an empire waist. She had a gracefully arched nose and her dark eyes were outlined in kohl black. Her cheeks glistened with sparkles of color. She was a classic subcontinent beauty, a vision drawn from an Indian silk painting. *No wonder they hide their women,* I thought.

I had been told not to offer my hand to a woman, to let her initiate a handshake. This lady didn't hesitate. She stuck out her hand to Sue, then to me. Her grip was strong and firm. I was impressed, and a little on-guard, by her brazen looks and forthright demeanor. All the Pakistani women we'd met were far more demure. *What's she selling?*

"How long will you be here?" she asked.

"We just arrived," I said. "We'll be here three years."

"Good. Then it's worth my time to get to know you."

I knew what she meant. Expatriates flowed in and out of Karachi like the Indian Ocean tides. Most were assigned to Pakistan for two or three years and then moved on. Even in a city of seven million people, the expat community was small and fluid. We were told there were more expats than usual, but still only a few thousand at most. There were expats from numerous countries working in Karachi for consulates, aid agencies, international banks, and companies that traded with Pakistan. Tony Horton said the administration and faculty at the American School were nearly all Americans.

It was the height of the cold war, the Soviet invasion of Afghanistan at full throttle, and the United States was nurturing its friendship with Pakistan. The U.S. had a number of diplomats in the country, along with drug control officers, cultural attaches and, I was sure, CIA operatives.

The other guests were quick to acknowledge our presence. For us, every unfamiliar face offered an opportunity to expand our circle of friends and to enrich the social mix. We exchanged business cards compulsively.[12] Some cards had directions printed in Urdu on the back to help one's driver find their residence. Everyone was remarkably inclusive and Sue and I quickly felt at ease. "There's so little pretense," Sue told me. "I can just be me."

"Are you on the school board?" I asked the subcontinent beauty.

"No."

"Do you have a child at the school?" Sue asked.

"No."

"Okay, I give up," I said. "What's your role in this drama?"

"I design clothing and decorative furniture and I've done business with nearly everybody in this room."

*Ah, ha.* I was tempted to check my wallet.

Sue said to her, "Let's talk," and led her off to a corner, delighted, I assumed, to find another source for furniture.

That evening we met more people from more places than we would meet in the lobby of the United Nations building in New York. There was the Consul General from Oman, his ample body draped in a white *dishdasha*, and a Turkish architect who was managing the construction of the Hilton hotel being built by a Pakistani entrepreneur. We met three bank executives: from London, Germany, and America. There were three airline executives: the man from Pan Am, a noble looking Parsi; the man from Air France, a debonair Parisian; and the man from Air Italia, an animated fellow with a gregarious, red-haired wife.

Sue and I talked with the Turkish architect, Ali Kosal, and his attractive wife, Cholpan, who wore big-stoned rings on several fingers and half-a-dozen gold bracelets. A gold, two-headed serpent coiled around her wrist. Colored jewels adorned her neck and hung from her pierced ears. Ali said, "Jewelry is our insurance. If we need to exit Pakistan quickly, we can start over with what Cholpan's wearing."

"You've lived abroad before, I take it?"

"Yes, I went to college in New York and spent my summers out on Long Island remodeling houses and learning to sail. I've worked for Hilton for years. Cholpan and I have moved around a lot."

"A red-headed Italian?" I asked, nodding toward the wife of the Air Italia executive.

"They're from Northern Italy," Ali said. "A place invaded by the Norwegians."

"She makes a luscious lasagna," added Cholpan.

"The fellow with Pan Am," I said. "I'm told he's a Parsi. What's that?"

"A Zoroastrian," said Ali. "Sometimes they're called fire worshipers.

You know that concrete tower on the side of Karsaz Road? You must pass it on your way to work. It looks like one of your American farm silos."

"Yes, I've seen it. I thought it *was* a silo of some kind."

"No, it's called a Tower of Silence. The Parsi put their dead up on top for the vultures. The bones drop through the grate. Even with all that, the Parsi are very progressive."

Everybody we met invited us to a party. For the next couple of weeks, three or four nights a week, we attended one function or another. Small dinner parties in private homes where we talked about our children, politics and international finance; larger gatherings of mostly expatriates; or mostly locals where the talk was polite if not probing; and catered events at better hotels thrown by international companies doing business in Pakistan—a couple of times with entertainment or music where Sue and I could dance.

After a few weeks of frenetic social activity, Sue and I were relaxing out by the hotel pool.

"I'm having fun and glad to get out of the hotel," Sue said. "but this social whirl is more than I expected. I'm exhausted. I need some down time."

"Me too," I said. "We can't keep this up."

"It's not fair to the kids, being gone so much. And we're always the guests, never the hosts. It's frustrating not being able to reciprocate."

We interrupted our conversation to watch Pascale, the hotel manager's wife, give her baby, Bambi, swimming lessons. She held him while he splashed and kicked and dunked him under the water so he would learn to hold his breath.

Another long-term hotel guest, the wife of a British bank manager, was sitting under an umbrella nearby, grumbling. "That baby's too young for that," she said. Then louder, "He'll drown." Then a shout, as Pascale held the baby under water for a couple seconds, "Don't do that." Then more grumbling, "Where do they get these irresponsible babysitters?"

Pascale ignored her and continued playing with the baby.

I turned to the woman and said, "She's the mother."

It was as if I had taken the cork out of a constipated alligator. The woman launched into one complaint after another. "She's a bad mother...This hotel is a disaster...The food's terrible...You'll catch something if you swim in the pool...Karachi's the armpit of the world...It's too damn hot...These Pakis just gawk at you."

She went on and on. I just stared at her. It was more encouragement than she needed.

Pascale never looked at the woman. After a few minutes she picked up Bambi and stepped out of the pool. She picked up a towel, patted herself and the baby dry, and left the terrace, never looking back.

When the woman paused for breath, I asked her, "Is this your first overseas assignment?"

"Bloody hell, no." she said. "I've been trailing my husband from one hell-hole after another for fifteen years."

"Where else have you lived?" I asked.

"Saudi, Kuwait, Egypt; all hell holes," she said.

Sue interrupted, "Honey, we need to get back."

"Excuse us," I said, as we picked up our things.

As we left the terrace I said, "A terrible, unhappy, angry woman."

Sue nodded. "I've run into her before. She's very unpleasant company. Please don't let that happen to me."

"She's been to a lot of interesting places," I said, "but she takes herself along wherever she goes. You don't have that much venom in you."

"Not yet," Sue said. "But watch out if I have to live in this hotel much longer. I'll start by murdering that organ player in the lobby."

# 13

# THE EXPATRIATE TAX

"Sue's going to kill me if we don't move soon," I said to Orville. "She's going crazy and so are the kids. So am I. We've been living in the hotel for six weeks."

"The house won't be finished until you move in," Orville said. "As soon as the air-conditioner is hooked up, you need to bite the bullet." As we got to know each other, Orville became more direct in his advice, and after weeks of delays and *Insha'lahs* at every corner, I was ready to listen.

"Another thing," he said, "you have responsibilities as rich expatriates living in a poor country. You can't run a household here without help. And when you hire them, you need to treat them right and pay them a fair wage. And while you're at it, don't bargain too hard in the market. Think of it as the expatriate tax."

"Let's set a date," I said to Sue. Mohajir had cleared the advance and the central air-conditioning unit had been delivered to the site. Installation was nearly complete. Our landlord said it would be operational within a day or two.

"The sooner the better," Sue said. "How about next weekend?"

"Agreed."

We asked around about finding household help and were referred to a middle-aged couple, Peter and Margaret Peters, who had been working for an expatriate family that moved to another posting. We invited them to meet us at the hotel. They looked Pakistani but

Sue and I were puzzled by their un-Pakistani names. Peter, who was to be our cook, was tall and thin, and fragile looking. He wore a white shirt over dark pants rather than a *shalwar kameez*. He had a star and crescent the size of a quarter tattooed to his forehead, partially hidden by a wisp of black hair—a half inch of gray showing at the roots.

"Why the tattoo?" I asked.

"I am Christian, Robert Sahib. My father was Indian but he took a British name. After partition I was afraid I would be killed. Men would pull down your pants to see if you were a Muslim." He glanced down at his lap. "I am not, but I could show this." His finger pointed to his forehead.

I swallowed hard as I recalled the mayhem that followed the partition of India in 1947. As the British stood by doing nothing, Hindus slaughtered Muslims and Muslims slaughtered Hindus, as refugees fled across the newly drawn borders in both directions. The killings were one of the reasons for the continuing animosity and distrust between Pakistan and India.

"And I can cook pork," Peter added, flashing a smile.

Margaret, who would serve as our bearer, our housekeeper, wore a *shalwar kameez* but no head scarf. "My mother was Indian and my father was British," she said. "I went to a Catholic girl's school,"

That explained her excellent English, I thought, and probably Peter's. Another shadow of the British occupation.

"And your home is very near where we live," she added.

We looked over their chits, their reference letters, and hired them on the spot, gave them a small advance, and set them to work cleaning the house.

A week later, two months after arriving in Karachi, we moved out of the Holiday Inn and into our new home.

The house was cavernous and our footfalls echoed off the terrazzo floors and concrete walls. The air-conditioner was working and the place was spotless but nearly bare. Our shipment had arrived two weeks earlier but was tied up at the docks waiting to clear customs.

None of the furniture we had commissioned had been finished. The house was a pick-up game of what Sue called, "warehouse eclectic." We had a bed in each bedroom made up with linens borrowed from the mother of one of Jennifer's classmates, plus a few chairs and a small table in the dining room that Mohajir had commandeered from an unused office. There were two lights in the house: a desk lamp on the dining room table and a floor lamp in the upstairs hall that cast a thin light into the unlit bedrooms. A stove and refrigerator stood lonesome in the kitchen, awaiting the company of cabinets and counter tops. There was no paint on the walls, no drapes on the windows, no rugs on the floors, and the garden, while no longer cluttered with construction debris or a stage for plastic-bag ballerinas, was as barren and desolate as a jail yard.

On the day we moved in, we were busy putting away our few clothes when we heard Margaret yell, "Sahib, Memsahib, come quick!"

We all came running, our shoes squeaking and clattering on the terrazzo.

"Look," she said, pointing out to the patio. A dark wet stain stretched across the tile—the flush from an upstairs toilet.

"Yuk," said Jennifer.

"Awesome," said David.

"Margaret," Sue said, with what I thought was amazing calm, "Please clean this up and we'll close down that bathroom until this is fixed."

That afternoon we talked to our landlord and decided to hire a contractor to finish work on the house. Within limits, my employer would pick up the tab.

The contractor, Sadiq, was a tall man with a round face, broad shoulders, and passable English. He had the unflappable disposition of an Indian fakir and was a bit too quick with his *Insha'lahs* to give me confidence that he would keep the work moving. But he came well recommended and we didn't have a lot of choice. To keep him on top of things, I asked him to come to the house each morning with his work crew, a couple of young fellows recently arrived from the countryside.

First things first, we had him look at the toilet.

"Rocks in pipe," he said. It seems that construction workers from the rural areas had used stones to wipe themselves and threw them down the toilet. He pointed out to the patio. "Pipe top left off." For accessibility, all the water and sewer pipes, and the electrical conduit, were mounted on the building's exterior walls, a common practice in Pakistan, and convenient when they needed service.

Sadiq's men fished out the stones and made the needed repairs. Sadiq also checked over the electric wiring and showed me the fuse box. "Electric go up, go down. Fuse blow." He made a popping sound with his lips. "Penny under fuse, not good. Fire maybe," he said, as he handed me a box of extra fuses.

Next, Sadiq brought in a crew of cabinet-makers who set up a workshop in the middle of the kitchen floor. They cut and assembled and mounted each cabinet by hand, trimming around the Italian appliances purchased by the landlord. Sue made some modifications so she could use the kitchen too—assuring that countertops were wide and deep and that cutting boards were in usable locations.

One evening I came home to see workmen moving the stove while Peter, laboring without complaint in the bedlam, was boiling a pot of spaghetti. In the weeks of chaos he served homemade pizza, spaghetti and meat balls, and his crowning glory: a dinner of roast beef, mashed potatoes, and canned corn—all delicious and a welcome break from hotel food.

At first Sadiq bristled at taking instructions from a woman. But after a few days it was clear that Sue knew what she wanted. She would point out a crack that needed to be filled before she would allow Sadiq's inexperienced workers to paint. Brush in hand, she showed them how to load the brush with paint and cut a straight line around a window or door frame, then watched as the workers practiced doing it themselves. She was polite but firm and I think Sadiq and most of his crew grew to respect her and they used their new skills with enthusiasm. It was a good thing. Sadiq and his men were in our employ, and underfoot, for more than ten weeks.

Sadiq's work force grew to a half dozen men, scattered throughout the house. They replaced a door frame that had been eaten away from the inside by termites, only the thin outer skin holding it togeth-er. Sadiq called in an exterminator who also took care of the cock-roaches, at least temporarily, that made us squirmy as they wiggled their antennae through the drains in the bathrooms, emerging at night to scurry across the bed linens. Sadiq's men wrapped leaking water connections with dental floss—a substitute for non-existent plumber's tape. They adjusted door hinges and hardware so the doors would swing freely. They repaired a leak in the roof.

It was the long list of kinks Orville had tried to warn us about.

With Sohir and Peter and Margaret and Sadiq, we had four em-ployees, not counting Sadiq's men—and there were more.

We hired a *chokidar*, Abdullah, who had been the security guard for our landlord and came with the house. He was a Pathan, from the same village as other *chokidars* in the neighborhood. He had a wife and children somewhere up in the Northwest Frontier Province who he sent money to each month. He spoke no English but he had a quick smile and seemed to anticipate our comings and goings—al-ways ready at the gate. To our relief, he didn't chew beetle nuts—the unsightly red spittle juice stained the walks and driveways of several houses we had visited.

Abdullah was short and stocky, only a little taller than David. With his white beard, Abdullah looked like Santa Claus; but that didn't keep David from tormenting him. David would climb out on the ledge that surrounded the house just below the second story windows and throw firecrackers down at napping Abdullah, round cherry bombs that exploded on impact. He bought them, without our knowledge, from the gunpowder *wallah* who came to the gate. Abdullah would shake his fist up at David and swear at him in Urdu—the first words in Urdu David learned.

Inexplicably, he and David became friends, with Abdullah teach-ing David Urdu; thankfully more than swear words, and David teach-ing Abdullah how to write his own name in English. In addition to learning to swear, David began to mimic Abdullah's habit of clearing his nose with a loud hacking noise. David walked around the house snorting repeatedly, testing the sounds he could make. We were re-lieved when the experiment fell away after a few weeks, but David and Abdullah continued their animated friendship.

Through friends, Sue found a gardening consultant who had de-signed many of the formal gardens scattered around the city before he retired as a professor of horticulture from Karachi University. Sue worked with him on a landscaping plan, visiting and photographing a number of gardens, both public and private. "You will never believe how beautiful this city really is," she said. "There are flowers every-where, and lots of trees I don't recognize. Some gardens are hidden behind those high walls, but there's a lot that's in clear view. More of the city parks would be beautiful if they had more water."

Sue relied on the consultant's advice for a variety of tropical plants and flowers: bougainvillea, frangipani, poinsettias and other unfamil-iar perennials that would do well in our yard. A dignified man, he dressed in a dark western suit and tie as he and his crew of *malis* brought in soil and plants and came each day to water and weed.

In only days, green sprouts were everywhere. "With that climb-ing bougainvillea, we'll hardly see those walls," Sue said. "It already looks less like a stockade."

Sue asked Margaret for a reference for a *dhobi*, a laundry man, after getting a warning from a friend about killer *dhobis* who mur-dered your laundry. "She's very fashionable," Sue told me. "She gave her lingerie to her *dhobi* until one day she saw all her frilly bras and panties draped over bushes, right next to the road, down by the river where all the *dhobis* were beating the clothes on the rocks. I think she was more embarrassed by having her underwear exposed than having it mistreated."

The *dhobi* Sue hired came to our house twice a week and did our laundry by hand in a wash tub. Everything was hung to dry on clotheslines Sadiq mounted inside the back wall, out of sight from visitors. There were no broken buttons and everything was ironed, even our underwear and socks were neatly pressed. We were told that the Brits had taught their *dhobis* to hot-iron everything to kill the larva laid by flies in wet laundry. I knew they had such problems in Africa and South America, but I didn't think we did in Asia.[13] Still, I wasn't about to tell the dhobi to stop.

While Margaret claimed there was not a caste system in Pakistan, there was a strict division of labor, and nobody who worked inside the house would think of sweeping up outside. In retrospect, asking Margaret to mop the patio after the toilet spill was probably a breach. She had not complained, but she insisted on hiring a sweeper, a boy of about ten or twelve who came each morning to tidy-up the driveway and the patio. He duck-walked on his haunches as he brushed away the accumulated leaves and litter with scythe-like sweeps of a handle-less broom.

One of Sue's new friends recommended a *dherzi*, a dressmaker, whose work was prized by the expatriate community and his availability closely guarded. Some expat had to leave town before you were allowed in on his rotating schedule. He came to the house and set up his sewing machine on a sheet spread on the floor of a spare room. He sat for hours with posture as straight as a Buddha and a demeanor as tranquil as a Sufi mystic. He made clothing from bolts of silk and cotton that Sue found in local shops, flawlessly copying designs she selected from photos in magazines. He made dresses and blouses for Sue and Jennifer and, if there was any time left, shirts for David and me. We signed him up to return every few months for the rest of our stay.

Sue made up a book to keep track of everyone on our payroll, their names and their wages. She felt she was managing a small business. "The Brits are better suited to this," she said. "I'm a simple Minnesota girl. I'm not used to having things done for me. And I'm uncomfortable having people in the house all the time."

"It will grow on you," I said. "You only have to cook when you want. Margaret will take care of the house. What's not to like."

"You're right," she said. "But once in a while I need a little quiet. Sometimes I like to lounge around in shorts and a tee-shirt. I feel like I have to hide in the bedroom."

# 14

# LIVING POSH IN PAKISTAN

Karachi's marketplace was rich but scattered. You could find most anything if you knew where to look. Or, as Sue and I soon discovered, the marketplace found you. We hadn't been in the house forty-eight hours when the *wallahs*, the salesmen, began showing up at our door.

The first to arrive was a carpet *wallah* with oriental rugs stacked precariously in the back of his small truck. With a practiced flourish he laid each carpet in turn on the patio, or on the bare ground, pausing long enough to explain its origin, its knot count, and the key features of its design. We had no idea what we were seeing or what kind of price was fair. "You are keeping them," said the *wallah*. "I will come back. If you are keen, you can pay then."

We picked out a couple of tribal carpets and laid them on the bare floor of the dining room. They livened up the room with color and texture. "Nana says you can't have too many carpets," Sue said, as her eyes swept over the surrounding expanse of naked and austere terrazzo.

My eyes widened as I mentally counted all the places in the house where a carpet might fit.

We already had a furniture *wallah*. Sue selected a Queen Anne dining room chair from one of his magazines. A couple of days later he returned with a full-scale drawing, rendered in pencil on brown wrapping paper, that would be used by his workers to craft a set of eight chairs, two with arms. "How high do we make the seat,

Memsahib?" he asked. "How deep? How much slant to the back? "

For several days Sue carried a measuring tape around to our friends' homes, sitting in their chairs and measuring those she thought were most comfortable. She went through the same routine for two sofas and a pair of lounge chairs for the living room. There were similar questions for a dining room table, "How high, Memsahib?" and for an oriental design coffee table, "Are you keen on carved feet?"

We both noticed that the Horton's home was especially well furnished—an eclectic array of furniture and cabinets, oriental carpets, and Asian accessories. "We've lived a lot of places," said Nana. "We've picked up pieces here and there and we bring them with us when we move. We're always adding more. It makes us feel at home, more settled and less like transients."

We found several other expatriate families who did the same thing. For some, their employers set up their households before they arrived. Not so for us.

"I didn't know I'd become a furniture designer," Sue said.

"And interior decorator," I offered.

Sue was getting helpful advice from a Pakistani interior designer, another independent woman like the classic beauty we'd met earlier, but not quite so zaftig. Together they designed hand block printed materials for window coverings, visiting the workshop to watch the stamping process and to assure the dye colors were just right. They found upholstery fabrics for the furniture we were having made and artwork for our bare walls.

Two handsome brothers also showed up at our gate, riding a motorbike with a canvas bag filled with brass. Again, they took items out of their bag one at a time: a scale with a set of weights shaped like elephants, two jars the size and shape of mangos, and a small pot with an intricate design engraved around its rim. They showed us an ornately carved beetle nut cutter, a pair of filigreed saddle stirrups, and a ship's chronometer that gleamed golden in its handcrafted wood box.

I was in awe of the endless number of treasures that emerged from their bag, like Strega Nona's bottomless pasta pot, and their ability to wrestle all that bulk and weight, and themselves, on their small motorbike. Sue and Jennifer seemed equally enthralled with the two charming young men. The girls eagerly accepted their offer to return in a couple of days with more prizes to choose from. "We will bring very special pieces, selected just for you Memsahib," they said, their dark eyes luminous as in unison they flashed perfect smiles.

There were other *wallahs* as well, hawking goods of all description. One was the never seen gunpowder *wallah*, who sold firecrackers to David. We bought tattered books from the book *wallah*, usually junk novels in English purchased from other expatriates, but occasionally one of the *Flashman* novels, stories of the British bully and coward who seemed to be present at several key historic battles in the British Empire's assault and retreat in Afghanistan in the mid-1800s.[14] And comics, mostly *Richy Rich*, that David collected by the dozen. A fruit and vegetable *wallah* came by almost every day, ringing a bell and pushing a two-wheeled cart loaded with whatever fresh produce he was able to buy at the market.

After a couple of weeks our shipment still had not cleared the docks. The shipping company's agent came by my office to discuss the matter. "We are having delays, Sahib. The dock workers have so very much to handle," he said.

He gave me other reasons, none of them too clearly defined, and lingered in my office even after I thought our conversation was finished. I went to Mohajir. "Can you help me with our shipment?" I asked. "Our stuff has been on the pier for weeks, baking in the sun."

Mohajir did a slow subcontinent head wobble that can be mistaken for no to the uninitiated, but really means yes, or I understand. "*Thika, thika*," he said. "No problem, Mister Robert."

Two days later, mid-morning, a truck backed into our driveway with a sealed metal container. Two men from Mohajir's office unloaded the truck as Sue and I supervised. The truck and the men were gone by noon.

The next day I went to Mohajir to thank him. "How did you do that?" I asked.

He smiled. "I have a man who does the needful."

I can be so obtuse. "Do I owe you money?" I offered.

"No, Mister Robert. It is my job, and my pleasure, isn't it."

It was like Christmas. It had been months since we had packed our shipment back in Minnesota. We had used generic labels for each box—kitchen, living room, master bedroom—rather than detailed inventories, so we opened each box with anticipation and surprise. We quickly found new clothing to break the boredom of our limited wardrobe, linens for the beds and bathrooms, pots and pans and kitchen utensils.

Jennifer unwrapped her boom-box, never used, and plugged it into an electrical outlet. It didn't make a peep and never would—its 110 volt circuitry was fried by Karachi's 220 volt system in a millisecond. We warned David before he made the same mistake and I bought a transformer before we plugged in the small stereo we had purchased for ourselves.

We had no trouble finding the four tubs of peanut butter. The tubs had exploded in the heat and rancid peanut oil permeated their cardboard box like stains on a brown paper bag filled with powder milk biscuits.

With our shipment unpacked, a growing inventory of furniture, a couple of rugs on the floor, and the house nearing completion, we were a bit awed by our new residence. "Rather posh," I said, in a poor British accent.

Sue and I had both read *Freedom at Midnight* and *Plain Tales From The Raj* and knew the legend that the Brits advised those traveling by ship from England to India to remember "POSH"—port out, starboard home—when selecting their cabin aboard ship so they could escape the worst of the tropical sun. True or not, the word certainly caught the flavor of living well in the subcontinent.

"Ain't we swell, though," said Sue, sounding more like a hillbilly moved to Hollywood than a Brit. "It is such a relief to be out of the hotel." She looked around the living room. "I have to say I like it. Now, if we could get the rest of our furniture delivered and a few more carpets, the house would be almost perfect."

"Almost?" I asked, stepping into it.

"We need to push our landlord for a telephone," she reminded me. "And we're always running out of water. Our new yard and garden are going to shrivel up."

# 15

# THE QUALITIES OF WATER

Aziz Currimbhoy was communicating with the gods on the tenth floor of a hotel in midtown Manhattan when he had an epiphany.

"I could see all these pipes," he told me. "There were pipes coming into the commode, and pipes going out. They were connected to other pipes, and to sinks and bathtubs and showers in every room, on every floor of the hotel. All the hotels and office buildings in Manhattan were the same. All over the State of New York, all across America was this network of pipes. Clean water flowing in, dirty water flowing out."

Aziz drew his hands together, his fingertips touching in contemplation, his slender face reflecting the delight of his insight. "This is the difference between America and Pakistan, isn't it." He milked the essence from every word. "Your plumbing works."

I had come to Aziz for advice about the problem we were having with water at our new home. Every few days Peter would say, "Sahib, I need to order another tanker."

Once more I had followed the well worn path to the office of Mister-Fix-It, Mohajir, and explained my frustration. This time there was none of his ever hopeful, "No problem," response. Instead, he twisted a hand in the air. "This is difficult, Mister Robert. Water is a big problem in Karachi."

So I went to Aziz, the project guru, the Professor, the font of knowledge on all issues local, corporate, and religious. A slender, middle-aged man with a quiet demeanor and gentle ways, he was cosmopolitan, wise, and easy to talk to—a calm presence in any room he occupied. I think Shamsh relied on his counsel at least as much as I did.

"We can thank the British for our water system," Aziz explained. "Water is clean and chlorinated when it leaves the water plant. But there is not enough water and its flow is not constant. It serves one section of the city, then switches to another, then another. There are no water towers, like in your country, so in-between the pipes are empty and do not stay clean." He leaned across his desk, his expression earnest. "At your home you have a cistern, do you not, and it should fill every few days, *Insha'lah*. You pump the water from the cistern up to the tank on your roof. You draw water from the roof tank for your house."

I knew the part about pumping water from the cistern to the roof tank, but not the reasons for the interrupted supply.

"But Karachi is growing very fast and you are in Defence, a new section. Maybe the water service is not so reliable. Maybe it will improve, but you will need to buy water until it does."

"So be it," I said, resigned to the inevitable. "Will we have the same problem here at the hospital?"

"That is why we have built big ground tanks. We are in an area that gets water regularly, but we don't want to take chances. That is also why we will have fish ponds; for landscaping, yes, but in case of fire."

"What about sewage?"

"*Accha*. A good question, isn't it. You must talk to Orville. He has made a discovery."

The next morning I was in Orville's office. "What's the issue about sewage from the hospital?"

"I'm glad you asked." He got up from his desk. "Come with me."

Orville led me outdoors to a sandal-worn trail that snaked through the sand and scrub to the back of the property, to a wall beyond the school of nursing. He opened a heavy gate. We walked through and onto a wide expanse of barren land stretching off into the dusty haze in both directions. "This is a city right-of-way. This is where the city sewer pipe is buried," he said, gesturing toward the open field.

"That sounds good," I said.

"Wait, there's more." Orville pointed to the base of the wall. "This is where the waste line from the nursing school comes under the wall and connects to the city's sewer pipe. It's a big pipe that will serve those apartment buildings over there." He pointed to a group of partially constructed high-rises about a quarter mile away. "It will also serve the hospital."

"Still looks good."

"Yes it does. But last week, out of curiosity, I walked the sewer line off that way." He pointed into the murky distance. "It goes about a half mile or so, and then comes to a *wadi*, a ravine, and pokes out of the ground, an open pipe. The *wadi* flows from there for another half mile before it joins a canal. The best part, there is a squatter's village along both sides of the drainage ditch."

"Holy shit."

"Exactly."

I had driven by a number of squatter villages, called encroachments, which were scattered around the city. From the road, the villages were an indecipherable jumble of shacks cobbled together with discarded concrete blocks and construction rubble, roofed with sheets of metal or plywood. Inside they were a warren of narrow dirt pathways that zigzagged among the buildings. The encroachments sprang up in any open space that was left unattended: abandoned building sites, government lands awaiting roadway construction, and on the banks of *wadis*.

Access to an abundant supply of water is *the* essential requirement for health, but whatever the compromises of the city water system, the encroachments had little water or none. I drove by one settlement of several dozen shacks every day going to and from work. Once, I saw a water truck, maybe an enterprising driver with a little water left over after a delivery, visiting a village. People lined up with jugs and buckets. I often saw women carrying water drawn from a spigot in a nearby community, and children pulling overloaded wagons, water sloshing from a hodgepodge of bottles and bowls.

Sometimes a *wallah* would hawk water drawn from five gallon carboys stacked on a wheeled cart. I assumed the water *wallah* drew his supply from the same sources available to locals, who paid for the convenience of having it brought to them. Buying bottled water had to be out of the question. Commercial water companies that controlled the production of bottled water kept the price high and probably exercised their influence to discourage other lower cost alternatives. One day I saw villagers washing their clothes in a drainage ditch. I was told they sometimes drew water from standing puddles.

If clean water was a problem, the disposal of sewage was worse. Much of the effluent produced by the city's seven million people moved through narrow channels usually covered with removable concrete slabs. Orville said that concrete sewer pipes, like the one buried behind the hospital, were an exception, their use more common in up-scale neighborhoods. The channels were designed to carry the waste to the nearest sewage treatment plant. I saw covering slabs that were missing or broken, providing easy access to rats and skittering cockroaches. Some neighborhoods perpetually smelled of raw sewage.

Encroachments more so. Squatter villages didn't have sewer systems and I saw men, women, and children throwing pans of gray water into the alleyways or hunkering on the banks of a *wadi* to relieve themselves. Some sewage channels drained into ravines, like the one down stream from the hospital, and the ravines drained into low hallows that after a heavy rain were overflowing with a reeking oily glut of sewage and floating trash.

*All they need is our medical waste added to that fetid soup.*

Once I saw the city bulldoze an encroachment to the ground and truck away the debris. Residents were forced to relocate, some living temporarily under cardboard lean-tos while others joined already crowded encroachments nearby. The bulldozed site remained empty for weeks, whatever project planned for the land delayed or canceled. More likely, the authorities were concerned that if left too long the encroachment could become too well established to be destroyed. I thought the city authorities were being capricious or just mean. In time, however, the bulldozed land remained empty too long and the squatters began to rebuild, one shack at a time, bending to the unrelenting pressure of in-migration from Pakistan's hinterlands. After several months I couldn't tell the bulldozers had ever been there. It was testament to the tenacity of the human spirit.

After Orville's discovery, the Project used its considerable influence to mobilize city authorities to fix the sewer pipe before the hospital came on line. Still, I had nightmares about that squatter's village clinging to the banks of the wadi.

At home, I told Peter to put in a standing order for a tanker truck every week. In the kitchen, Peter and Margaret were meticulous about straining the water we used for food and drink through a ceramic filter to remove grit and then boiling it for several minutes. Peter washed everything that came from the market in "pinky," a sterilizing solution of water and potassium permanganate. Once, when the water in the house began to smell funky, we sent Sohir up on the roof. He found a dead bird floating in the water tank. It reinforced Orville's admonition to "shower with your mouth closed."

We bought long-life milk in half-liter trapezoid containers. We kept flour in the freezer to kill bugs, and cereal in the refrigerator, and Peter sifted it all to screen out insect carcasses. On occasion, though, I suspected he added caraway or fennel seeds to hide weevils in the bread dough. Really harmless and high in protein, I rationalized. In hotels and restaurants we ordered bottled water and checked to see that the sealed cap had not been broken, and we never ordered ice. We never ate cold salad or fruit we couldn't peel ourselves, only dishes that were cooked. We seldom bought from street vendors except barbequed chicken *tikka*, and *nan* hot from a *tandoori* oven, which we couldn't resist, and soda pop which we drank from the bottle through a straw, leaving the last inch or two in the bottom so our lips didn't have to touch the rim. And those crisp kettle-fried potato chips were just too tempting.

We still got ill on occasion, but less often and less severely than in those first few weeks. I asked a doctor if we wouldn't eventually get used to Karachi's fauna if we just ate what locals ate. "Probably so," he advised, "but we get sick too. And every day people die here with loose motions. And what makes them ill might kill you. Better you be careful."

Once in a while, when there was a shortage in the nearby shantytown, women would line up outside our gate asking for water. At first Margaret refused, telling Sue, "Memsahib, you pay too much for water to give it away."

Sue was insistent, "They need water, Margaret. We can spare a little."

We bought our water and shared it. It was all we could do. And I had too much to do at work to spend any more time fretting about it.

# 16

# DISTANT AND DISCONNECTED

Shamsh called me into his office. It was mid-October, shortly after we moved into our house. "I know you're planning a trip next year," he said, "but I want you to fly to Boston to see Tom Payette, our architect, and review the hospital plans. You can also swing by Minneapolis while you're there, see your family, and maybe get something going on recruitment."

I hadn't anticipated traveling so soon.

I talked to Sue. "I'll be gone a week, no more. Are you okay with that?"

"I've got a lot to do to get this house in shape," she said, "but I think I've got things under control here." She was busy selecting paint colors and picking out upholstery fabrics.

"I'll write a letter you can give to my folks. They'll be as upset as I am about this terrible shooting in Egypt. Anwar Sadat was a brave man to make peace with Israel." We had just read in *Dawn* that Sadat had been assassinated. "They'll be worried about us. They think the Middle East is right next door."

The next week, when I boarded my flight out of Karach, I picked up a copy of *Time Magazine*, eager for some unfiltered news from the outside world. The lead story was about the assassination. "The Middle East is in a mess, right now," I said to my seatmate, another American expat. "They say some of this hatred is pointed at America for supporting Israel. I'm glad we're in Pakistan, not there."

"Me too," he said. "The climate in Pakistan couldn't be friendlier." Sue had said the same thing in her letter.

The weather in Boston was clear and crisp when I arrived, a pleasant change from Karachi's heat and humidity.

"We started all this nearly ten years ago," Tom Payette told me when we met at his office. "Before we drew a line, we spent months with a team from the Aga Khan Foundation visiting examples of Islamic architecture. The Foundation even published a book on what we learned and His Highness helped establish a school of Islamic architecture at Harvard. It has been a fascinating experience both personally and professionally, and a great opportunity to see the world."

We were standing in front of several renderings—drawings of the hospital and medical school under construction in Karachi.

"There really isn't such a thing as Islamic design, per se," he said, as we walked over to a rendering of the hospital's front entrance. "But there are features we found that are commonly used throughout the Muslim world." He described grand, arched entryways that reveal the interior slowly, enticingly; and secret inner courtyards, moist and glistening with fountains and pools, surrounded by shaded colonnades. Tom pointed out details on the drawings. He stretched his arms out wide as he said, "The walls are thick and textured to create streaked shadows on their surface. Deep set windows protect against the unrelenting sun. Stone and wood jalousie partitions, that allow air to circulate, are carved in intricate lace patterns that both hide and reveal." He paused, giving me time to study the illustrations.

The features he described were exotic and sensual and didn't jibe with my notions of the Islamic world's reputation as repressed.

"We incorporated these ideas into the design of the Aga Khan University," Tom said, "but we've kept it all functional and on a human scale. We wanted a place where people can be impressed but not overwhelmed, a peaceful environment that promotes quiet contemplation."

"You sound like a Sufi poet," I said.

We spent the day going over the schematic drawings of the hospital and medical college, reviewing the function and layout of each space. I took extensive notes. It was information vital to the operational forecast and budget planning, and more background and detail than I had access to back in Karachi.

Earlier in my career I had worked on other major hospital design projects and it was clear that Tom was an experienced hospital architect. He also had an acute sensitivity to Pakistan's environment and culture. I left his office with a new appreciation for the thought and care that had already gone into the Aga Khan's ambitious scheme.

I called my mother before I got on the airplane to Minneapolis. "Your dad's in the hospital," she said.

My father had been frail and had been hospitalized a few times with periodic bouts of heart fibrillation and efforts to control his late-onset diabetes.

"I haven't sent you a letter yet," she said.

I went straight to my parents' house from the airport. There was a chill in the air and the fall colors were past their prime, bare branches stretching forlornly beneath the gray sky. Yellow and brown leaves covered the ground and skittered in the streets.

My mother looked worried. "He's pretty sick," she said. "It's not his heart, it's colon cancer."

"Oh, damn," I said. I had not been expecting anything so serious. He was seventy-eight years old and had been sick for years. I assumed he would just stay in a state of limbo, not getting any older or any sicker until we returned. *What was I thinking?*

"I'm really sorry Mom," I said. "We are so out-of-touch over there. We don't have a telephone yet and letters are so slow."

I made a couple of Presbyterians, Bourbon with ginger ale and soda, my mother's favorite at-home drink, and we sat in front of the fireplace and talked, and sipped, and cried. After an hour or so she said, "It's too late to see him now. But go tomorrow. Late morning is best."

I drove to my hotel; a downtown location that I thought might give me a chance to scout a venue for the interviews we planned for early next year. It now seemed too far from Mom's place. But it was close to the hospital where Dad was a patient.

Late the next morning, I stopped by my father's room. As I poked my head in, the attending nurse said, "I'm done here. He's all yours."

Dad was in an observation ward with a glass wall to the corridor and monitors pulsing above his head. An intravenous drip was stuck in his arm. He was lying on his side, awake, but looking at the wall. "Who is it?" he asked, with a weak voice.

"It's me, Bob, your number one son."

I heard a quiet gasp and I saw his shoulders shake. With some effort he rolled over on his back, looked at me and smiled. "Thanks for coming," he said. "I'm glad you're here."

For ten minutes, with determination that surprised me, he brushed off my questions and peppered me with his own on Pakistan and my new job. "How do you like it there? How's Sue? Tell her thanks for the letters. How are the kids doing? Are they treating you right at work?"

After his questions were satisfied, we settled into reminiscing about our lives together as father and son.

"I remember a time we were driving from Minneapolis down to Spring Valley, to the farm, just you and me," I said. "We stopped at a cheese store and you asked the salesman if the limburger cheese was ripe. I remember his drawl, 'Mister, ain't nothing more gonna happen to that cheese.' You bought a sizeable chunk and the car stunk for a month. Mom thought something died in there."

Dad nodded his head. "Maybe it was the same trip. You were twelve or thirteen, painting the chicken coop, and you told me you knew why I wanted you to go to school."

"How could I forget? It was a hundred degrees in the shade and I was sure I didn't want to do that the rest of my life. You should have been ashamed of yourself, abusing the child labor laws like that."

He chuckled. "It was good for you."

"Do you remember the first time you took me pheasant hunting out at Buffalo Lake?" I asked.

"I let you use a single-shot 22 loaded with BB shot."

"I thought I was big stuff."

Dad was kind-hearted but taciturn. At times I'm not much

different, a product of my less than effusive Scandinavian/English/ German heritage. But that morning we had a better conversation than we'd ever had, except about business. We laughed and cried together until I could see his eyes droop.

"I'll see you tomorrow," I said, but he was already asleep.

That afternoon I called Sue's folks and invited them out to dinner, a little Chinese restaurant that was one of their favorites. I was disappointed when they declined, but Adelle asked if I'd pick up some take-out on my way to their place. When I arrived, Adelle met me at the door and gave me a hug. "How's your dad?" she asked, as she took the bag of food from my hand. "Wait, let me dish this up and you can tell us both. Go talk to your father-in-law for a minute."

Nate was in his bathrobe and looked pallid. "How you doing?" I asked.

"Good," he said, but his voice lacked its usual sonority. "I'm due for dialysis tomorrow, so I'm a little slow. I really don't like this."

I was about to press further when Adelle called us to the table. I'd always known them to relish eating but now they picked at their food. I told them about my father but didn't dwell on his illness; they both seemed so down already.

I changed the subject. "Here's a letter from your daughter. It will bring you up to date." Adelle took it and set it aside.

"You know," I continued, "we are all doing really well. I'm sorry we're so far away. When we get a telephone we'll be able to talk more often." I also told them that I thought the move had been good for Sue and me. Sue and I didn't often discuss our relationship, but I thought the adventure of it all, our struggling together in a challenging place, had brought us closer together. It *felt* right.

I paused. They didn't respond except to nod their heads. "Jennifer's got a boyfriend," I said.

That caught their attention. "Where's he from?" Nate asked.

"Good question," I said. "He's American, but his folks are in the foreign service, and in his whole life he's only lived in the States for a couple of years."

"Where does he call home?" Adelle asked.

"He's adopted Texas, he says. He's never lived there but it seems as good as any. Maybe it's because they have a strong football tradition. Jennifer's also working on a school play, *Blithe Spirit*."

"Is she acting?" asked Adelle.

"No, she's working on the set design, and really enjoying it."

Nate and Adelle nodded their heads but didn't say more.

"David's at the school pool a lot and he's become a pretty good swimmer. He's also joined the Boy Scouts."

"They have Boy Scouts over there?" Nate said, a quizzical look on his face.

"Sure, why not? It's for the boys at the American school. I said I'd help out at Scout meetings."

They seemed pleased to hear about the kids but it was disconcerting to see their lack of spark. They were usually more animated. I was disconnected myself, my father's illness weighing heavy in my thoughts. I wasn't very well tuned to Nate and Adelle's needs that evening. They were both obviously depressed but I didn't offer them much support.

The next morning I went back to visit my dad, to pick up where we left off. After an hour of more reminiscing, I said, "I'm scheduled to leave early tomorrow. I'm thinking I should stay a little longer."

"No." he said. "You've got a family waiting for you and a life to lead. Get on with it."

I was taken aback. He was so emphatic.

"Did I ever thank you for being a great dad?"

"Yes, a few times, one way or another. You've been a good son."

"I love you," I said as I kissed him on the forehead.

"I love you too," he said. I knew he did, but I think it was the first time I'd heard him say so.

It was an interminable flight back to Pakistan. I arrived in Karachi in the middle of the night, expecting to be assaulted by the sultry heat. But when I stepped off the airplane I was greeted by a cool and dry breeze, a welcome change of season that had arrived while I was out of town.

Sohir met me at the airport and drove me home. I crawled into bed. Sue acknowledged my return with a mumbled, "Hi," and went back to sleep. I lay awake staring at the ceiling, listening to the chirps of a gecko that had staked out our bedroom window as its territory, until jet lag and exhaustion overwhelmed me.

Over breakfast I told Sue and the kids about my dad. That day Sue and Jennifer wrote him letters.

Sue told me what she had written. She said she had always been grateful to my father for how he had welcomed her into the Taylor family. She wrote how helpless she felt being so far away and hoped he could feel the "love messages" we were sending out from the other side of the world. She noted the many good times they had shared.

Jennifer wrote, "I remember when we went to Moose Lake for the weekend last year. I really enjoyed myself, mainly because I got a chance to know you a little better. I hadn't known you had a farm before, and the stories you told were really interesting." She added, "It means a lot to know that whatever choices I make you will still love me and not pass judgment."

With colored pens, David made a get well card. It had a checkerboard on the front as a reminder of the game they played together. Inside he drew a red heart pierced with arrows and wrote, "I Love You."

We sent the letters and card by Pakistani mail because we didn't know anyone who was traveling to the States anytime soon.

A few days later, in the first week of November, too soon for our mail to have arrived in the States, we got a telex that Dad had died. I had a hard time understanding what had happened. I'd gone from not knowing he was really sick, to his dying, in just a few days. The gap between Minneapolis and Karachi was not just distance, it was time. Communication was painfully infrequent and slow.

We were so wrapped up in living our new lives that I expected everything back in Minnesota to stay the same, unchanging. I wrote my mother, "It's difficult for us to really feel that he's gone because, in so many ways, we feel we're the ones who have gone, and that all of you will be there when we return."

Jennifer wrote a poem, "Grandfather:"[15]

> It's funny to remember with a start
> One I loved not so long ago
> His wrinkled lips puckered in greeting
> And I tried to learn so much
> But never spent enough time
> He sat quietly—unobtrusive
> While we noisily ran about,
> But now I know his chair is empty
> And not that much remains.
> Oh, Grandfather, where are the memories
> Of an entire childhood,
> And where did your innovations flee
> When no longer sitting.
> You were sent to lie
> Under conifer branches swaying.

We didn't go back to Minnesota for the funeral, a decision I still regret. Dad and I had said our goodbyes and I was at peace with that. Still, I felt uneasy for not staying on in Minneapolis a few more days. Going back for the funeral would have given Sue and me the chance to reaffirm our relationship, to reestablish our place in our larger family, and to answer everyone's questions about our new life. We should have been there.

# 17

## CHILDREN OF ABRAHAM

"My condolences on the loss of your father," Aziz said.

"Thank you. I'm glad I had the chance to see him before he died. I'm going to miss him."

"You know this is a time of mourning, the first week of Muharram. Muslims mourn the martyrdom of Imam Hussain, the Prophet's grandson."

"We were warned not to go downtown," I said, "something about demonstrations and tensions running high."

"It is good that you are cautious," Aziz explained. "During Muharram, some Shiits march in the streets and flagellate themselves with sharp knives or slap their chests with their hands until they bleed. It can go on for days. Sunnis mock the marchers and fights break out. Sometimes the fervor gets out of hand."

"Fervor I've heard of," I mumbled, "unprecedented fervor, actually."

Aziz looked puzzled but I didn't bother to explain. "I've read about the animosity between Sunnis and Shias," I said. "They're both Muslim, but what's your take?"

"Yes, you are right," said Aziz. "But belief in the one God has not been any more of a unifying force for Muslims than it has been for Christians or Jews. The split started shortly after the Prophet's death, with a dispute over who should be his successor. It was complicated by the fact that Mohammad, peace be upon him, had no sons, only daughters. The result was two broad denominations, Shia and Sunni.[16] And there are sub-groups in each. We Ismailis are Shia, for example, but we are different from other Shia. It is like Christians, isn't it. How many protestant denominations are there?"

I had heard that some Muslims thought Ismailis were so progressive they weren't really Muslim. I was sympathetic. Some people felt the same about Unitarian Universalists, that we didn't have dogma. We were too liberal and not really a religion.

We had been in Pakistan a short time and I was only beginning to learn about Muslim history and traditions. And ever since Nazia gave me that strange desk calendar, I wanted to know more about the Muslim holidays.

"I know the Islamic year is based on a lunar calendar," I said to Aziz. "But I'm confused. Every time I turn around, there seems to be another holiday."

"Every year the holidays fall on different dates, based on phases of the moon. Now it is Muharram, the start of the New Year. Our holiest month is Ramazan.[17] This year it was in July, before you got here. Next year it will start eleven days earlier, sometime in June. It is a month of fasting and charity—one of the pillars of our faith. We are to experience the hunger of the poor and then give generously to charity."

"You can't fast for a month."

Aziz looked amused. "No, no," he said. "We fast all day, from sunrise to sunset. We take nothing by mouth—no food, no drink, no smoking. We break fast after sundown. There are many dinner parties." He tilted his head upward as if capturing a thought floating near the ceiling. "It is all very practical, isn't it, but sometimes not too much work gets done."

"Ramazan ends with Eid," he continued, "a day of prayer and celebration."

"Wait," I said. "Didn't we celebrate Eid just a few weeks ago? I got several Eid Mubarak cards."

"Eid means festival, so there are many. The Eid after Ramazan is Eid ul-Fitr and only lasts one day. The one last month was Eid al-Adha, the Festival of Sacrifice. That was the Greater Eid. It is like your Thanksgiving. Each family sacrifices a goat, or some other animal, depending on their wealth."

For several days, driving home from work, I had seen men at the curb selling young goats, half a dozen tethered together, frightened and silent. Each kid's coat had been sprayed with a splash of iridescent paint, a branding, I guessed.

"It is acting out the story of God testing Abraham by commanding him to sacrifice his own son. As Abraham is about to obey, God tells him he can sacrifice a goat instead. It's right out of the Old Testament."

I wasn't surprised to hear Aziz cite the Bible. Mohammad had given a lot of respect to the earlier prophets such as Abraham, Moses, and Jesus. In essence, Christians, Jews, and Muslims worshiped the same God, all children of Abraham. They just didn't agree on how to do it.

Our own American holiday season, our first away from home, was fast approaching.

A precursor to the holidays was the Marine Ball, a celebration of the founding of the United States Marine Corps on November 10, 1775. Formal dinner parties are thrown in every city where Marines are stationed, including Karachi, where the Corps provided security for the American Consulate.

The Karachi Marine Ball was held in the gardens of the Counsel General's residence and Sue and I were among two-hundred invited guests, U.S. officials and business people. The grand estate was elaborately decorated with strings of colored lights and green up-lighters shining into the high fronds of a row of towering royal palms. The guests were dressed in their finest and Sue looked resplendent in a long silk dress. It was our first formal party and I didn't have a tuxedo. Even in my best dark suit, I felt a little under-dressed and I vowed to have a tux made before the next invitation arrived. I could have one tailored in one of the local shops for the price of a pair of slacks back in the States. Whatever the cost, I didn't dare usurp that much of our *dherzi's* scarce time.

After an elegant sit-down dinner, Sue and I headed for the tennis court dance floor where we swayed and jived to the music of an excellent expatriate band. "This is nice," I said, as we finished a slow number.

"Hm," Sue replied, her head on my shoulder.

During the next set, as the band played an old rock and roll tune from our high school years, Tony and Nana Horton joined us. "Oh," Sue said, after watching them for a moment, "you dance just like us." That evening we cemented our growing friendship, shuffling our feet on the concrete court. We craned our necks in awe at the nearly full Pakistani moon, and helped each other pick out faint but familiar star clusters in the unfamiliar southern sky.

The next morning over breakfast I was disoriented. "I have this hollow feeling," I said. "I feel like I'm supposed to call home and talk to my dad. I don't think I've had more than two telephone conversations with him in my life, it's always my mom. It's strange, now I wish I could."

"Let's try to get through to your mom this evening," Sue offered. "If we're lucky, maybe we can reach my folks too. Our friends said we can use their phone whenever we want. I'll send Sohir over to their place with a note after he drops you and the children."

Every week or so, we asked our friends if we could come by to use their telephone. We spent the evening with them, enjoying their company, while we alternated using their rotary phone. We repeatedly dialed a long string of numbers; listening eagerly for the telltale clicks and hisses that preceded the hollow sound of a distant telephone coming alive. If I got a ring, I counted them like Lily Tomlin's Ernestine, "One ringy-dingy, two ringy-dingy," each ring increasing my optimism for a successful connection. We got through about half the time.

When Sohir picked me up that evening, he had a note from our friends saying we were welcome to come. We went to their place after dinner, all four of us taking turns dialing. We tried for more than an hour but we couldn't make a connection.

# 18

# THE AGA KHAN'S LOFTY
# EXPECTATIONS

The Sunday before Thanksgiving I was up in Islamabad, sitting in the vast hall of parliament. The cavernous space accentuated the hollowness I'd felt since my father's death.

I was attending a conference co-sponsored by the Aga Khan Foundation and the World Health Organization. A banner stretched across the front of the auditorium: "The Role of the Hospital in Primary Care." The work sessions were to be held in Karachi but the Aga Khan had flown a hundred guests into Islamabad, a thousand miles to the north, just so President Zia-ul-Haq could address the opening ceremonies.

The Aga Khan and several of his cohorts had arrived from Paris and Geneva. Heavy-hitters from the World Health Organization, WHO, were on the podium and scattered among the audience. The Pakistan Minister of Health was there, along with several of his staff. Representatives of the military, and the military health services, sat in the audience in their crisp ribboned uniforms. It seemed like an exorbitant expense for the Aga Khan to bring all this classy company together, but having recognition from the national government and a nod from WHO were seen as prestigious and strategic endorsements for the Project.

President Zia, dressed in a light-colored tunic with a Nehru collar, kicked off the program. It was the first time I had seen Zia in person. With his dark, deep-set eyes, and black slicked-back hair, he reminded me of a movie villain from an old black and white melo-drama. I wouldn't have been surprised to see him twist the end of his mustache if somebody in the audience failed to nod appreciatively. He was shorter than I expected; a Napoleonic presence. Zulfikar Ali Bhutto had appointed Zia Chief of Staff of the Army because he thought Zia was harmless. Zia returned the favor by hijacking the elected government and hanging Bhutto. *Be careful whom you allow to drive a big truck.*

Zia spoke in English, complimenting the Aga Khan for his fore-sight and commitment to all the people of Pakistan. When he fin-ished, he was applauded enthusiastically. He turned from the podium and was embraced by the Aga Khan as a swarm of journalists popped flashbulbs to record the event for posterity.

As the Aga Khan assumed the podium, I realized it was the first time I'd seen him in seven months, since my brief introduction at his estate at Aiglemont. He seemed regal, taller somehow; although I knew he was only about my height, five-ten or so. He too was dressed in a light-colored tunic, the formal attire for Pakistan's high society.

The Aga Khan was a complex man. He was born in Geneva, Switzerland, but was a true cosmopolitan, a citizen of the world. He was revered by his followers and a respected statesman, but he stayed out of politics. His work in education and healthcare convinced me he was committed to doing good in the world. He also lived big, like the wealthy businessman that he was, with a stable of race horses he inherited from his grandfather, Italian racing yachts, and an array of grand estates and luxurious retreats scattered near Paris, Geneva, and Sardinia and who knew where else. I'd heard he was demanding and unrelenting in his expectations, but so far I hadn't experienced those traits personally. I still had a lot to learn about him.

His Highness was energized by the crowd. He said Zia's pres-ence confirmed the President's commitment to improving health care delivery. He thanked the President for encouraging the exten-sion of the Aga Khan's health services into the most remote parts of Pakistan, as well as the creation of the new Aga Khan University of Health Sciences. "As the Imam of a Muslim community spread over twenty countries," His Highness said, "I have, of necessity, become something of a student of health care. To me, basic health, education and housing are crucial stepping stones in the process of personal and national self-realization and growth."[18]

Dr. Henry Mahler, the Director General of WHO, had been a prime mover in developing the declaration, "Health for All by the Year 2000," that emerged from a 1978 Primary Health Conference held in Alma Ata in Kazakhstan. He commended the Aga Khan for supporting a network of primary care clinics in five countries. He described the sorry state of health care in so many parts of the world, the unnecessary deaths of delivering mothers and their newborns, and the untimely deaths of young children from dehydration, malaria, and infectious diseases. He diplomatically noted Pakistan's progress in fighting polio and tuberculosis, but pushed for more to be done. He applauded the Aga Khan for his efforts to help address these critical needs, and for his effort to train nurses and to emphasize primary care in the new medical college.[19]

Mahler's remarks added substance to my growing job description. I had spent several days before the conference helping Shamsh draft a report he would deliver when the conference moved back to Karachi. I was glad to help and it proved a useful exercise—I learned a lot about health care in Pakistan, the ambitious plans for the Aga Khan University, and the challenges I faced in commissioning the hospital.

I knew Pakistan's health system was an example of chronic government neglect, a criticism Mahler had leveled at many developing countries. Pakistan had a few better financed government hospitals, mostly military, but community hospitals and clinics were consistently under-funded. There were only a handful of private hospitals, mostly small, with limited services. Urban areas were better served than rural, but that wasn't saying much. Many rural areas weren't served at all. The net result was deplorable maternal and infant mortality statistics. I had heard reports that in some regions in the north a newborn's umbilical cord was severed by pounding it between two stones—too often resulting in tetanus and death. In some remote areas, goiter was endemic, a swelling of the thyroid resulting from no iodine in the diet. A century earlier, goiter had been prevalent in America too—until iodized salt was introduced.

I was convinced there was room for an institution like the Aga Khan Hospital, a place that would provide quality inpatient services and could play a role in supporting primary health care services. I knew we were building comprehensive outpatient facilities and planned to serve the poor as well as those who could pay. But it is one thing to build impressive facilities with the potential for great things. It is quite another to create an institution that would think and behave differently than most other hospitals in the world. It was going to take a long-term commitment, and a continuing source of money, to make all the Aga Khan's up-front investments more than just nice architecture.

At lunch, I sat with Cheves and Winnie.

"Hospitals don't get much respect among these World Health folks," I said.

"WHO is devoted to primary care," Cheves said. "Mahler and the others think hospitals get all the money and have the power, and primary care gets the leftovers."

Winnie leaned forward. "They're right. Some of the money could be better used to support basic health services that serve more people, such as immunization, child care, and maternal health. We want our nursing students to understand all that, so we give them experience working in the poor sections of Karachi; even in some of those squatter villages you've seen."

"It will be the same with the medical school," Cheves interjected. "We want our medical students to understand the importance of primary care. But it's going to be a struggle to get them into general practice. Our graduates will be the best trained in Pakistan and they'll be able to pick their residencies anywhere in the world. Most will want to go into a medical specialty, because that's where the money is. You can't blame them. We hope they stay sympathetic to primary care."

That afternoon we all flew back to Karachi for four more days of presentations and work sessions. The Aga Khan was generous in inviting some of the most notable names in health, but demanding in his expectations. Over the week, I spent long hours monitoring several work groups that were developing recommendations on how the new medical center, the hospital I was supposed to commission, could fulfill its potential in supporting the development and delivery of primary health care services.

The implications gave me palpitations. My job was to figure out how the Aga Khan's lofty expectations could be converted into a functioning hospital, an institution that performed in a manner and at a level unprecedented on the subcontinent. I hadn't realized how remarkable the culture was back at Hennepin County Medical Center—a super-specialty teaching hospital that also emphasized outpatient services and served as a safety net for the poor. As part of my previous job I had been responsible for a handful of clinics that targeted poor neighborhoods in the Greater Minneapolis area. Could I help create that kind of culture here, at the Aga Khan Hospital?

At the closing session of the conference, Thanksgiving Day on the American calendar, His Highness commended the participants for their hard work and the quality of their recommendations. He noted that the Aga Khan Health Services, because it included both hospitals and a broad system of rural health clinics, had a unique opportunity and obligation to lead the way in bridging the gap between hospitals and primary care.[20]

Was he looking at me when he said that?

I was no longer feeling hollow when I went home that afternoon. Dad would have been proud. He had great respect for painting chicken coops, but would have thought building a grand hospital in a poor country was also worthwhile.

Still, I had a lingering sense of disquiet. The challenges I faced were daunting.

# 19 | HOLIDAYS INTERRUPTED

I had flown back from Islamabad the Monday before Thanksgiving. I arrived at the house just in time to greet Peter carrying several rag-tag strings of colored light bulbs. Also, to my dismay, he had a five foot high white star made from parchment stretched over a wooden frame.

The overt celebration of non-Muslim religious holidays was not much favored in Pakistan, and the public display of non-Muslim religious symbols was illegal. As a result, Christian and Jewish expatriates from America and Europe did most of their celebrations in closed venues: private homes, churches, and hotels.

Even so, it wasn't uncommon for houses and restaurants and office buildings to be strung with lights in celebration of one Muslim holiday or another, so I thought we could get by with a tasteful, understated display at our home.

"Our son made the star for you and Memsahib," said Peter. "It lights up."

"Thank you," I said, biting my tongue. *So much for understated.* With the high walls surrounding our house, not much would show to the street anyway.

Early the next evening, as Sue and I dressed for a reception honoring conference delegates, Peter and his son hung the star and strung the lights around the house. Using duct tape, they secured everything to the ledge that surrounded the house just below the second story windows.

"Robert, Sahib, come see the lights," called Peter. I joined him in the yard as his son switched on the power. The star glowed softly in the rapidly fading daylight.

Only half the lights came on. Peter and I were talking about how to fix the problem when we heard a sharp crack, like a stick breaking, from up on the ledge. Instantly, the star and the colored lights, and every light in the house, went dark.

"Oh shit," I said, and ran into the house and upstairs to David's room and out the window to the ledge. David was flat on his back. The acrid smell of ozone and burnt insulation was in the air.

"David!" I yelled, as I kneeled down beside him, my heart pounding.

His eyes fluttered open and he looked up at me. "Wow," he said, his voice slurred. "I got zapped."

"Are you all right?" I asked, with as much calm as I could manage.

"Yeah, I think so." He sat up and studied his hands. "My fingers hurt."

Even in the dim light I could see blisters on his finger tips. "Anything else?"

"No, I think I'm okay."

"Look at me." I held up three fingers. "How many?"

"Three."

"Can you stand?"

He got to his feet but was a bit unsteady.

"I saw some lights were out," he explained. "I saw two wires and I wanted to help, so I picked up one in each hand."

I put an arm around his shoulder.

"I felt a shock down to my feet but I couldn't let go. I couldn't help it. I curled up in a ball. Then everything went black."

I held his arm as we climbed back through the window. Sue was in the darkening hallway. "What happened?" she asked. "I'm trying to put on my makeup and all the lights went out."

"There's been an accident," I said. "David almost got electrocuted."

Sue reached out her hand toward David. "Are you all right?" she asked.

"I'm fine, Mom," David said, dropping his eyes to look at his fingers.

I walked David downstairs and into the kitchen. Peter was lighting candles and had found a flashlight and the box of fuses left by our contractor, Sadiq.

As David retold his story to Peter and Margaret, I took the flashlight and checked the fuse cabinet. Nearly every fuse was blown. With each fresh fuse I took out of the box, I blessed Sadiq's Muslim soul. And for good measure, *Bless Mohammed, may peace be with him.*

The lights back on, I returned to the kitchen and sat down heavily on a chair, suddenly feeling like I had been run over by a silver-toothed Pakistani truck. For a moment I couldn't speak, my voice caught behind the pomegranate-sized lump in my throat. I finally croaked, "David, let's bandage those fingers."

The next evening, the outdoor lights now successfully aglow, we assembled and decorated our plastic Christmas tree—a little early in the season, but we wanted the house to look festive for Thanksgiving. We had shipped the tree over in a box, along with strings of lights, a transformer, and a few ornaments of sentimental value we thought would survive the trip.

David pulled branches from the box with his bandaged fingers while Jennifer straightened needle clusters and bent each stem into a graceful arch. Sue sorted the branches by length, handing them to me as I inserted them into holes drilled in the wood trunk firmly clamped in a red and green stand. We ate popcorn, drank warm apple cider, and listened to a Bing Crosby tape playing on David's boom-box.

We took turns hanging ghosts of Christmases past on the tree. Sue attached a green wire hook to her old ski season pass from our year in Vail. David hung a miniature knitted ski cap with "Colorado" sewn into its brim. Jennifer hung a glass ball that had been given to her by Sue's folks. I hung a string of small oriental lantern lights that had adorned my mother's tree for years.

Sue and I were both raised in households that celebrated the holidays with gusto and we loved the tradition and inspiring imagery. As Unitarian Universalists, we were more humanists than Christians but we celebrated all the holidays even if we sometimes interpreted their messages with a different bent.

Sue's father was a non-practicing Jew and her mother a lapsed Norwegian Lutheran. In addition to Christmas, we celebrated an occasional Passover and kept a menorah around the house as a nod to Chanukah, a reminder to rededicate ourselves to family and friends.

We loved the Christmas story legend, the birth of every child a celebration of hope, the true miracle of the holiday. I had always been tantalized by the twenty-fifth of December, an auspicious day in pagan tradition. It's the first day after the winter solstice that you can see that the sun has stopped its retreat. The promise of spring's new life *will* come around again. No wonder it was chosen as the symbolic birthday of Jesus. Conveniently, December twenty-fifth was also celebrated in Pakistan as the birthday of Mohammad Ali Jinnah, father of the country.

When we finished decorating, our house looked like my mother's place—a Norman Rockwell scene from a thirty-year holiday tradition, except for the Bedouin kilim Sue circled around the base of the tree waiting an accumulation of gaily wrapped packages.

The evening before Thanksgiving, I headed home after a full day of conference meetings. When Sohir picked up the kids at school, I was feeling melancholy. I was staring out the car window daydreaming when we stopped at an intersection and my attention was drawn to a woman sitting next to the roadway. Her head was hooded by a dark shawl, her eyes cast down toward the ground where a baby lay dirty and crying. She held out her hands, palms up, the universal request for alms.

I had seen her before but hadn't paid her much mind. "Look there," I said as I pointed out the woman to Jennifer and David. "Have you noticed her before?"

"She's there almost every day," Jennifer said. "I wrote a poem about her. It's called 'The Beggar.'"[21] When we got home she read it to me:

*As black as death*
*The shapeless figure squats*
*In eternal mourning.*
*Her outstretched palms*
*Scream in pain*
*For the face no one will see,*
*Allowing her to claw into me*
*And nuzzle her heavy*
*Darkness*
*In my chest.*

"I didn't know you were so moved," I said.

"My photography teacher has been helping me see things," she said. "And I've been writing more. One of my teachers suggested I publish a book of my poetry. He said I can use my photographs and my book as part of my college application when the time comes."

"If this is an example, you'll get in anywhere you want."

For Thanksgiving, we invited a few of our new expatriate friends, plus a couple of young American servicemen stationed aboard a ship in the Karachi harbor, for as close to a traditional meal as Sue and Peter could muster.

Peter couldn't find a turkey in the market so he bought two chickens. Sue found canned corn and retrieved a can of cranberry sauce and a bag of wild rice she'd directed me to pick up on my trip to the States. Peter prepared mashed potatoes and baked a couple of authentic American apple pies using a traditional Betty Crocker recipe, substituting Crisco for non-existent lard in the crust.

We all sat on our newly delivered chairs, around our newly delivered dining room table, praising the fine food and taking turns telling stories of thankfulness and reminiscing about absent and lost loved ones.

"Most of you know that my dad died a couple of weeks ago," I said, raising my glass of wine. We'd gotten a bottle as a gift from the Hortons. "I want to toast to him. He was a good man and lived a good life." *All of us here have a better life than we know,* I thought, as an image of that woman begging on the street floated behind my eyes.

David said he wanted a dog for Christmas. I thought he'd ask for a bike to replace the one that had been stolen before we left Minnesota, but there wasn't anyplace in the Defence neighborhood where he could ride.

"A dog? Well, why not," said his mother.

"What about your allergies?" I asked her.

"We have an enclosed yard," she said. "It wouldn't need to live in the house so I should be okay. I'll ask around. Somebody must know where we can find a puppy."

A few days later, David, Sue and I stood outside the gate of a house being barked at by an angry looking bitch, obviously still nursing, and who was, praise god, inside the compound. We were told the home owner had puppies for sale and we showed up unannounced—there was no way to call ahead.

The owner came to the gate and we told him our interest in the puppies. He nodded his head and snapped a leash on the dog's collar "Sorry for the barking," he said.

If any of us had a clue about dogs, we might have been more attentive to the bitch's pi-dog heritage and gnarly personality.

David picked out a cute puppy with a white coat dappled with tan—all puppies are cute it seems, a pact with the devil. David named her Carrie, after a girl friend of Jennifer's back in Minneapolis who I think he had a crush on. I knew it was also the name of a Stephen King novel, but I didn't say anything.

Mid-December, the American Women's Club threw a formal holiday party at the Counsel General's house and invited every American in town. The grand residence was even more elaborately decorated than for the Marine Ball, with pine wreaths and colored lights and several Christmas trees hung with silver and red bows and twinkling glass ornaments. Sue looked radiant in a long gown trimmed in gold sequins. I looked proud in my new tuxedo. I had picked out the style from a thumb-worn magazine at the tailor's shop. As we posed in front of a Christmas tree, the photographer on duty said, "You're a fine looking couple."

A few days later, as we made plans for Christmas and a short family vacation, we received a Telex from Stuart Hanson, my brother-in-law, every word printed in capital letters as if he were shouting, "NATE IS IN A COMA. WE THINK YOU SHOULD COME HOME."

We knew Nate was struggling, but we weren't prepared for the news. *Could I have seen this coming if I'd been paying closer attention when I saw him back in Minneapolis?*

We visited our friends who had a telephone to call Stuart. "I hope we get through," Sue said. Her hands were shaking and I offered to dial. Stuart was a highly respected physician in Minneapolis. He didn't doctor anyone in the family but he kept track of everybody's health status. I was relieved when the call connected and I immediately gave the receiver to Sue.

"Yes," Stuart told her, "Nate is in the hospital and is still unconscious. Your mom is worried sick."

"We'll make arrangements right away," Sue said before hanging up, a stricken look on her face. "We can't lose both our fathers like this, can we? I need to go back."

"We'll all go," I said.

Sue flew to Minneapolis the next day. The rest of us followed a couple of days later, flying straight through, three flights and twenty-three hours. We arrived late into Minneapolis, jet weary and anxious.

Sue was blurry eyed and exhausted. "I've hardly slept since I left Karachi. Dad's awake but he almost died. Mom's mad at him for not taking care of himself. He's not eating right. Mom complains to me but she's so angry she won't talk to him."

We stayed the night at Sue's folks' place and the next morning visited with her mom. Adelle echoed what Sue had said. "He doesn't take care of himself," she said as she looked down at her lap and wrung her fingers. The skin on the back of her hands was spotted, thin and transparent. I had never seen her look so fragile. She raised her gaze to ours, her eyes damp. "He's better. You need to go see him."

We went from the house straight to the hospital. Nate was sitting up in bed reading the newspaper. His color was good and his normal resonant voice was near full strength. "I guess I had a close call," he said. Sue let out a sigh and went over and kissed him on the cheek.

That evening we visited Stuart and my sister, Gail. "Nate kind of did it to himself," Stuart said. "He has not been careful with his diet and he hasn't been keeping his fluids up. His blood got toxic. I think he's fighting dialysis. It doesn't help that he's still smoking."

After we got back to our room, Sue said, "I don't blame Mom for being angry. It's almost like Dad did this thing on purpose."

I was thinking the same thing. I remembered my abbreviated conversation with Nate a few weeks before. Nate had always been socially garrulous, most alive when he had a drink in one hand and a cigarette in the other, working the crowd at whatever gathering he attended. Sitting at home was not his style and I had never known him to favor television. He had told me he didn't like dialysis, but I hadn't opened myself to listen more carefully. I'd been too tied up with my dad's illness.

"It's possible," I said to Sue. "But that's a pretty drastic measure. It could be a cry for help."

"I know, and it frightens me. And then I get angry with him for scaring Mom like that, and for scaring me too."

When we visited my mother she told us, "We got your letters after Dad died. We all read them. It was as if you were here. We were really touched."

"I'm glad," I said. "I wasn't sure they'd get here at all. A few weeks ago they arrested a postal worker in Karachi who had been hording undelivered mail in his yard. We try to send letters with friends."

Mom handed me Sue's letter. I opened it and absentmindedly scanned the pages. I choked up as I read a passage Sue hadn't told me about, "This peculiar move of ours has been a good one for us as a family," she wrote. "We needed a change in space and lifestyle and this choice appears to be a healthy one for all of us. I thought you might feel better if you knew we are all doing well and that Bob is being cared for."

I reached out and took Sue's hand and looked into her eyes. She smiled and squeezed my fingers.

When Nate stabilized, David and I flew back home. I was delighted to have a little time with my son, just the two of us. It turned out to be an adventure. Waiting for our connecting flight out of Chicago, we watched a panel truck get tossed off its wheels in the backwash of a taxiing jet. "Awesome," David said, as the truck settled on its side and the driver climbed out the door window, apparently unhurt. The driver stood looking at his topsy-turvy truck, scratching his head.

On the white-knuckle flight into New York, we started our descent in a thunderstorm, the airplane bucking and swaying. On our final approach there was a bright flash of light and a deafening crack of thunder. The airplane lurched and I threw my arm across David's chest, just like my mother used to do when I sat in the car at her side, in the days before seatbelts. "Awesome," David said again.

We caught a 747 out of New York headed for Frankfurt. Halfway across the Atlantic, just past the point of no return, we felt a jolt as one of the jet engines flamed out. The pilot announced, "We've lost one engine, but please don't be alarmed. This airplane can fly just as well on three engines as it does on four. We are continuing on into Frankfurt."

*Stay calm for David.*

David tapped me on the arm. "Dad, he could have said it flies as well on two engines as it does on four."

"You're already a seasoned traveler," I said. "I didn't take my first flight until I was twenty-one."

"Was it a bi-plane?" David asked.

"The whole world hates a smart ass," I said, mussing his hair.

"You should talk," he said, moving quickly to the far side of his seat to avoid any blow that might come his way.

Sue and Jennifer stayed on in Minneapolis another two weeks, and it's a good thing. Jennifer had not been feeling well when she got there. A day or so after David and I left she was diagnosed with mononucleosis.

She was still dragging when she returned to Karachi in mid-January and suffered more than usual from jetlag, sleeping a good part of five days in a row.

"Isn't mono the kissing disease?" I asked her.

"Oh Dad," she said, without further explanation, and went back to sleep.

With rest and medication, she was back on her feet in a week and already caught up on her missed homework. She was six pounds lighter, still sluggish, but clearly on the mend.

Jennifer and David were both glad to be back at school, in part because of the warm welcome home they received from their friends.

Sue came back emotionally spent. "I feel conflicted for being so distant from my folks and so unreachable," she said, "but I am so relieved to be back in Karachi."

She bit her lower lip and winced.

"You look like you're in pain," I said.

"It's menstrual cramps. They're just a little worse than usual."

She dismissed the problem, much more upset about her parents.

I was glad we were all back in Karachi. I looked forward to several weeks at home—together with family, in our own space, in our own house, before my recruitment trip to Canada and the States.

# 20

# CHEESECAKE AND PURDAH

"I love cheesecake," said Zaher Lalani as he took another bite of his dessert. Actually, it was my dessert, a three-inch square of creamy confection with a graham cracker crust sitting in a shallow cup. He had finished his and, in response to his puppy dog glances at my tray, I offered him mine. It was early February, 1982, and we were on a flight to Toronto, the first leg of our recruitment tour.

Our visit to Toronto didn't start out well. We rented a car at the airport and Zaher asked if I would drive. I said, "Sure," and opened the door and got in on the passenger side. "Right," I mumbled, recalibrating my mind to switching back to driving on the right. I got out and walked around to the driver's door as Zaher watched with a benign smile on his face. I started to back out of the parking space and scraped the car's front left fender against a concrete column.

"Let me start over," I said, as Zaher remained diplomatically silent. It took us a little extra time to drive to our hotel because of my now overcompensating caution. *Stay to the right, stupid,* I repeated to myself every half block.

That evening we ate dinner at the hotel, overwhelmed by an extravagantly rich, luscious and diversified buffet. We gorged ourselves on foods forbidden in Pakistan: cold salads and fresh vegetables. We filled our plates with lasagna and chicken Kiev. We returned for seconds of rare roast beef and fresh asparagus.

"Where do they get all this stuff," I said, shaking my head in wonderment.

Too soon I was stuffed, but Zaher took two pieces of cheesecake from the dessert table, one with a blueberry sauce, the other with cherry. "I *really* love cheesecake," he said.

"So it seems," I said, as he licked the last dollop from his spoon and I watched his eyes dart back to the dessert table.

"Why Toronto?" I asked Zaher, as we lingered over coffee the next morning.

"A lot of Muslims, and a lot of Ismailis, have settled in this area; across the border in Detroit too," he explained. "There are several hundred thousand Muslims in Canada and the States—maybe a hundred thousand Ismailis. They're scattered all over but the biggest concentrations are in New York, Chicago, Vancouver, and here in Toronto. Canada was especially hospitable when the Ismailis were forced out of Uganda by Idi Amin, back in 1972. His Highness worked with Prime Minister Pierre Trudeau to help ease the immigration."

"That explains why your associates have done such a good job lining up candidates." We had several promising prospects for a couple of key management positions, plus a few doctors who were considering returning to Pakistan and wanted to know more about the Project.

Later that day, one of the doctors we interviewed told us he left Pakistan to attend medical school in Canada. He stayed on after his residency, joined a hospital-based practice, and started a family. I asked him why he wanted to return to Pakistan.

"I have been successful here but I would like to return home," he said. "But there has not been anyplace to practice good medicine over there."

His response gave me hope that we could recruit qualified repatriates: Pakistan natives who had gotten their credentials and experience elsewhere and were willing to bring their professional skills back home.

"Will the Aga Khan hospital allow non-Ismailis on the medical staff?" he asked.

"Absolutely," said Zaher. "We will serve the whole community and we need doctors of every persuasion."

"Good," he said, "very good." Then he added, "My two daughters are now twelve and ten. They were born here in Canada. I want to bring them back to Karachi so they can become good Muslim women."

That evening, over dessert, Zaher was shaking his head, a perplexed look on his face.

"What?" I asked. "Isn't the cheesecake any good?"

"It's not that," he said. "It's that doctor we talked to today. He wants to put his girls in purdah, to cover them up and confine them to the house. They've been raised in Canada and are used to all the freedoms here. His wife too. He wants to keep doing what *he* does here, but he wants to lock up his women."

"Are you saying that just because he's not an Ismaili?" I asked. "I can understand he wants his daughters to be good Muslims."

"They don't have to be in Pakistan to be good Muslims. No. I've seen it before. It's the way he talked about his daughters."

"Does that make him a poor candidate?"

"No, but I cry for those girls."

We were both quiet for a few minutes. I had an image in my head of a young girl hiding behind the partially closed door of an austere house, peering out at an empty yard surrounded by high walls. As the image faded I changed the subject. "What about that guy for personnel, the Ismaili?"

"Zahir Janmohammed?" replied Zaher.

"Yeah, Janmohammed. He seems well qualified, very personable, and he's done his homework. He already knows a lot about the Project."

"I agree." said Zaher. "But we have to be cautious. Every Ismaili would love to work for the Aga Khan. Not every Ismaili is qualified."

"You could've fooled me, based on those I've met so far."

"Janmohammed *does* look good," Zaher said. "He's a modern man, with a modern wife, living in a modern world."

"Point taken."

The next afternoon, after a round of interviews in the morning, Zaher and I were sitting in a cafeteria at the Toronto airport waiting for our flight to Minneapolis.

"Excuse me a minute," said Zaher, as he walked over to a bank of vending machines. He came back with a plastic fork and a piece of gray green cheesecake on a cardboard plate. It had a gob of blue jelly and a wilted flower of whipped cream on top.

I tried not to grimace. "I didn't know you could get cheesecake from a vending machine."

"It's one they fill from the back," explained Zaher, "an automat. They put the food in from the kitchen side. Out here, on the tray line, you open the door and take what you want to the cashier."

"How convenient." *He must have the metabolism of an Aga Khan race horse*, I thought. *I would have gained ten pounds on what he eats.*

Minneapolis was a mix of family and business. I had been home briefly over Christmas, when Nate was sick, but had to rush back. This time my mother insisted on having a party, inviting everyone over to her house for champagne.

"Champagne" might be a bit of an overstatement. For years my mother kept a case of cheap sparkling wine in an extra refrigerator in the basement. She thought it was the height of luxurious living. "You never know when someone might stop by," she said. She would instruct her guests, "Bring a snack." Her core rule was, "There's always room, when you're willing to share."

I invited Zaher to join me. I knew he'd be welcome.

I come from a big family, with two older sisters and three younger brothers. Sue's family is smaller: her parents, who didn't attend, and her one older brother, who did. You add in their spouses and significant others, and their children, and a couple of aunts, and a few close friends of the family, and you have a crowd.

I introduced Zaher to my mother, and then to another relative, and then he was gone, disappearing into the throng. It was an hour before I saw him again. There was no cheesecake to be found on my mother's table, so I thought he must have enjoyed the company. I certainly did.

Driving back to our hotel, Zaher said, "I like your family."

"I'm glad. I like them too."

Three outstanding prospects came out of our visit to Minneapolis.

John Cushing had told me months earlier, before we moved from Minnesota, "Think of me when you start hiring." He was an ideal candidate for the Associate Administrator post. In addition to his excellent experience, he had the perfect attitude and demeanor. I first met John fifteen years earlier when he served as a graduate school intern at the hospital where I was a fledgling manager. Belying his red beard, he was as gentle and kind-hearted a man as I had ever met. I had invited him grouse hunting up north, near Brainerd where my in-laws had their cabin, the one now sold. He joined the hunt with his camera and a sensitive eye. We walked leaf-covered back roads at morning light, sipping thermosed coffee and Snow Shoe Grog to ward off the chill. In the evening we sat around the fireplace reading aloud the wilderness poetry of Robert Service and the canoe-country philosophy of Sigurd Olson.

In addition to their two daughters, John and his petit and vivacious wife, Martha, had adopted two Korean boys, one of whom they named Garrison, after Garrison Keillor. John and Martha were responsible for introducing Sue and me to *A Prairie Home Companion*, early in Garrison Keillor's career, inviting us to a live performance broadcast from the Unitarian Society in Minneapolis.

Neen Lillquist was my prize candidate for nursing director. Neen was strong, able, and had a history of working in developing countries—in Brazil for the World Health Organization after graduating from nursing school. I first met Neen when she was a nursing supervisor at a Minneapolis hospital where I was an administrator. She earned the respect of the medical staff, as well as her nursing colleagues, for her intelligence and fearlessness. She was good at planning and helped coordinate our effort to improve our budgeting procedures and control costs.

She also had her ear to the ground and was a reliable source of scuttlebutt that kept me, on more than one occasion, from stepping on a land mine. I think I earned her respect when she invited me to a hurriedly called meeting of the nursing staff who were very angry with the Director of Nursing. I walked into the room and could feel the tension. I had no idea what to do so I asked, "Can you tell me what's wrong?" And then I listened for more than an hour, probing occasionally for clarity, repeating what I'd heard to assure I understood. I learned a lot in that meeting, about the value of listening when tempers are high, and it was the start of a valued friendship with Neen.

Neen's husband, Art, was laid back and unflappable, a retired automobile service manager. They lived on a small farm near Bemidji, Minnesota, where Neen ran her own consulting business working with a nearby Indian reservation as well as other clients. "Art and I are ready to travel," Neen said as we made our goodbyes.

Steve Rasmussen was a surprise. Steve was a graduate student in health administration at the University of Wisconsin and invited himself into our interview schedule after seeing a notice posted on the Wisconsin campus. He showed up on the pretense he wanted to learn more about the Project. Steve had been raised in Northern Pakistan, the son of a missionary, and spoke fluent Urdu. We didn't know where he fit in but I said, "Stop by the Project on your next visit to Pakistan. There are some people that will want to meet you."

"That went pretty well," I said, as Zaher and I sat in an airport restaurant, waiting for our flight back to Pakistan.

"I think we found some good people," he said. "I really like Cushing and Lillquist."

"I think Janmohammed is a real find, and Ismaili to boot," I added.

"I'd like to see more of this Rasmussen fellow," said Zaher.

"Me too," I said. "And we met several qualified doctors. I don't think we're going to have too much trouble recruiting when the time comes; your concerns about purdah notwithstanding."

"It's a cause for celebration. I'm going to have a piece of cheesecake."

It was the twenty-first piece of cheesecake I'd seen Zaher eat in thirteen days. He ate two more in the traveler's lounge on our layover in London.

Was that all? I never saw his bill for hotel room service.

# 21 | FROM BEHIND THE VEIL

While I was in America counting desserts, my wife and daughter were escaping purdah. Sue took Jennifer to New Delhi for her sixteenth birthday, a festive girls' holiday out-from-under the constraints of Pakistan's conservative society. Sue remembered how her folks had made her sixteenth a special occasion, a coming-out party at a local country club. Sue and several girlfriends had been dressed to the nines in strapless, full-skirted gowns. Sue didn't think she could pull off something similar in Karachi. But a trip to India would be memorable. The two women thought it would be great to spend some quality time together.

Pakistan wasn't the venue for such a celebration, but India was. Shamsh, my boss, had told us a story that illustrated the difference. "There were two dogs," he said, "one was from India and one from Pakistan. They met at the border between their two countries. The dog from India was thin, its coat infested with lice and patched with mange. The dog from Pakistan was well fed, its coat smooth. The dog from Pakistan says, 'Why are you coming to Pakistan?' The dog from India replies, 'It must be obvious. I am hungry and looking for food. But why do you want to go to India?' The dog from Pakistan says, 'Sometimes I want to bark.'"

In addition to the birthday celebration, Sue had good cause to want to bark. She was still smarting from a recent article in a local newspaper where she was characterized as a complainer, when she hadn't uttered a peep. The offending journalist had called me and asked if he could come by our home and interview *me* about living as an expatriate in Karachi. We met in our living room. Sue said hello and then excused herself and went upstairs to read. The reporter wasn't very probing. "How is it to live without TV?" was one of his first questions.

"I kind of like it," I replied, rather flip. "In fact, having a television is a little like introducing typhoid into your house. I can live without it."

He asked other questions of equal depth. I didn't expect a very insightful article. When the piece was published a week later, I wasn't surprised that I sounded vapid. But I was dumbfounded to read several quotes from Sue. She came across as culturally insensitive, not as bad as the angry woman we'd met months earlier by the hotel pool, but whiny and tetchy.

Sue read the article and I could see her cheeks redden. "That jerk," she said. "I never talked to him. Yes, I don't like how women are treated here. Sometimes, when I'm in this house too many days in a row, I feel these high walls closing in like I'm locked up in purdah. But I wouldn't dream of saying those things in public." She paused to catch her breath. "What's he trying to prove?"

The journalist obviously had his own agenda but we were not sure what. Under President Zia all the newspapers were censored with a heavy hand and I was sure journalists prickled at the controls. Still, why would he want to embarrass an expatriate or an American in particular? Did he want to howl at the government and used Sue to do his barking for him?

Several acquaintances saw the article and were not happy with Sue for her alleged indiscretions and her protests of innocence didn't carry very far. It wasn't until the reporter repeated the offence with another expat that Sue's version got much traction. The reporter was cut off from further interviews, but the damage and hurt had already been done.

Eager to bark for real, and desperately wanting some time with Jennifer before she fled our nest for college, Sue arranged for David to stay with a friend while she and Jennifer flew off to India. When I got back from my recruitment trip, they filled me in.

"New Delhi is so lively," Sue said, while Jennifer nodded her head. "There are so many restaurants, shops of every description, and great art galleries and museums. And women on the streets, dressed in beautiful silk saris in gay colors, or fashionable western cloths. They're everywhere, hurrying about their business, their heads uncovered, brushing shoulders with men."

It sounded titillating and scandalous compared to Karachi.

"We visited all the sites," Jennifer said, "and we took a lot of photographs. I think I got a couple I can use in the show."

Jennifer shared her mother's passion for photography and they were both getting ready for a spring photo exhibit that was being planned by the Pakistan International Photo Club. Sue had helped organize the club when she discovered other expatriates and several Pakistani friends who were also avid photographers. Sue also helped organize field trips and workshops. She said, "I'm learning so much, The others are pushing me to see beyond the exotic. I think I'm getting better at seeing the poignant and humane." From what I'd seen of both Jennifer and Sue's work, I thought their photos were going to stand up well in competition.

"And we did some shopping," Jennifer continued, batting her eyes innocently. "I got this blouse there," her fingers running down her sleeve, "and a couple of skirts."

"What a surprise," I said.

"It was nice being with Mom," Jennifer said, glancing at her mother. "We talked about school and college. We had fun, didn't we? It was a great birthday."

"I'm sorry I couldn't be there. But I did bring back some goodies from the States, belated birthday and Valentine's Day gifts." I handed them each a box of Swiss chocolates and a card.

"Thanks, Dad," Jennifer said, giving me a hug.

"That goes for me too," Sue added, following up with a hug of her own.

A few days later, on our way home from another unsuccessful attempt to call her parents on our friend's telephone, Sue said,

"Tomorrow I'm going to get us a telephone. We've been in our house six months and the landlord still hasn't installed one. Even if it didn't work any better than our friends', we could try longer and we wouldn't be such an imposition. We could try every evening if we had to, until we got through. And we could call our Karachi friends. The novelty of sending Sohir with a written note has worn off."

"It's worth a try," I said.

The next evening Sue told me about her visit to the telephone agency. "It was so frustrating. The guy was giving me the run around and I got mad. I finally told him I wanted a firm date. Raising my voice went over really well." A smile cracked her bemused look and she chuckled. "He told me, 'Whatever you are wanting, I am not giving.' He said it will be *seven years* before we see a phone. So much for throwing my weight around."

"I'll talk to Mohajir," I offered. "Maybe he can do something."

When I stopped by Mohajir's office, he smiled and waggled his head. "No problem, Mister Robert. I will have my man do the needful straight away."

We had a telephone within the week.

"I am a slow learner," I said to Sue.

She didn't argue with me.

One of the first telephone calls we got was from Nana Horton reminding me I had volunteered to help out at the Karachi Olympics, a day of food and silly games held on the grounds of the American School each February. Parents, teachers and students, with other friends of the school, were invited to form national teams: the Americans, the Canadians, the Brits, the Pakistanis. And where there were too few from one country, regional teams were encouraged: the Asians, the Africans, and others. Tony even invited the Russians, construction workers isolated at a building site outside the city, but they declined. I couldn't blame them given the tensions between the Soviet Union and the U.S. over the Afghan war.

That weekend, the Olympics opened with a parade around the school's football field, each team dressed in matching t-shirts and carrying a flag. Tents were set up to serve a variety of ethnic and re-gional foods. The Swiss imported sausages. I manned the American hotdog grill, wearing an apron and white chef's hat. Sue helped ladle bowls of homemade American-style chili. Teams competed at old-style picnic games such as sack races and the balloon toss. At the end of the day, ribbons and trophies were awarded based on ill-defined criteria.

The event raised goodwill and a good deal of money for the school.

In April, when the weather in Karachi changed from pleasant to unrelenting hot, a national strike was called to protest the bombing of a mosque in Jerusalem. President Zia was measured in his response and called for calm, but the American Consulate and the Karachi American School closed for a few days.

Shortly after the strike, Neen Lillquist, our Nursing Director prospect, and her husband, Art, came to visit. While Neen and Art impressed my colleagues at the project, Sue and I gave them the razzle-dazzle. We showed them the sites and introduced them to our friends at dinner parties.

We also took them bunder-boating in Karachi's harbor. Late one afternoon, we bundled into two cars—Jennifer and David wanted in on the fun—and drove down to the East Wharf. There were a dozen forty-foot, flat-bottomed dhows with lateen sails lined up along the pier, their captains hawking rides. We signaled a skipper we had used before and when he nodded, we clamored aboard, each of us choosing a seat on one of the cushions that lined the ornately decorated gunnels. The captain gave orders to his small crew to cast off the lines and we drifted out into the busy harbor. For thirty minutes we sailed under a clear, moonlit sky, serenely tacking our way among the sea-scared cargo liners that hovered above us. The crew kept busy baiting drop lines with over-ripe chicken parts and laying a charcoal fire in a metal tub set into the wood deck just aft of mid-ship. As we reached the outer edge of the harbor, where the water was a bit less murky, the captain furled the sail and the boat began to drift, our signal to dangle our drop-lines over the sides.

"What's the trick to this?" asked Art.

"Lower your bait until you feel it touch bottom," I said. "Then bring it up an inch or two and wait until you feel a gentle tug. Then raise your line very slowly so the crab doesn't drop off. When you can see it just below the surface, ask a crew member to net it for you."

Sue chimed in, "I had Peter put together a picnic basket, just in case we don't get enough crab. I had him add side-dishes and soft drinks too."

"Got one," David said.

"Me too," said Neen.

A member of the crew put a pot of water on the coals to boil and in half an hour we had enough crabs for him to start cooking. He put several crabs in a metal colander and lowered it into the boiling water. In a few minutes he withdrew the colander and dumped the steaming crabs on a tray. He smacked each crab a couple of blows with a fist-sized rock to crack the shell before throwing it into a bowl. He sprinkled them all with a spicy seasoning and handed the bowl to the captain, then went back to cooking another batch in his bubbling caldron. The captain walked among us and, starting with the ladies, plucked a hot crab from the bowl and lowered it onto an awaiting plate.

We pried apart the cracked shells, pricking our burning fingers on the sharp spines, and plucked out the sweet and spicy meat.

"It's a tough life you lead," Art said, as we sailed our way back to the wharf. The evening air was cooling.

"It's considered a hardship post," I said. "It's all brutal living and unrelenting stress."

We sent them back to Minnesota thoroughly bamboozled and eager to return in the fall.

Sue was looking forward to fall as well, anxious to find employment after summer break. Getting the house decorated, traveling to India, and entertaining visitors had kept her occupied and distracted for several months, but running the household had become routine. She had recently finished editing the book she co-authored on earth-sheltered architecture and had a brief job helping the Pakistan society of architects organize a conference. But those tasks were at an end.

I was apprehensive. Tony Horton told me that finding work for expatriate spouses was difficult in many foreign postings, and was a major source of stress and marital conflict among the school faculty. Whenever possible, he hired couples who both were teachers.

In Karachi, work opportunities of any kind were scarce, and work permit requirements often closed off jobs that might be available to foreigners. Sue had been promised work when I was recruited, but working for the hospital would be problematic. Even if I wasn't her supervisor, I would still be her boss, no matter how remote the line of command. There were unavoidable overtones of nepotism and conflict of interest.

Conflict or not, an opportunity came to knock when we hosted John Cushing, our candidate for Associate Administrator, and his wife, Martha. Like the Lillquists, I introduced the Cushings to my colleagues and oriented them to the Project, while Sue showed them the Karachi American School, arranged visits to prospective houses (with clear cautions to find a place that was broken-in and near the school), and lined up visits to the bazaar and other sites. She hosted a dinner party in their honor, invited them along to several social events, and set up an evening of bunder-boating.

Martha Cushing came to Karachi with her professional portfolio in hand. She was an experienced manager in her own right, with an advanced degree in finance, but I had cautioned her that finding work might be difficult, citing Sue as an example. Martha lined up several job interviews during their visit and was hopeful something would turn up when she returned. Sue and I admired her industriousness.

The Cushings were well received by all and when they left they were enthusiastic about moving to Karachi.

"When they move here," Sue said, "we can't let them go through what we went through. They need to have a house and furniture ready when they arrive. They need to be able to get household help quickly and know the rules for staying healthy. The same for the Lillquists, and there will be others."

"I agree," I said. "It would be hard on them and a distraction at work."

I talked to Zahir Janmohammed, the personnel director we'd recruited from Canada who was already well settled in Karachi's Ismaili community. "We need a recruitment package and plans for helping new people settle here."

"Good idea," he said. "I've been thinking about that too." To my surprise, he added, "Would Sue be willing to help me put together a program?"

"I'm sure she'd love to," I said, "but I can't ask that of you."

"She could work for me as a consultant," Zahir suggested.

"Well, if the job is narrowly defined and limited in time, maybe it would be okay. But I have to stay out of it."

"She could be a great help. I'll check it out with others," he said.

It wasn't entirely kosher, but Sue needed to work.

# 22

# EVERYBODY'S HERO

While Sue waited word from Zahir, she immersed herself in planning our trip home for our annual summer leave. In late May, right after school adjourned, we flew to Kyoto.

If you fly from Karachi to Minnesota you can go either east or west. If you over-fly Minneapolis you're on your way back to Pakistan. We had come over through Europe, so for our first home furlough we decided to visit Japan, and then on to Hawaii on our way to the mainland. We planned to spend a few days in Colorado, visiting friends and maybe looking at property, before heading on to Minnesota.

Sue booked an upstairs room in a traditional ryokan in old Kyoto where we slept on tatami mats and had our breakfast sitting cross-legged at a low table. We ate fried eggs with chopsticks, washed down with a pale tea, and watched a huge spider clinging precariously to the ornately carved beams above our heads. Every one of its multiple black glistening eyes seemed focused on us.

With sign language and a smile, locals helped us decipher the Japanese hieroglyphics so we could catch the correct train up to Nara. We walked manicured forest pathways and watched, amused, as ducks, tame deer, and Japanese tourists repeatedly bowed their heads at each other, exchanging formal greetings all around. We gazed in awe as a woman caretaker, rubber boots up to her knees, carefully swept fallen leaves off the shimmering surface of a stony creek bed.

We sat on a rock wall under overhanging trees and slurped noodles from bowls of fragrant soup.

In Tokyo, raven-haired school girls tested their English on Jennifer. "Hello. What is your name? How old are you? Do you have a boy-friend?" They giggled as they tried to touch David's blond hair and asked us to take pictures of them on *our* camera. David enjoyed the attention and we celebrated his birthday at a Shakey's Pizza parlor, the menu in English and Japanese, a precursor to the global economy. David tried to eat one slice for each of his eleven years.

We spent hours in the Kabuki theatre watching in fascination as the iconic, two-sword samurai Ronan, Miyamoto Musashi, dis-patched his enemies in splendidly choreographed battle. He was the sixteenth century marshal arts icon who wrote *A Book of Five Rings*, a classic guide to management strategy that was part of my personal library. I bought his fictionalized biography, *Musashi*, by Eiji Yoshikawa, to keep me company as I sent everyone onward to Hawaii and Minnesota and I flew back to Karachi, alone, my plans to join them interrupted by the pressing need to work on the "Forecast."

Back home in Karachi, I looked up from my breakfast mango to watch the water gushing out of the roof scuppers, splashing onto the terrace, spilling over into our already flooded yard. It was the third day of miasmic weather, heavy clouds and unceasing rain.

The summer monsoons were sweeping up from the Indian Ocean, pushing clouds over-loaded with moisture. Usually the clouds lum-bered farther to the north, aiming their payload on Pakistan's ver-dant agricultural mid-section, the steppes that slope upward toward the northern mountains. Apparently, the clouds rumbling and spark-ing above my head couldn't hold their water that long. They were relieving themselves onto Karachi's desert lowlands with a tropical vengeance.

At first the rains were welcome. Trees and bushes once again re-vealed their sumptuous greenness too long hidden beneath winter's dusty shroud. The accumulated grit of winter was washed from the roof tops. All over the city the deep ditches that lined every roadway were flushed clean, their accumulated flotsam spewing out into the *wadis*. Along our street, I saw shoots of new growth tentatively poking up in cracks and crevices, checking to see if conditions favored making an effort for a new beginning. I saw grown men dancing in puddles, like kids on a hot summer's day back in Minnesota frolicking in the wash of an open fire hydrant.

Peter poured me another cup of coffee and cleared the empty shell of my mango, the best part of a summer in the tropics. I lingered for a few minutes sipping my coffee, reading several pages in my book, *Musashi*, listening to the water running from the roof. I was easing into my day, getting centered, just like the samurai, or my mother, might recommend. When I was a child at home, one of six, my mother got up each morning an hour early, made herself a cup of coffee and read the newspaper. It was a few minutes of her own before the house came alive. I adopted the habit. I much preferred getting up a little early, the day still unsullied and full of promise, taking my time instead of sleeping late and having to rush.

About seven-thirty Sohir drove me to work, skillfully maneuvering the car around the water hazards with what mariners would call local knowledge. Excess water had pooled in every low spot, including many street intersections, hiding usually obvious perils that now lurked beneath the surface. Potholes that could swallow a car up to its windows, and six-foot-deep manholes, their covers harvested by enterprising metal *wallahs*, lay in wait.

At work, Zaher Lalani said he saw a man wading through the water gripping a long sturdy pole. "He held the pole horizontally, across his chest with both hands like a tightrope walker. I think he did it in case he stepped into a deep hole, so he could pull himself out."

"Maybe he was a good Samaritan," I said, unsure I was right. On the drive to work I had seen an upright stick in the middle of the road where I knew there was an invisible manhole. The stick looked like a river channel marker, intended to warn off the unwary or unfamiliar driver. *Was there a guy at the other end, down below the roadway?*

Shaking off that disturbing image, I went back to working on the Forecast. Shamsh said His Highness was getting impatient. I was deep into studying hospital floor plans, gathering intelligence from my colleagues, cranking away at a calculator, and drafting tentative projections and conclusions.

I was puzzled by one inconsistency. My boss, and others who should know, repeatedly stated that the hospital would have 721 beds. I needed to have more details in order to project staffing needs and to estimate costs and revenues. I started tabulating beds by service, checking the numbers against the floor plans. How many beds in obstetrics? How many in pediatrics? When I added up all the inpatient services, I could find only 654 beds, sixty-seven beds fewer than claimed. The difference was critical to the forecast. Staffing needs, costs, and revenues were all impacted significantly.

I pointed out the discrepancy to Shamsh. He was circumspect. "His Highness expects 721 beds and that's what we're planning for."

"I'll keep looking," I said lamely. "But I can't imagine we're going to cram in extra beds just so the numbers come out right."

"I'll look into it further," Shamsh said.

Ramazan was due to start any day but I wasn't sure exactly when. I asked Aziz. "Officially, it doesn't start until the appearance of the first sliver of the new moon," he said. "On your calendar, that will be on the twenty-third of June, cloudy or clear." He repeated what he'd told me earlier. "We fast from sunup to sundown. Nothing by mouth—no food, no drink, no smoking. Other than that, people go to work and life goes on."

Two or three days into Ramazan, it was clear to me that Aziz had understated its impact on life in Karachi. There were fewer people on the streets. Traffic was thinner and less frantic. Sohir, our driver, showed up at the house on time, but he seemed listless.

"It is because he can not drink his chai," Peter said.

I was sympathetic. Chai packed a double whammy stimulant: heavily caffeinated tea boiled with a generous dose of sugar. If I missed my morning coffee, my IQ never got above ninety and I had a headache by noon. The whole town, the entire country, was under-caffeinated and running on idle.

So was the office. People came to work late, nobody scheduled meetings, the telephone was quiet. I loved it. It was a gift of uninterrupted time to work on the Forecast.

With no clear direction from Shamsh, I continued to plan for the number of beds I knew were being built. Maybe I'd find another wing of beds behind some grand Islamic archway, a temptress hidden from my view but ready to reveal her glorious presence as soon as I stepped beyond the intervening barrier.

My days were quiet, but productive, and my nights were lonely. Most evenings I dined alone at home or went to the American Club, a modest hole-in-the-wall recently opened at the American Consulate, for a beer and pizza. On the weekend, when the skies permitted, I visited the pool at the Karachi American School; swimming and reading, mostly alone, every expatriate with any sense having abandoned the city. Back in Minnesota we called it going "up north," or to "the lake." In Pakistan, the British and well-to-do locals went to a "hill station" such as Murree in the mountains above Lahore. I would have been happy to be anywhere else.

As a distraction, I took up painting. I found oil paints and canvas in the local market. No surprise, since there were many artists in Karachi. Gulgee, whose work I'd seen at the Horton's, was a prominent example. One canvas I modeled after a photo of my in-law's former cabin, taken in the fall, yellow leaves contrasting with white birch trees. The other was a prairie partridge copied from a photo I snipped from *National Geographic*. The results were uninspired, the product of my listless boredom and loneliness. I missed my family, I was going to miss my brother's wedding, and I was going to miss the fireworks on the Fourth of July. I resigned myself to a long, hot, and wet summer. Poor me.

At the end of June I got word that a candidate I was pursuing wanted to talk. He could meet me in Minneapolis in a week. The Forecast be damned. I telephoned Sue to tell her I was coming to Minneapolis. It was the first time I'd been able to get through since she and the kids had arrived there.

"Great," she said. "Everyone will love to see you." She spent ten minutes telling me how much they had all enjoyed Hawaii.

I was envious. "How about Colorado?"

"Sorry, how could I forget? I found a lot. You'll love it. It's down valley in Edwards, next to a creek, with views of the Eagle River and the mountains beyond. I took some photos. Colorado is so beautiful in the summer. I'd love to live there again."

"Let's see if we can make that happen," I said. "I'm eager to see the pictures. We'll talk about it when I get there. What else have you been up to?"

"I went to a wake for the Equal Rights Amendment over at the Capitol in Saint Paul. It was an amazing scene, both sad and beautiful." Under President Regan the atmosphere supporting the constitutional amendment had waned and, even with an extended deadline, the vote fell three states short of the thirty required when time ran out on June 30, 1982. "All these women were out in public, singing and waving candles. I felt proud to be an American citizen, and privileged to have the freedom to express my opinion even though we didn't win."

I was about to say goodbye when Sue said, "Be warned, my dad is sick again. And right now it's kind of rough for Mom too."

I was on an airplane for an extra long day, gaining hours as I flew across a dozen time zones. In New York I transferred to an evening flight bound for Minneapolis. For the duration of the flight, I sat in a window seat peering at the ground as the light faded, hoping, unsuccessfully, to see a bursting plume of fireworks. It wasn't until I got to Minneapolis that I realized it was already the fifth of July, not the fourth.

I arrived into Minneapolis late evening and took a taxi to Sue's parents' home.

Sue met me at the door looking distraught. She gave me a hug and held on.

"What's wrong?"

"Mom tried to commit suicide. She and Dad are both in Methodist Hospital. It's been awful."

"Jennifer's staying with a girl friend," she said. "David and I have been staying here. We spent the Fourth over at White Bear Lake in St. Paul." Good friends of ours had a place there. "I asked Mom if she wanted to go along and see the fireworks but she said, 'No. Go and have a good time.' I was sorry she didn't want to get out of the house but she seemed fine. We got back late and didn't want to disturb her so David and I went right to our bedroom in the basement. This morning we got up a little late but Mom was still in bed. Dad called from the hospital and I told him Mom was still sleeping. He was surprised and he told me to go wake her up."

Sue's voice cracked as tears ran down her cheeks. "I tried to wake her up but I couldn't. She was breathing but she wouldn't wake up. David, bless him, had his head on straight and called an ambulance. Then I found an empty pill bottle in the study. When the paramedics arrived I showed it to them. I guess it helped them know what to do."

I nodded and held her hand. "How are *you*?" I asked.

"Shaky, for sure, but better now that you're here. Dad's been neglecting his diet again and Mom was really mad at him, and frightened too. She talked to me in the hospital this afternoon but clammed up when Dad came by to see her."

"I'll stick around for awhile until things settle down."

Sue gave me a full-bodied hug. "I am *so* glad you're here."

The next morning over coffee, Sue said, "I forgot to tell you last night. I went to the doctor and asked about these cramps I've been having. He said I have a fibroid tumor."

"What?" I said. I'm sure I looked stricken.

Before I could say more, she added, "It's nothing to worry about. He said they sometimes go away on their own. He said we should watch it. If the pain gets worse, or if I have heavy bleeding, he can do surgery the next time I'm in town."

"We're living in Pakistan, for crying out loud. Does the doctor know that?"

"Yes, yes. He said there's no real danger. I can live with a little discomfort."

"Sometimes you take this 'I am strong, I am invincible, I am woman' stuff too literally." I said. "If you're uncomfortable, don't keep it to yourself. I'm supposed to protect you. It was in our wedding vows."

I think Sue thought I'd come home just for her. I wasn't about to tell her different.

The next weekend, my youngest brother got married. I had written to say I couldn't make it. When I showed up, my brother and his bride thought I'd flown back just to surprise them. That's what my Mother thought too. I didn't tell them different either.

My interview was successful. I ended up with another hire.

A week later I flew back to Karachi, everybody's hero and feeling not quite so lonely.

On the airplane I picked up a copy of the *International Herald Tribune* and was disturbed to read that David Dodge, the acting President of the American University of Beirut, had been kidnapped by pro-Iranian Shiite Muslim extremists.[22] Years earlier, a colleague of mine back in Minnesota had been an administrator at the American University Hospital of Beirut Medical Center. He had raved about Beirut being the "Paris of the East."

*Now they're targeting Americans? What next?*

# 23

# PILLARS OF ISLAM

It was the middle of Ramazan when I got back home to Karachi. Sohir looked tired, with dark circles under his eyes, when he picked me up at the airport a little after midnight. On the drive into town I was sitting in the back seat watching his eyes in the rearview mirror. Halfway home they fluttered shut and his head drooped.

"Sohir," I yelled, and grabbed his shoulder.

"Yes, Sahib," he said, as his eyes popped open.

"You're falling asleep."

"No, no," he protested. "I am fine."

I talked to him the rest of the way home, touching his shoulder once in a while to keep him alert.

Sohir and I were welcomed at our gate by Abdullah, who waved a friendly hello, and by David's dog, Carrie, who snarled and barked loudly until she recognized our car. I greeted Abdullah with *A'Salam A'Lakum* and a smile and patted Carrie on the head, her tail now wagging vigorously. I told Sohir to sleep the rest of the night on the *charpoi* in Peter and Margaret's room.

Over breakfast the next morning I was re-reading the newspaper I picked up on the flight into Karachi. The kidnapping in Beirut was blamed on Islamic extremists. I had been dismissing the events in the Middle East—Sadat's assassination last fall, for example. And then in February, Syrian authorities had killed tens of thousands squashing anti-government riots. Those incidents seemed closer to us now, increasingly ominous and threatening. The purposeful targeting of Americans made it all more personal.

*Who are these people?*

The Muslims I knew in Karachi were anything but extreme. Yes, there were occasional squabbles between people in some of Karachi's poor neighborhoods, and Aziz had told me about the tensions between Sunni and Shia during Muharram, but where were the extremists coming from?

I had read that more than seventy percent of all the Muslims in the world were Sunni, and fifteen percent Shia, with the balance a smattering of smaller groups. Sunnis were a majority in most Muslim countries: Saudi Arabia, Egypt, Jordan, and others. Sunnis were the vast majority in Pakistan too, but Shia were still such a sizable minority that they amounted to one of the four largest Shia populations in the world, right up there with Iran and Iraq—and Lebanon, where the American had been kidnapped.[23]

*Were the Shia to blame?* Aziz had said that the Nizari Ismailis, the followers of the Aga Khan, were Shia, a small sect with fifteen to twenty million members worldwide. From what I had observed in my first few months in Pakistan, the Ismailis were pacifists and progressive and actively engaged in the modern world. For a minority within a minority, they seemed to have prominence beyond their numbers.

I went to Aziz. "Remember, I told you Muslims are as diverse in their beliefs as Christians or Jews," he said. "We've got our fundamentalists and extremists just like you do." He paused and took off his glasses, rubbing the bridge of his nose. "Are you familiar with the pillars of Islam?"

"A little," I said. "There are five, right?"

"Yes, if you're Sunni. But we Ismailis are Shia and we have seven pillars." He started to count them on his fingers. First, there's love and devotion to God; second, the oneness of God; and third, prayer.

"Doesn't every Muslim believe in one God?"

"Yes, Shias and Sunnis both."

"That's like Unitarians," I said. "We got the name a few hundred years ago when we rejected the idea of the trinity. We said Jesus was a divinely inspired human, not a god, and we were called heretics because of it."

"And all Muslims believe in prayer," Aziz continued. "But there are many different ways to do it. The way we do ablutions, how we face Mecca, how we kneel, how we bow our heads, the prayers we say—they are all the same, yet different."

"I read somewhere that Allah wanted people to pray fifty times a day," I said. "But Mohammad flew up to heaven on a winged white horse and negotiated the number down to five."[24]

Aziz waggled his head. "Very practical, isn't it."

"Indeed."

"Then we have charity, what we call Zakat," Aziz continued. "Then fasting, like now during Ramazan. Also, you've heard of *Hajj*, the pilgrimage to Mecca?"

I nodded.

"Finally, there's *Jihad*, the struggle."

"I hear a lot about jihad."

"Jihad is very important but Muslims disagree on what it means," said Aziz. "For Ismailis, and many other Muslims, it is the Greater Struggle. We Ismailis are pacifists and we believe the biggest threats to Islam are internal; our personal and social weaknesses and misbehaviors. We look inward for answers; the struggle to become a better person. For some other Muslims *jihad* means confronting the *external* enemies of the faith."

Some extremists were practicing *jihad* by striking out at other Muslims. It reminded me of the animosities between Catholics and Protestants. But lately there had been attacks by Muslims against Americans.

If the Iranian Revolution and the taking of American hostages wasn't the start of it, it certainly brought the hostilities to the forefront.[25] I'm sure Iran saw us as colonialists, occupiers, akin to the British. And the bombings and kidnappings in the Middle East made it clear that our steadfast support of Israel hadn't made us many friends in the Arab world.

Still, I suspected there was more to it than all that. For some demigods, we were just a convenient scapegoat, an easy way to consolidate power by deflecting pent-up frustration, anger, and festering discontent.

I didn't have a firm grip on why, but it was clear that hostilities against Americans were escalating.

There was a beggar I passed regularly on my way home from work, not the mournful woman Jennifer had written about, but a man who sat on a raised platform next to the roadway, his severely crippled legs drawn up beneath him. He stood out from other beggars because of his radiant smile and friendly wave. Mindful of Aziz's instruction on *Zakat*, charity, every few days I'd ask Sohir to stop so I could give the man a few rupees. Once I stopped to talk, asking Sohir to help interpret. The man had become ill with what I guessed was polio when he was a boy. When his parents died, he had to make it on his own and claimed this choice corner as his place of business. Charity was his only source of income and he'd done well enough to get married and put two children through school. He said he had a number of people who stopped regularly, like me. Most were Pakistani.

Aziz said that most of Pakistan's infirm and elderly were cared for within their extended families. From what I could see, many of those who were without family, or who had been cast out for some offense or another, were on their own. Too many of Karachi's maimed and mentally ill ended up on street corners, knocking on your car window with an upturned palm, or in the bazaars, pulling at your sleeve.

There was no government safety net but there were a few private organizations that tried to help. The Aga Khan had a number of charitable programs, the most prominent being health care, and other Muslim groups did as well. The Red Crescent, for example, worked like the Red Cross, providing assistance especially in times of disaster.

Cheves told me that President Zia-ul-Haq had once tried to capture some of the *Zakat* money for government, to be used, he pledged, for charity. The people scoffed and Zia backed off.[26]

I asked several of our Muslim friends if they had gone on Hajj, made a pilgrimage to Mecca, in Saudi Arabia. "Not yet," was a common reply. "But I hope to go soon."

All Muslims are supposed to make the pilgrimage at least once in their lifetime, if they are physically and financially able. The trip is made during the second week of *Dhu al-Hajjah*, the twelfth and last month of the Islamic calendar. While on Hajj, a pilgrim is to perform several rituals, including walking seven times around the *Kaaba*, a black cube-shaped building, purported to have been built by Abraham. All Muslims, wherever they happen to be in the world, are supposed to face the *Kaaba* during prayer.[27] When we were staying at the Holiday Inn, there was a *gibla*, an arrow glued to the top of the bedside cabinet, which pointed in the right direction

A couple of weeks after Sue and the kids returned from the States, Sue and I visited the home of a friend who had a photograph etched on glass mounted on his wall, a scene looking down on the crowds surrounding the *Kaaba*. We were examining the photo when our host flipped a switch and the crowd appeared to move counterclockwise, slowly circling the holy cube. It was technology I had only seen in bars, like an illuminated Hamm's beer sign with a Minnesota lake or waterfall flowing peacefully. Our friend said he had been on Hajj a couple of years earlier. "It was very inspiring," he said. "I was humbled to walk on the same ground where the Prophet walked. It must be the same for a Christian or Jew visiting Jerusalem."

I left their home that evening thinking how little I really knew about Islam. The occasional incidents, the recent kidnapping in Beirut, for example, were puzzling. Such events didn't jibe with the thoughtful and friendly Muslims I was getting to know.

I played poker once a month with a few guys: a mix of Americans, Europeans and Pakistanis. We played nickel, dime, quarter stakes and dealer's choice which meant we played an unpredictable jumble of straight poker and wild card. It didn't matter. It was just for fun and some good conversation.

Sheikh was one of two Pakistani fellows who played with us. He was in his late fifties, I guessed, and had a successful jewelry business. He was articulate, well traveled, warm hearted, and no better at poker than the rest of us. We were all fond of him.

Sheikh took his cards and conversation seriously and held both close to his chest. Sometimes he talked about his concerns for his country. "This war in Afghanistan is bad for us," he told us one evening, a few days after another incident of neighborhood violence. He said that guns had never been common in Karachi but now they were being brought to the city by refugees fleeing from the north. "We used to fight our battles with sticks and stones. Now it is guns."

# 24

# LAST TENDER

Pascale looked ravishing in a low-cut party dress that showed her slender and curvy form to good advantage. A gold necklace with a single emerald set in a square of small diamonds embraced her neck.

It was mid-August, 1982, and Jennifer and David were back in school. I was still immersed in preparing the Forecast. Sue was busy drafting the next issue of the newsletter for the American Women's Club and, blessings be, Zahir Janmohammed had asked her to write up a script for a recruitment slideshow and a settlement plan for new arrivals. Karachi life was back to its normal frenetic pace.

Pascale and her husband Chris Windfur, from the Holiday Inn, were at our house for a dinner party, just the four of us, celebrating Sue's return from her summer retreat to the States and our upcoming twentieth wedding anniversary.

Sue asked Pascale about their baby. "How's Bambi?"

"Healthy and talking," said Pascale.

"I'm curious," asked Sue. "You're French, Chris is German; what language do you use with Bambi?"

"When I am alone with my Bambi, I speak French. When Chris is alone with him, he speaks German. When we are together, we speak English. And Bambi's *ayah* speaks Urdu."

"Isn't that confusing?"

"So far he seems to keep it straight. We will see."

Sue couldn't constrain herself any longer. She leaned in close to get a better look at Pascale's necklace. "It's gorgeous."

"Try it on," said Pascale as she unhooked the clasp.

"Oh, I can't possibly," said Sue, as she turned and put her hand on the nape of her neck.

Sue also wore a low cut dress, a clinging black number and one of my favorites. "You really look good in it," I'd said, when she was trying to decide which outfit to wear for the evening. *The neckline's perfect.*

Pascale helped Sue with the clasp. "Let me see," she said, as Chris and I stepped forward to get a good look.

Sue did a slow pirouette. The emerald rested just below that enticing little indentation in her breastbone that is as good a reason to believe in God as I know. If God created anything, he created that little dimple with love and infinite wisdom, using the tip of his finger.

"It's stunning on you," said Chris.

Sue walked over to a mirror hanging in the hallway. "Wow," she said.

"You may keep it," said Pascale.

"Very funny," said Sue. "But it is lovely."

"You *can* keep it," I said. "It's yours."

Sue looked at me with a puzzled look on her face, her mouth half open. "Really?"

"Yes, really. Happy anniversary."

She gave me a kiss and a lingering hug. "Thank you," she whispered in my ear.

"You're welcome. You can wear it next week, on our cruise." Sue knew about the three day cruise to the Greek Islands, since she'd helped research the options.

"I've got the perfect green dress to wear with it."

The expense was a stretch, well beyond what I'd ever done in the past, but it was also in recognition of our being back together for more than a year. This struggling together against adversity was working out pretty well. Normal and boring, it wasn't.

Peter and Margaret moved into the house to watch over the kids during the week we were gone. Friends with the State Department agreed to help out in case of an emergency.

We had a half day and an overnight in Athens before we had to catch our cruise liner. We had visited Athens before, back in 1964 on the same trip when we'd puttered our way through Europe and so enjoyed Paris. Back then we were traveling on the cheap and committed to seeing every Greek antiquity in the guide book: the Parthenon, the Acropolis, the works.

On this trip, hungry for night life, we focused on Athens' funky Latin Quarter. We had a great time, retired late, and got little sleep.

Late the next morning we boarded our cruise liner, a modest-sized boat with room for about two hundred passengers. It was our first cruise and we were determined to take full advantage of all that was offered. At noon we lunched at a sumptuous buffet served outdoors on the upper deck. In the afternoon we swam and lounged in the Mediterranean sun near the pool. At supper we overate at a formal sit-down dinner hosted by the ship's captain and that evening danced to the music of a band accompanied by a cigarette-voiced torch singer.

When we awoke in the morning we were anchored off Mykonos, our first stop.

After breakfast we prepared for the short boat ride to the island. As we departed the ship we were asked to take the tag with our cabin number off its hook on the "Onboard" column and put it on a hook on the "Off Ship" column. Only a few dozen tags hung from the "Off Ship" hooks. The attendant said many people never left the boat.

"Two hundred yards from Mykonos and you never leave the ship?" I said to Sue as we stepped into a small boat with about a dozen other passengers, one of several tenders ready to shuttle people from the ship to shore. "That's hard to believe."

As we neared the dock, the man at the helm, dressed in crisp whites, said, "Tenders will be here all day to return you to the ship when you're ready. The last tender will depart at five-thirty sharp. Don't miss it or we'll leave you here."

As we walked along the quay I checked my watch. "We should plan to be back a little after five. That gives us over seven hours on the island."

In the piazza, we sat for an hour over a second cup of coffee, served with a plate of assorted cookies. Shaded under a blue umbrella, we watched brightly painted boats rock gently on the translucent water. A fisherman pounded an octopus on a rock and hung it on a wire among others to dry in the bright sun. We walked hand-in-hand among white buildings, their doors and windows painted in lively indigos and reds. We lunched on feta cheese, olives, and spanakopita in a small taverna by the sea, drinking retsina. We walked some more in the afternoon, touring a few antiquities. We lingered in small shops on narrow streets, intrigued by the goods on display for the mostly tourist buyers. "Just looking," was a phrase we repeated endlessly.

A few minutes before five, I said, "It's time we start wandering back." We walked at an easy pace, enjoying one last look at the whitewashed buildings and the boats in the harbor. The tables on the sidewalks were beginning to fill with locals: sunburned, craggy faced, mustached men smoking cigarettes, snacking on olives and dolmas, and drinking ouzo.

We arrived back at the pier about five fifteen, we thought well before the last tender was scheduled to leave. One other couple was just stepping down into the empty boat. The tender captain was unhappy. "You are the last. Everyone is back on board. We must hurry."

I turned to the other couple. "Did we have the time wrong? I thought they said five thirty."

"They did," said the man. "The captain said they all went back early so they wouldn't miss dinner."

"I can't understand that," said Sue. "I'd think everyone would want to stay on the island as long as possible. We came back a few minutes early because we thought we might not have seats."

"Go figure," said the woman. "I didn't want to miss a minute."

On the brief ride back to the ship we got to know our boat-mates. They were about our age, from California, as yet unmarried but thinking about it, the Greek islands one stop on their several-week European adventure.

When we stepped aboard the cruise liner the attendant was stern-faced. I checked the "Off Ship" board and, sure enough, there were only four tags still hanging there. "Are we late?" I asked.

The attendant said, "Everyone's at dinner. The Captain wants to leave for our next destination."

"Yes," I said. "But we were told the last tender was at five-thirty. Were we wrong?"

"Well no," said the attendant, "but everybody came back early."

"You tell us when we must be back and we will be on time. But we won't come back early. There's too much to see and do. That's why we're here."

The attendant kept her stern face but said, "Yes sir."

We weren't back to our cabin before we heard the ship's engines rumble. We were well underway by the time we'd cleaned up and got to the dining room. Sue wore her green dress and emerald necklace. She looked tan and scrumptious.

There was only a smattering of people left in the main dining hall, but more than enough food. We sat with our new friends and lingered together over a light dinner, refusing the waiter's suggestion of rare roast beef or lobster but accepting his offer of soup and bread and the freely flowing champagne. We lost ourselves in laughter and conversation, bonding with kindred spirits. Later in the evening we poked our heads into the ship's bar, had a nightcap, and joined hands with our new friends and a handful of others in a spirited interpretation of a Greek line dance, weaving and spinning up and down the ship's canted dance floor.

The next morning we looked over the ship's railing toward Santorini, a procession of tourist-laden mules already ascending the pathway that wound its way up the island's steep slope. Small white buildings, some with low round domes, clung to the precipitous hillside. Our cruise ship was anchored in a basin of calm green water surrounded by a circle of vertical-sided islands, the perimeter, we were told, of a huge volcanic crater from eons ago.

Again, as the day before, we were shuttled to shore with the admonition that the last tender would depart the island no later than five-thirty. We joined our friends and spent the day doing all the usual tourist things: riding the mules to the top, seeing the sites, visiting tourist shops. This time we did succumb to temptation, purchasing a rug in patterns of gray and white; very Greek, and very cheap.

"You can't have too many carpets," Sue said, repeating the advice she'd gotten from Nana Horton back in Karachi. "I know right were it will go."

We lunched in a little taverna perched on the edge of the hill, shaded by an overhanging arbor, looking down at the stunning view of our cruise ship resting in the azure water. At four-thirty we stopped for a cold beer in a bar, again overlooking the captivating view.

"This is pretty nice," Sue said, covering my hand with hers. She leaned in close to my ear and whispered, "Thanks for making this happen."

"Are you saying all I needed to do to win you back was to take a job in Pakistan?"

"Yeah, something like that, if you throw in the Greek Islands now and then."

"I don't know why it didn't occur to me years ago," I said.

"Happy Anniversary," she said, giving my hand a squeeze.

The four of us were at the pier by five-twenty, again the only passengers on the last tender returning to the ship. This time, as we boarded the ship and dutifully moved our tags, the attendant smiled and said, "Welcome aboard."

"Thank you, we had a great day," I said.

We were underway before dinner, heading back on an overnight leg to Athens. We had a good meal, a good conversation with our new friends, we never did run out of topics; and a little slow dancing before retiring early.

We spent two more days in Athens with our friends. We revisited some of the antiquities, but spent a lot of time walking the city or sitting at street-side tables watching the world go by, munching on Greek food and sipping cold beer.

We said goodbye to our friends at the airport with promises to keep in touch.

Sue and I held hands most of the flight back to Karachi. I was feeling mellow and happy. My job was the last thing on my mind.

# 25

# PING-PONG WITH
# THE AGA KHAN

My mellow mood was quickly overcome by the press of work. Shamsh wanted me to complete the Forecast so it could be presented to His Highness at the October quarterly board meeting in Aiglemont, only a few weeks away. The Owner's Representatives Board had given my projections their tentative nod of approval, with a few alterations.

I was preoccupied preparing a revised draft when our eagerly awaited Director of Nursing, Neen Lillquist, and her husband, Art, arrived in town. To my great relief, Sue helped get them oriented and settled into their new home.

In addition to the Forecast, the Project sent numerous special papers and routine reports to Aiglemont in advance of the meeting, including a report on the status of hospital commissioning, which I prepared. I kept tabs on all the issues we were dealing with: management recruitment, planning, budgeting, and the like; and started drafting my report a month early to allow time for the inevitable edits and rewrites after Shamsh and others offered their comments.

The anxiety was always palpable around the office in the weeks leading up to a meeting with His Highness. Shamsh insisted that any change in any document submitted to HH, even a word, required a retype; no small task in the days before computers. I kept Nazia busy typing and retyping my reports. I wrote the first draft in longhand, building a pencil callus on my middle finger as leathery and large as a polo pony saddle, and Nazia would type it up. I'd edit the first draft and give it back to her for retyping. I'd review that draft before sending it on to Shamsh for his review. Shamsh always had a number of helpful suggestions which I'd incorporate into a third draft which Nazia would retype before I sent it back to Shamsh for a final review.

Except there never was a *final* review. It took me a while to devine that there were always additional comments, with decreasing importance and relevance to be sure, but still requiring another edit and another retyping by Nazia. The cycle was repeated as long as there was still time for the retyping before the deadline for shipping the pouch off to Aiglemont. When I caught on, I didn't stop preparing my report well in advance, but I got a little slower sending it on for comment, and a little slower yet submitting the final version. I was becoming a case study in passive-aggressive behavior.

As I learned more about my job and the dynamics of the environment, I became less passive in accepting Shamsh's suggestions to soften my analysis or alter my recommendations. I tried to be sensitive to Cheves' admonition that, "It's their project." But he also said, "We were hired to tell HH the truth. Sometimes his followers paint too rosy a picture or don't want to tell him bad news."

Sometimes Shamsh went too far, inserting his own view into my text. If I didn't agree, we'd talk about it, or I would talk to Aziz, seeking his counsel. Most often Shamsh and I reached agreement, but not always. Once he made a change in my report that I didn't discover until it had been sent off to Aiglemont. I didn't agree with the change and I was pissed. I told him, "You don't have to agree with what I say, but I think you and HH deserve my best advice. You can always tell His Highness you think differently."

We did think differently, at least on some issues. Shortly after I was hired Shamsh said to me, "Because we both received our degrees in business from the University of Minnesota, you think we have the same management philosophy. We don't. When you delegate, you describe the assignment, set out your expectation, and say, 'Report back to me.' I do the same, but I say, 'See me before you make any decisions.'"

I smiled and nodded in assent. "That about captures it."

"Here you have to be very clear about what you want and you have to check up on people constantly. If you don't, they think it's not important to you and so it's not important to them, and they let it slide."

I thought that was good advice and I nodded my assent, even if I thought he overdid it. If he was anxious about something, he would pace and hover about, frequently dropping by my office. Sometimes I found it hard to sort out what he really wanted me to attend to from the litany of ideas and ruminations he threw out. His creative brain was usually working in overdrive. I was learning to focus on what I thought were the real priorities, with a little help from Aziz and Cheves, and then feed them back to Shamsh. If he brought up an idea a second time, I gave it more credence.

As I worked on the Forecast, the discrepancy in the bed count continued to nag me. A forecast is built up from numerous assumptions. I prefer to start with a projection of demand—the number of expected patients, the services they might require, their ability to pay—and then plan facilities and services accordingly. If such an exercise had been done before the hospital was designed, I wasn't privy to it. I was starting from the other end, an "if you build it, they will come" approach. If I knew the bed count and array of services, then I could plan how the beds and services could be phased in, project the number and kind of staff needed, and calculate the costs involved. To justify my projections, I still had to estimate expected demand.

I talked to Shamsh again about the bed count. "We are not building all 721 beds right now," he said. "We will build an additional private patient wing when we are confident the demand is there."

"I can live with that," I said, pleased to have a concrete answer.

Since there was no comparable hospital project ever attempted in Pakistan, my forecast assumptions were often based on guesses, I liked to think educated guesses, but guesses nevertheless. I researched demographic statistics for the area, as thin as they were. I consulted with everybody for their advice.

One challenge was divining where hospital patients would come from. The hospital would have no trouble filling the charity wards, although covering the costs was an issue. But what about paying patients? How many people in Karachi could afford to pay for their health care? Where did they get health care now? What were people willing to pay? How many people had health insurance? What do other hospitals charge?

I stopped by Cheves Smythe's office to get his take on the numbers of well-to-do in Karachi. "There are more here than you think'" he said. "They hide their wealth behind those high walls."

A clap of thunder rattled the tin roof over our heads. I leaned forward so I could hear. "For one thing, they don't want to attract the tax authorities," he continued. "A doctor I know here in town has a very successful private practice. He owns a flat in London, but here he lives modestly. He told me the tax man came to his office demanding he pay more taxes. The doctor asked how much the wealthiest doctor in town paid. When the tax man told him, he wrote him a check for one rupee more. They're out there, but the essence of our problem is how do we attract them?"

The ceiling clattered.

"Did you say essence or putrescent?" I said in frustration. "Sometimes this stuff is like gathering the sour juices of our collective ignorance."

I put the parts together and looked at the Gestalt of it all, with some dismay. If there was even a small error in each of my assumptions, when they were cobbled together the small errors might cancel each other out. But I feared they might join their dirty little hands in a conspiracy to form a significant misdirection.

Every time I changed an assumption, I had to recalculate its impact on everything else. All I had to work with were legal pads and a hand-crank calculator—no computer models, no interactive Excel spreadsheets.

I eventually got the Forecast to a point where I could project with some confidence a range of possibilities and to identify the factors we needed to monitor. I presented the projections to Shamsh and the Owners Representative Board. They were justifiably concerned about several issues and we had lengthy discussions about the validity of each assumption and the implications of my estimates. I had no quarrel about their concerns, but I found it increasingly frustrating as the debate continued with no resolution in sight. ORB wanted to explore how each strategy would play out over the long run, examining and rejecting each option in turn until no options were left, and then they would start all over again.

The process was time consuming and I was eager to get on to other things. At the end of one wheel-spinning session I said to Cheves, a safe audience, "If Marco Polo tried to plan every step along his journey he would have been an old man before he took his first step out of Venice. We can't stand still. We need to know where we're headed and the range of performance we think is acceptable. Then we need to act. We need to move forward and make adjustments as they're required."

Eventually, ORB approved the Forecast and Shamsh wanted me to make the presentation to His Highness. I was pleased to have his confidence, but I couldn't shake the feeling that he and the members of ORB were not sure how HH would respond and they wanted to keep it all at arm's length.

In truth, I was more sympathetic to Shamsh's anxiety than I let on. In several meetings with His Highness I'd seen him live up to his reputation: probing, persistent, and constantly escalating his expectations. I was a little nervous myself, not sure how my presentation would be received.

When I first heard I'd be attending board meetings at Aiglemont, Sue and I fanaticized about flying off to Paris, staying in a comfortable little hotel downtown, maybe on the Left Bank. I'd take a taxi out to the Secretariat to visit with His Highness for the day. Then I'd come back to Paris for a night on the town, just the two of us, before flying back to Karachi.

We were wrong. Sue never saw Paris, nor did I, not once. Sue didn't seem resentful, maybe because we had visited so many interesting places since we'd moved to Karachi. Still, to minimize any hard feelings, I gave her blow-by-blow accounts of my visits to France and said it was all work. I lied only a little.

Aiglemont was thirty miles north of Paris. The surrounding countryside was rural, with low rolling hills, a scattering of farms and timber groves, and small villages with narrow streets winding among picturesque chateaus and quaint houses with red tiled roofs.

I stayed in a little country inn nowhere near Paris. The inn had enough rooms to house everyone, usually six or eight of us: Shamsh, Aziz, members of ORB, Cheves Smyth, and me. Sometimes others would join us, depending on the agenda. The rooms were small and tastefully furnished and decorated. The walls were covered with floral-patterned linens that were cushy to the touch. The inn also had a small dining room, five or six tables, and served a simple breakfast of strong coffee with hot milk, juice, and a fresh baguette or croissant, with unsalted butter and orange marmalade on the side.

The dinner menu depended on what was available in the market that day and the creativity of the owner-chef. In the evening, when we returned from the Secretariat, I tried to guess what was going to be served by the rich smells of onion and garlic that wafted from the kitchen. I never got it right. It was in that small inn that I was first introduced to *moules*, mussels, steamed with shallots in a red wine sauce, lamb with fresh figs served in a tangine reduction, with a baguette to sop up the juices.[28] Another evening it was roast duck with a raspberry glaze served with white asparagus and oven-baked potatoes. All that and a glass of French wine. I seriously doubt I could have eaten better in Paris, at any price.

About mid-morning we'd leave the inn for the short drive to Aiglemont. The estate was meticulously landscaped and capped the broad knob of a low hill like a French beret. His Highness had a chateau on the estate, stables for his thoroughbred horses, and the Secretariat, a corporate office complex where some of his chief advisors and their staff holed up, and where he presided over our meetings.

I was told by a colleague at the Secretariat that His Highness had built a jogging trail that meandered through the grounds. HH had been on the track team at college. My friend said there was a legend of mythical proportion that one morning His Highness was running along the trail in a green jogging suit when he came across one of the grounds keepers, a fellow who had worked there for years. HH paused to say hello and ask about some shrub or tree. The elderly grounds keeper looked HH up and down, admiring his green outfit. He pushed back his floppy hat and said, "Your Highness, you look like a Leprechaun." HH, greatly amused, replied, "Not a Leprechaun, the *Aga Khan*."

When we arrived at the Secretariat we made our way to a small lounge adjacent to HH's boardroom. The lounge was furnished with cushy chairs upholstered in understated fabrics and had a quieting view of a courtyard with gardens beyond. Just outside the window was a fountain where the water flowed peacefully over all sides rather than spraying brashly in the air.

In spite of our comforting surroundings, we were not a tranquil group. We often waited for hours, reviewing the agenda, drumming our fingers or pacing the floor, hanging on a call from His Highness. Sometimes we were told that HH was delayed and we should come back after lunch. HH was known to be a voracious reader and I suspected one reason for the delay was that he was taking a second look at all those papers we'd sent him.

When we were called, we all filed into the board room which shared the serene view of the outer courtyard and gardens. We took chairs at the twenty foot long table hewn from a rare light-colored wood, sandalwood perhaps, that dominated the space. For most meetings I found a chair discreetly to the side and distant from His Highness, leaving room for his senior advisors and board members to sit close. For this meeting, however, when I was to present the Forecast, every chair was already occupied when I entered the room, save two: the chair at the head of the table where His Highness would sit and one at the far opposite end where I took my seat and looked down the long gauntlet of faces toward the Aga Khan's empty chair.

Shortly after we were all settled, HH entered the room, all smiles and nods and pleasant greetings. He was dressed in a dark western suit, a mass of documents clasped to his chest. He spread his papers on the table, unbuttoned his suit jacket, straightened his tie, and sat down.

His Highness glanced at the ceiling, then reached under the end of the table to raise the lights. He had an array of hidden controls at his finger tips that he could use to adjust the lighting, call his secretary, or god knows what else. Cheves and I joked that he had a lever that would open a trap door. If somebody misspoke, he'd drop them in and we'd never see them again.

The Forecast wasn't due on the agenda for what I guessed would be half an hour or more, so I watched the others perform with a bit of detachment. His Highness was very astute at asking questions. He was brief, probing, and to the point. He was impatient with longwinded answers and would interrupt if he thought someone was off-message. Occasionally he would ask one of his advisors, both non-Ismailis, who sat at his immediate left and right, for their view on the issue at hand. Firm decisions were rare but his comments often included an admonition to do more, to do better, or to dig deeper, always pushing for a higher level of performance. I could see why those who worked with him closely said that he was unrelenting in his expectations.

His Highness looked up from his papers. Every head turned toward him expectantly. "Mr. Taylor. I've read your report," he said. "What about the wealthy in Pakistan? Now they travel to London for their health care. Can we keep them in Karachi?"

Every head turned in unison toward me. "Maybe we can," I said, "but not in the short term. We will attract them for routine services, but we need to build a reputation they can trust before they'll stay in Karachi for anything serious. And even then, well-to-do patients go to London for the restaurants and theater as much as for the health care. It will be hard to compete."

Heads rotated back to His Highness as he asked, "How can we control start-up costs?"

Heads turned toward me. "We have a strategy to build up our services slowly, deliberately. We need to anticipate increased census, but we can't get too far ahead of the curve."

All heads swung toward HH as he asked, "How long will it take to fill all the beds?"

The heads turned back in my direction. "After the buildings are turned over by the contractor, it will take six months to admit our first patient, and another forty-two months before inpatient services are fully operational. Outpatient services will open earlier and volumes will increase more quickly." I had used 654 beds in my projections and didn't raise the issue of the miscounted 721 beds. I had a sense HH knew the real number or he would have pressed the issue.

We went on that way for twenty minutes. Nobody in the audience broke in to ask a question or offer a comment. They just kept swinging their heads in unison, back and forth, back and forth. Out of the corner of my eye it looked like a crowd watching a Ping-Pong match. At least in this game, unlike when Sue and I were separated, I didn't feel like the ball with no control over the game. I had a racquet and I could hit the ball back.

Finally, His Highness asked, "What if your projections are wrong?" He was leaning forward in his chair, peering down the table at me as if he could see into my soul.

"They *are* wrong," I said. I heard a muffled gasp or two in the audience, but I was focused on His Highness. "The projections are our best, educated guess, but the reality will be different. Not all factors are under our control. We must be prepared to make adjustments as needed along the way."

His Highness ended play with a glance at the pile of papers in front of him. He didn't give me any direction or offer any further words of concern or praise. He just raised his eyes and asked about the next item on the agenda.

I sat through the rest of the meeting light headed and unfocused, trying not to get lost in the hypnotizing view beyond the windows. I was unsure how I'd done or where I stood. Somehow, I felt the game wasn't over. Afterward I got a few comments that I had done well. Shamsh was quiet and noncommittal. I think he was waiting to hear feedback from HH that would not be offered in my presence.

Cheves said, "At least he didn't pull the lever on you."

# 26

# FRENCH BEACH

Ghulam cradled the fishing lure in his hands like an injured pet. It was at least a foot long, scarred with teeth marks and nearly devoid of paint. One of its treble hooks was gone; the others bent and corroded from salt water.

Broad across the chest and shoulders, he had thick-fingered hands that reminded me of my Swedish uncles, outdoor people back in northern Minnesota. He looked at the lure thoughtfully. "Need new, Mr. Robert," he said. "No buy here. You buy? Me pay."

Ghulam was the chief of a Chandio[29] fishing village built on the rocky flats overlooking Baleji Beach, which expats called French Beach, a small emerald cove on the Arabian Sea protected by a semicircle of black volcanic rock, less than an hour's drive outside Karachi. The village had two dozen low houses, all facing inward toward a central courtyard. The conclave's most prominent feature was a small mosque with a green dome that rose just above the flat roofs of the town's other buildings. The village also had a fleet of five or six wooden fishing boats, once brightly painted but now weathered gray and showing the wounds of heavy use. It took several strong men to muscle one up onto the beach above the tide line.

Ghulam and his people took their fishing seriously but that wasn't their only source of income. In a stroke of economic genius, the village had built a dozen simple concrete huts that stretched along the beach and were rented to expatriates who lived and worked in Karachi. No locals were allowed, except an occasional snake charmer, a lobster or fish monger, or a man hawking camel rides. Ghulam permitted their presence for our amusement. The villagers kept to themselves.

Our hut was like the others: a simple, one story building made of concrete block, with a flat roof. We had two windows facing the sea, holes in the wall really. The vertical wooden slats in the open windows gave the place the charming look of a Tijuana jail. The windows bracketed a central doorway that was secure against everything except wind and sand and lizards and snakes and any other intruder that might wish entry. It did keep out the *pi* dogs, mongrel pariah dogs common throughout Pakistan, that lazed about in the shade, scrapped among themselves, and ignored us tenants. The dirt floor inside our hut was arrayed with a few mismatched chairs, a rickety table, and a couple of *charpois*, stringed cots, scattered about in no particular order.

The only private space in the hut was a cinder block toilet stall in the back corner with a spigot fed from a salt water tank on the roof. We'd fill a bucket with salt water and pour it in the toilet to flush. There was a septic tank or drain field out back somewhere. When the water *wallah* saw us arrive, he would ride up on his camel burdened with plastic carboys sloshing with salt water. He wore an inverted funnel on his head like Dorothy's tin man, and filled our roof tank, one bucket at a time, making repeated trips up and down a handmade ladder.

As one wag said, "No fresh water, no electricity, no telephone, no TV, this place has everything."

It had the ocean.

In the summer, the southern coast of Pakistan was pummeled by heavy seas that built up across the long fetch of the Indian Ocean, driven by the northward-bound monsoons. In the winter, the seas were calmed by off-shore breezes. Gentle swells rolled in off the azure waters to caress the shores of Hawkes Bay and the long curve of beaches that stretched in a golden crescent several miles to the west of Karachi. Close to the city the water was muddy and polluted, a mix of silt-laden water flowing into the sea from the Indus River and the noxious effluent from Karachi's busy harbor. The city beaches were littered with flotsam and stained with blotches of oil. Several miles out from town the waters were clear and the beaches wide and inviting. Still farther out, toward the Iranian border, old ships were run up on Ghadani Beach and dismantled for scrap iron; their telegraphs, compasses, and chronometers scavenged and polished by brass *wallahs* and sold to Karachi's expats and tourists.

On weekends and holidays the beaches of Hawkes Bay were populated with local families, walking the sand or picnicking. Up on the flats, young men played endless hours of the inexplicably popular cricket, one of the few legacies of colonialism that had been wholeheartedly embraced by locals. Only a few Pakastanis knew how to swim and they ventured into the water fully clothed, careful to stay in the shallows. They demurely shielded themselves with hands and arms as they emerged from the water with their wet clothing clinging to their bodies.

Once, we read in *Dawn,* several members of a local cult drowned, floating out to sea in flimsy boats following a visionary who promised nirvana just beyond the horizon.

The few foreigners who visited the public beach often drew unwelcome observers, local men and women who sat on the sand, their backs to the water, and ogled the strangers in their swimsuits playing Frisbee or basking in the sun.

French Beach was an emerald in the golden crescent. Its sand was fine, the water in its sheltered cove calm and clear. The view out to the sea was ever-changing. Tide pools among the rocks captured alien sea creatures. The beach huts provided shelter from the sun. And it was private, designed to protect the sensitivities of both expatriates and locals. Ghulam in his wisdom had created a sanctuary where expatriates could lounge about in their swimsuits, or drink beer, away from prying eyes. In the spirit of free enterprise, it was a money-making scheme catering to the privileged rich.

I never thought of myself as among the privileged rich until we rented a hut on French Beach, as unpretentious as it was. Our expatriate neighbors, disturbingly true to cultural stereotypes, included an

English couple who sat quietly for hours in their canvas beach chairs facing out toward the water, their heads covered in floppy hats, reading their books and sipping tea. Another hut was shared by a group of darkly tanned Parisians who dressed in breathlessly small swimsuits and laughed and shouted as they drank wine and threw steel Bols at a small wooden marble. An Italian family played operatic arias on their battery-driven boom-box, gestured expressively in every conversation, and served lavish picnic meals few others could assemble in their homes with a full staff of servants. We Americans swam, wind surfed, and played hotly contested rounds of backgammon, Tony Horton the inevitable winner.

Our collection of children enjoyed the beach as well. One day David came running back to our hut yelling, "Dad, Mom, come quick! We caught an octopus." It was one of those mysterious sea creatures caught in a tide pool until the next high water.

I taught Jennifer to drive on the narrow roads that snaked among the nearby sand dunes, a belated gift for missing her sixteenth birthday. Both of us risked whiplash from the lurch and brake inherent with a stick shift novice.

As often as we could, we invited one of the kid's friends to join us for the day. Once at the beach, the children all but disappeared, free and on their own, a luxury they didn't have back in the city.

In late October, after my ping-pong match with His Highness, when the heavy surfs of summer subsided and the weather turned predictably glorious, Sue sat up from her beach chair and said, "Next weekend let's have a progressive party." She solicited the support of the Cushings and Lillquists, whom we had invited to share our beach hut as soon as they arrived in Karachi, and the Hortons, our most immediate beach hut neighbors. Everyone up and down the beach was enthusiastic.

"We need to warn Ghulam," Tony said. He told me he had learned his lesson when he invited two busloads of teachers out to the beach, a break from a conference being held at the Karachi American School.

"They swam, and picnicked and drank beer, too much beer," Tony said. "At sunset, a dozen teachers ran to the beach, shedding their clothes as they plunged into the water. They made a noisy ruckus."

Tony shook his head. "They hadn't been in the water more than a few minutes when first one, then another, felt bites, like underwater no-see-ums. They all rushed out as one, brushing their bare skin vigorously. They didn't see the lineup of men from the village sitting at the top of the beach quietly enjoying the moonlit show."

"I wonder what bit them?" I chuckled.

"Who knows," Tony said. "It seems funny now, but I am not eager to repeat the experience."

The weekend of the progressive party the French brought the wine, the Italians baked an exquisite homemade lasagna, and the Hortons' brought coolers filled with iced imported beer, and sodas for the children. I barbequed an undercut of beef and others brought cheeses and olives and breads and desserts from sources unknown. It was a wondrous stone soup assemblage. We drank and ate, talked and laughed, played Bols, and took turns singing songs from our home countries.

We all behaved, of course, like responsible adults; visitors sensitive to the mores of the local culture. Still, it was probably best that Ghulam's villagers were no place to be seen, as if they had all gone off for the weekend to visit relatives.

On the drive back to town, Sue leaned her head against the back of the seat and laid her hand on my elbow. She smelled of sunshine and sea salt. "Another perfect day in a hardship post," she sighed.

In November, the superb winter weather now firmly established, we decided to stay overnight at the beach. In the late afternoon, after a day of windsurfing, we set up *charpois* outside where we could get a clear view of the sand, the sky, and the fading light over the water. As we settled in, the community mutts lay down in a semicircle around us as if they were our protectors. Just before sunset three men in army uniforms walked along the beachfront carrying guns. The dogs raised their heads and growled as the men glanced our way before continuing past the village and down the beach.

"Patrolling for smugglers?" asked David.

"Maybe so," I replied.

In the tropics, the sun sets quickly with no lingering twilight as we had back in the northern latitudes of Minnesota. And on French Beach there was no ambient light. An hour after sunset the sky was overfilled with stars, the Milky Way a bright swath from horizon to horizon. Out on the water we could see fringes of luminescent foam from breaking waves. Several hundred yards from shore an invisible fishing boat puttered by, its wake a serpentine trail of eerie green. We lay on our backs for hours, awed by the density of the heavens, thrilled by the fiery streak of the occasional shooting star.

About the time my eyes grew heavy, the green dome on the village mosque began to glow. At first I thought I was hallucinating or it was a reflection off the moon, except there wasn't any moon. I touched Sue's shoulder. "Do you see that?" I whispered.

"Maybe they're having a town meeting," she said.

"Or a dance," Jennifer said.

"Look out there," said David, "out on the water. That light."

Our eyes turned toward the beach. About a half mile out to sea a single light blinked dimly. We watched for half an hour before the blinking stopped. A little later the dome light went out as well. Then all was quiet and we slept.

Over my morning coffee I asked, "Was what we saw last night another example of Ghulam's entrepreneurial spirit?"

"Pure conjecture," said Sue.

"Right," said David.

The road out to the French Beach wound through a crowded section of the city, continued past Hawkes Bay, then narrowed to a strip of broken tarmac stretching on toward the Iranian border.

One weekend, as I drove along a heavily trafficked section of the road, two young men riding a motorbike whizzed by us on our left side. As they passed our window they waved and smiled, carefree and full of life. The traffic was moving in fits and starts as they darted between cars to the center line, then back again to the margin, and then out of sight.

A moment later, about fifty feet ahead of us, I saw a body flying through the air well above the car tops.

"Did you see that?" said David from the back seat.

"Oh shit," I said.

Traffic stopped and it was several minutes before we began to inch forward.

We came to the motorbike first, a distorted crunch of metal lying limp beneath the dented grill of a Land Rover. Twenty feet beyond the wreck, one of the young men lay flat on his back on the tarmac, unmoving, his *shalwar kameez* splattered red. The other lay on the side of the road, one leg bent in an unnatural arch, his face contorted with pain and disbelief, his mouth open in a silent scream.

A crowd had already gathered, a mix of helpers and gawkers. Excitement and agitation were palpable as onlookers vied for a better view or rushed about with their arms in the air. We had been warned never to stop for an accident because any gathering can become unruly and belligerent. Another reason not to stop was the police might show up. "They're not your friends," we had been told. "If you're in an accident, leave if you can. If the crowd doesn't turn hostile, the police will bleed you dry. They make their living with fines and petty graft."

Reluctantly, all of us rubbernecking, I drove on, the image of a flying body sandblasted into my brain.

We were warned not to drive back to town after dark, but not because of the traffic. The beach was notorious for smuggling, and army patrols and roadblocks were common, especially at night. To emphasize the danger, we were told that *dacoits,* highwaymen, were known to stop cars and rob and sometimes injure the passengers.

One sunny day we invited a friend of David's to join us, along with a visiting consultant who was staying with us for a few days. Jennifer was busy with field hockey practice. Sohir never drove us to the beach, that was my job. There were five of us jammed into the car. The weather was perfect. We swam and windsurfed, walked the beach, picnicked, and visited with friends. We lost track of time and headed back to the city after the sun had already set.

It was dark while we were still on an isolated stretch of road, several miles yet to the relative safety of city streets. I was driving fast when two figures appeared in the distant fringe of my headlights, one on each side of the road, both of them with large weapons at the ready. I was too close to stop and turn around. I figured that would surely invite gunfire. I had no idea what to do. I shifted into a lower gear and steadily reduced my speed as we approached them. Someone in the car turned on the inside light. We were at a near standstill as both men peered into the car and lowered their guns.

I stomped on the accelerator and sped away, as fast as our over-loaded and underpowered car could muster, and said, "Keep your heads down," as if that would have made any difference if the men had decided to shoot at us.

Everybody was mum until we approached the outer fringe of the city. Then David said, "They must have been cops."

"Why do you think that?" I said.

"Because we'd be dead if they were decoits."

We agreed we wouldn't write home about it. The consultant said he wasn't going to tell his wife. He left town and we never heard from him again.

"It's a shark," said Tony Horton, with no equivocation. "Look how the dorsal fin cuts through the water. A big one."

About a dozen of us, expats and several villagers, including Ghulam, were scattered along the beach and up on the rocks watching the dark shadow make slow circles in the small cove. We all knew there were sharks lurking out there, and poisonous sea snakes, and razor toothed moray eels, and sting rays, and other creatures that were higher on the food chain than we humans. Mostly we never saw them and gave them less thought than bad news in a foreign country. But on that otherwise pristine afternoon, our complacency evaporated.

"I'm glad I didn't go swimming," said a Turkish diplomat standing at my shoulder, a weekend guest of Ali and Cholpan Kosal. "People back home would understand if I was shot by an Armenian, but they would have no sympathy if I was eaten by a shark."

"I don't think any of us are going swimming today," someone else said, stating the obvious.

I excused myself and approached the village chief. "Ghulam," I said, "I have something for you. Do you have a minute?"

"*Achaa*," he said.

"Please, come with me," I said, as I led him back to our hut.

I retrieved a box from our car and handed it to him. He looked at it, puzzled. "Open it," I said.

Inside were two giant Rappala fishing lures I had purchased at Harrods on a recent trip to London.

Ghulam slowly shook his massive head as he looked down into the open box. "*Thika, thika, Shukria*. I will pay," he offered.

"No. They are a gift." It was a few days before Christmas, but I didn't think I could explain that to Ghulam.

"No rent."

"No, they are for you and your village, with our thanks."

He made a half bow and placed his hand on his heart, then turned and walked away, carrying the open box in front of him as if it might spill. As he neared the village his pace quickened, his huge frame moving with more grace than I imagined possible.

Later that afternoon, when Sue and I had changed from our swimsuits into our city clothes and were about to drive home, Ghulam came by our hut. "Come," he said. "See my village."

Sue smiled and elbowed me in the ribs as Ghulam escorted us to his village and into the central courtyard. Here and there women, their heads and faces uncovered, bent over low fires, the aroma of charcoal and grilled fish filling the air.

Ghulam invited us to sit on low stools and introduced us to his children. A small group of other children stood nearby, quietly taking us in. When Sue smiled in their direction, they giggled and covered their grins with their hands.

I smiled too, as Ghulam's wife served us chai.

# 27

# THE BEST

My mother arrived in Karachi with a large suitcase full of presents and a small suitcase full of clothes. She flew over with a couple from her home town, Bemidji, Minnesota, the parents of a young American woman we'd met who was married to a successful Pakistani business-man. It was our second Christmas in Karachi.

Among the presents was a bag of avocados, which we couldn't find in Pakistan. Sue immediately made guacamole. The rest of the presents we placed under the heavily decorated branches of our plastic tree to await Christmas Eve.

Outside, in our garden, Sue's partnership with the horticulturalist and his team of *malis* had transformed our yard into a verdant oasis. The day after my mother arrived, we took a family photo—Carrie, David's dog, included—with a backdrop of eight-foot tall red and white poinsettias that grew bountifully in one corner.

We took Mom to a Christmas concert held at the Holy Trinity Cathedral, and to the holiday gala at the merrily decorated Counsel General's residence. Christmas Eve day we were again invited over to the Counsel General's residence, along with all the kids from the Karachi American School and their parents. The weather was clear and warm. Anne Post's two donkeys were tied up in the yard, along with a camel. A small flock of lambs huddled inside a fenced pen. A skinny Santa Claus, bearded and sweating in his traditional red fur-trimmed suit, arrived in a white Victoria pulled by two white horses.

He tossed handfuls of Tootsie Rolls and Tootsie Pops to the screaming throng of children. I got one of each.

After a quiet Christmas Eve opening presents around our tree, we drove to a nearby Jesuit monastery where we heard they were going to stage an outdoor Christmas pageant.

The monastery was located on a wooded estate at the edge of the city. We followed directions to an unmarked entrance and turned onto a narrow gravel roadway that curved through a stand of trees hiding the buildings beyond. The parking lot's blackness was blinding as we exited our car. The sky glowed luminous, awash with stars.

A few kerosene torches provided a dim yellow light, guiding us to wooden benches set in a semi-circle. The night air smelled of straw and animals, with the ever present hint of burning charcoal. After the pleasant day, it was surprisingly cold, and we shivered in spite of our Minnesota sweaters and wool socks, our hands deep in our pockets.

"Who would'a thought it could get this cold in Karachi?" I said.

"I wish I'd brought my long underwear," said Sue.

"Me too," I said. "Mom, are you warm enough?"

"Just fine," she said, her Minnesota constitution impervious to anything short of thirty below zero.

Inside the circle of chairs, a menagerie of donkeys, goats, and sheep were tethered among bales of hay, surrounding a canvas tarp suspended on four wood poles. An illuminated white parchment star hung above.

I looked at the star. *Ours is bigger,* I thought.

That uncharitable reflection was immediately followed by a memory of my mother saying, *"Robert James Bobby Jim, count yourself again."* It was a chastisement she gave me as a child when I puffed myself up. "There's only one of you," she'd said. "You don't count for more than anyone else."

*Anything else you want to complain about?* I asked myself. "My feet are cold," I said.

After the crowd settled, an amplified voice began to recite the Christmas story as told in Luke. "In those days Caesar Augustus issued a decree that a census should be taken of the entire Roman world. And everyone went to his own town to register..." As the voice read, a disturbingly fair-skinned young Joseph, in turban and smock, led a donkey toward the tent with an equally fair and expectant Mary, dressed in blue, riding on its back.

The couple settled under the tent and the lights dimmed while the star shown brightly. Off to the side a spotlight illuminated two shepherds with long staffs pointing at the star as a half dozen lambs lay at their feet. The voice read, "And there were shepherds living in the fields nearby, keeping watch over their flocks at night." A horn trumpeted as the voice said, "An angel of the Lord appeared to them... and suddenly a great company of the heavenly host appeared with the angel, praising God."

The lights on the manger came back up as three wise men walked in from the wings, leading live camels, to pay homage to the newborn. The disembodied voice faded and the re-enactors settled into the scene, forming a life-sized crèche as a recording of the *Halleluiah Chorus* began playing over the loud speakers.

We walked back to the car, stomping our numb feet and slapping ourselves with unmittened hands to regain circulation in our cold limbs.

David said, "That was neat."

"I never expected to see that in Pakistan," Jennifer added. "A Christmas story. All those animals. It was really well done."

When we got back to our unheated house, Sue invited us into the kitchen where we huddled around the open oven door massaging our hands. My mother looked on, shaking her head. "Your blood must have thinned since you left Minnesota."

That night we slept under heavy blankets, visions of sugarplums dancing in our heads.

The day after Christmas the five of us flew to Bombay, the start of a two-week tour of India. Mid-morning, driving from the airport to our hotel, we passed miles of squatters living along the road's margins, adults and children hunkering in the shade of canvas lean-tos and dented sheet metal, or lying on string *charpois*, hemmed in on all sides by rushing traffic. "How desperate," Mom said. "How sad."

When we arrived at the Taj Mahal Hotel we were struck by its overdone palatial façade, an uncomfortable contrast to the desolate squatters. In the lobby Mom looked around at all the opulent luxury. "What a privilege to be here," she said, putting things in perspective. "We *must* enjoy ourselves," she added, as if it were an obligation.

As obedient children, we tried to do our duty, touring the shopping arcade that adjoined the hotel. Midway through the afternoon, though, Sue doubled over, obviously in pain. "You all go on," she said. "I'm going back to the room to rest."

"Are you sure you're all right?" I asked.

"It's nothing new. I'll be okay, but I need to lie down for a little bit."

By evening Sue had recovered and we decided to dine in the hotel's fine restaurant. We were escorted to our table by a tall turbaned Sikh, his dark beard cradled in a black silk bib. Mother followed in his wake as if she were the Queen of England. "This is nice," she said, as we settled in. "Do you think they can make a Manhattan?"

"Let's see," I offered, as our tuxedoed waiter approached. "Can you make a Manhattan?"

"Please allow me to check, sir," said the waiter. When he returned he said, "I am regrettably sorry, sir. We have sweet vermouth but we do not have American whiskey."

"Tell him to use brandy," I suggested. "And please ask him to be sure to put in a Maraschino cherry and some of the juice." After our cherry pie adventure at the Karachi Holiday Inn I was confident they had cherries. "Make it three, please," I added.

The waiter returned and slid a tray of drinks onto the corner of the table, three generous highball glasses and sodas for Jennifer and David.

"Here's to a great trip," I said, as we all took sips from our drinks.

Mom looked admiringly at the glass in her hand. "This is the best Manhattan I've ever had."

We flew on to Udaipur, where we boated out to the Lake Palace, a filigreed vision of white marble floating in the middle of Lake Pichole.

A sari-clad woman greeted each of us as we disembarked, pressing her painted finger to our foreheads and adorning our necks with leis of marigolds. The next day we toured the ancient sites, bought darkly weathered silver necklaces and clunky bracelets fashioned in the style of Bedouin nomads, and bumped and rattled our way back to our hotel boat launch on the thinly-cushioned bed of a two-wheeled tonga.

After a nap we went to dinner. "I really enjoyed the day," Mom said, as we settled at our table.

Sue and I were impressed with how well she'd stood up at the bazaar, and climbing all those steps, and the rough tonga ride.[30]

"I'm glad you're here," I said. "I feel we're so far away from you and Sue's folks and the rest of the family. Your being here makes me feel more connected."

"Me too," said Sue. "I wish my folks could travel. They used to enjoy going places, doing things. They would really like all this living big."

"I'm so glad you invited me," Mom said. "This may be the last overseas trip I can do. I intend to squeeze it to death." She looked around expectantly. "Do you think they can make a Manhattan?" A pattern was emerging. Her at-home drink was a Presbyterian. A Manhattan was for a special night on the town.

We went through the now familiar routine with our waiter. This time the bartender could only offer Scotch as an alternative to bourbon or brandy, a Rob Roy, actually. No matter. After a couple of sips my mother looked at her glass and said, with a twinkle in her eye, "This is the best Manhattan I've ever had."

From Udaipur, Jennifer flew back to Karachi to spend New Year's with her boyfriend. "They'll be well chaperoned," said Sue. I wasn't fully convinced, but what does a father know? Jennifer seemed so mature and self reliant. In six months she would be moving back to Minnesota to spend her senior year; she was running out of classes she could take at Karachi American School. *She's already a big girl*, I mused.

The rest of us flew on to Jaipur and the Rambagh Palace.

In the morning light, we drank coffee on the hotel's terrace, admiring the expansive lawns, invitingly green and rimmed by flowers in reds and yellows. A small group of women, dressed in orange and saffron saris, sat on the grass nearby smoking *charas*, hashish, and threading flowers in long garlands for that evening's New Year's festivities. It was easy to imagine ourselves as British colonialists, at the height of the Raj, sitting in these same lush gardens, sipping tea and feeling entitled. I was thrilled and, my mother's boy, feeling fortunate.

Like good tourists, we visited forts and palaces and historic oddities. "That was fun," my mother enthused. "I've never ridden an elephant before."

New Years Eve we ate and partied under tents on the Palace lawn. The bartender served Manhattans. Sue and I won a dance contest as we welcomed in the New Year, 1983.

From Jaipur, I hired a car and driver and we drove east to Agra, a longer trip than we expected, me riding up front in the suicide seat, none of us with seat belts. In those days the road was a two-lane ribbon that stretched through one of Rajasthan's fertile valleys, cutting through a smattering of small towns along the way. The road was heavily traveled and our driver was constantly beeping his horn as we passed horse drawn carts and motorbikes, or hugging the shoulder as heavily loaded trucks and buses sped by.

Every few miles we passed the burned-out hulk of a wrecked truck or bus, reminding us how easy it would be to become extinct traveling these treacherous roads, especially at night.

We were still an hour from Agra when daylight began to fade. In the dimming haze, we drove slowly through a small village, an irregular column of simple homes made of concrete block and clay tile pinching the highway. Acacia trees lined our path, their overhanging branches and white painted trunks forming a cloistering tunnel. Within feet of our car, women tended cooking fires, the smoke an ethereal mist in our headlights. The aroma of charcoal prickled our nostrils. "This is so India," I said, more to myself than anyone.

As the road opened on the other side of town, the traffic moved faster. Oncoming traffic emerged from the now dense black into the dim glow of our headlights. We seemed to be the only vehicle with our headlights on. As trucks roared out of the dark and rumbled by I could feel hands pressing against the back of my seat while I created craters in the dashboard and floor. I was thankful our driver was moving slowly and maintaining a cautious intimacy with the shoulder of the road. Even so, by the time we reached our hotel at Agra we were all frazzled. That evening at dinner I had the best Manhattan I've ever had. Mom and Sue said so too.

The next day we visited the Taj Mahal, lingering into the evening to see that magnificent shrine to love glowing in the starlight. From Agra we drove onward to New Delhi where David and I flew back to Karachi. Sue and Mom stayed on a couple of days to bark at the New Delhi moon.

One cloudless day after the girls got back to Karachi we took Mom out to French Beach. She was right at home in the simplicity and grandeur of the place. She watched silently as the water *wallah* led his camel to our hut, took the funnel from his head—his long dreadlocks cascading down his back—and climbed his rickety ladder to fill our roof tank.

In the late afternoon she stood with me at the water's edge, our bare toes mingling with the sand. "After all the places we've visited, what's the most exotic thing you've seen?" I asked.

She looked at me and smiled. "I think your water *wallah*."

She was quiet for a moment, sifting the sand with her foot. "You and Sue seem happy," she said. "I've always loved her."

"Me too," I said, and squeezed her hand.

Looking out at the blue-green water, she added, "And you're living pretty well."

"Yes," I said. "It's a hard life."

A week later Mom flew back to Minnesota. At the Karachi airport she said, "Thank you for a lovely visit," and gave me a hug.

I hugged her back. "You're the best mother I've ever had," I whispered, and then waved her goodbye.

# 28

# WOMEN ON THE STREETS

"Have you seen this," Sue said, waving a copy of *Dawn*. "They're beating women on the streets in Lahore."

The article was sketchy. Several women had been marching in the streets, protesting changes in the law. When they wouldn't disperse, they were beaten by the police. We were frustrated that we couldn't learn more from the local media, but the incident drew wide attention and eventually was written up in the international press.

The Women's Action Forum, organized shortly after we arrived in Karachi, had joined arms with the Pakistan Women Lawyers' Association to protest the unequal status of women as witnesses in legal cases. Zia had introduced the Hudood Ordinances, which were restrictive interpretations of Sharia law. Under the ordinances it took the testimony of two women to equal that of one man, and often that was inadequate. It was nearly impossible to convict a man of rape without the testimony of other men as eye witnesses.[31] Worse, the ordinances failed to distinguish between rape and adultery. In effect, a woman who complained of being raped was confessing to her infidelity.

"Either Zia believes this stuff," I said, "or he's pandering to the Islamic conservatives."

Later Sue told me the incident in Lahore was *the* topic of discussion among both expatriate and local women. Sue asked a Pakistani friend if she could help their cause, but she was warned off. "We want your encouragement, but not your help. It would be seen as foreign interference."

"Memsahib is upstairs," Margaret said one evening when the kids and I got home. It was a week or two after the beatings in Lahore.

Sue was sitting up in bed, propped up on pillows, with a book in her hands. She looked tired and pale. I sat on the edge of the bed and took her hand.

"What's up?" I asked.

"I feel terrible. It's my period. It's never been this bad.

"Whoa," I said. "Do you need to see a doctor?"

"No, I don't think so. But I'm tired of this. I want to have this taken care of this summer when I'm back in Minneapolis.

"For sure," I said. "How are you feeling now?"

"A little better. I took a nap. I think I slept for a couple of hours. I'm glad I won't have to face this in two weeks when we're traveling."

I was planning a business trip to Malaysia and Singapore with John Cushing and Neen Lillquist. Sue, Martha and Art were coming along for the ride.

"Do you want me to bring you something to eat?"

"No. I'll come down and join you for dinner."

# 29

# SILVER JUBILEE IN MARBLE AND STONE

It was a beautiful March morning, my first day back after our trip to Malaysia and Singapore. On my way to work I noticed several men hunkering along the side of the main road, painting the curbing a fresh white.

"*Bara* sahib coming," said Sohir.

"Yes, big man. The Aga Khan, and President Zia too. They're coming to see the hospital."

The trip to Malaysia and Singapore had turned out to be a fun junket, but not very useful for work. Neen, John, and I had wanted to find training hospitals we could emulate, but those we visited were either secretive or didn't keep close watch on such things as staffing patterns and budgeting. We also wanted to evaluate the potential for recruiting experienced nurses and technicians, but the prospects proved minimal. In Kuala Lumpur we were disappointed to learn hospitals had recently switched from teaching in English to teaching only in Malay, mimicking the call in Pakistan for classes in public schools to be taught only in Urdu, which excluded them as sites for advanced training for our nurses.

Our disappointment was mitigated by a magical drive down the Malay Peninsula and an overnight in the old Portuguese port of Malacca. Along the road we stopped at a Hindu temple and paid homage to a beatific Yogi who sat on the floor, buried to his waist under a mound of earth carpeted with green sprouts of grass—still smiling after fasting unmoving for nine days.

The mystic reminded me of an incident back in Minneapolis. A decade earlier, Sue and I were invited to attend a dinner sponsored by the local followers of the Maharishi Mahesh Yogi, the guru to the Beatles. I was one of three people being honored for our contributions to peace.[32] I had no idea what I had done to deserve the recognition other than one of my students was a yoga practitioner. Over dinner, Sue and I sat across from an earnest young man. He said he had visited the Yogi's University. "What was it like?" I asked.

"I was so thrilled," he said. "We practiced Transcendental Meditation and levitation."

"Levitation?" I asked, trying very hard to keep a straight face.

"I sat with a dozen others in a gymnasium with my legs crossed beneath me. My arms were folded across my chest and we practiced levitating."

"Really? How did it go?"

"To an outsider, it probably looked like hopping," he said.

Sue laid her had on my knee, a familiar sign to restrain my smart-ass impulses.

In the years after, I did learn to meditate in my own way, my favorite being a cup of coffee and a slow start in the morning. Practice as I might, I have not yet been successful at levitation.

On our flight back from Singapore, Sue and I were distressed to learn that Karachi's new Air France office had been bombed a few days earlier. No one was hurt but the interior was gutted. The reports said some Iranians were responsible, punishing the French for selling arms to their arch enemy, Iraq.[33] To our knowledge, it was the first terrorist incident in Karachi instigated by outsiders. The bombing had sparked street fighting in Karachi. Public schools were closed for a couple of days and a curfew was imposed. The military had been called in to restore order.

Sue and I missed all the excitement. Like other times we'd left town, Peter and Margaret had moved into the house, and we were grateful we had friends with the State Department who would have stepped in if needed. We were reminded how easy it was to be out-of-touch and relieved that the incident hadn't been worse.

"Everything looks good for the Aga Khan's arrival," I said to Sohir as we continued toward work. Oleander trees, in flamboyant pinks and reds, were blooming along the roadway where the curb painters toiled. Karachi's spring weather was lovely, blue skies and pleasant temperatures, and was likely to continue for a few more weeks. It all had a tranquilizing effect and I was feeling serene, like a Sufi equivalent to that Hindu Yogi we'd seen in Malaysia.

It was not as tranquil inside the project office. Everyone had been preparing for the Aga Khan's visit for several weeks—countless meetings, writing papers and picking up the grounds, a frenetic bustle of activity. The focus of this visit was the Aga Khan's Silver Jubilee, a celebration of his twenty-fifth year as the Ismaili Imam. President Zia was going to grant the charter to the Aga Khan University. His Highness also planned a walk-through of our construction site. Most buildings were now up, out of the ground, including the hospital, even though the structures were bare skeletons. Shamsh expected to take some heat because construction was behind schedule.

When I arrived at work, I checked in with Nazia and told her, "I'm going for a walk. I'll be back in an hour." I wanted to relish my mellow mood before I jumped back into the office fray.

I made it a habit to walk the campus regularly and I hadn't done so since before my travels. It wasn't my job to supervise construction but I wanted to become familiar with the buildings so I could imagine the flow of patients and staff. When finished, the campus would have a million square feet of enclosed space, a daunting size taken all at once. If I could get a feel for the parts, I felt I could better understand the whole. I found it helpful to look at the smaller spaces: a patient room, a nursing station, the radiology department, the kitchen, and such. I hoped it would all come together in the Forecast.

The sun was warm on my face as I ambled across the sand toward the dramatic archway that would be the entrance to the medical college. The college had started accepting applicants the previous fall, with classes to start the coming September. Because of construction delays, Cheves had given up having the facilities ready in time. Instead, he planned to hold classes off campus until our own space was available.

As I neared the site I could hear the whine of a power stone cutter and I saw a small plume of pink dust floating in the air.

"How's it going?" I said to Farouk Noor Mohammad, an upbeat and talented young Ismaili architect who served as Tom Payette's man-in-Karachi. Farouk's job was to assure the buildings were being built the way they were designed. He worked closely with the British construction contractor who was responsible for assuring that the quality of the construction was up to international standards. Most of the construction crew were Pakistani.

"Look here," Farouk said, as he showed me a polished tile made of rose-colored marble, about a foot square, that was being cemented to the façade of the archway that towered over our heads. "Each piece has to be cut to fit."

"It's going to be beautiful," I offered.

"And see here," he said. He held up another marble tile, its surface masked with a glue-backed material except for some lettering that had been cut from the middle. "We'll sand blast the lettering into the surface of the stone."

"Fascinating," I said. "I wondered how that was done."

"There's more," he bubbled, as he led me to a nearby concrete wall, the exterior of the medical college.

A workman was pouring a few cups of a rose colored slurry into what looked like a pastry bag a chef might use to decorate a cake, except the bag had several closely aligned piping tips, like the udder and teats of a mechanical nanny-goat. A workman held the tips up against the wall while another milked the bag. The slurry oozed out the spouts with an earthy aroma of cement and water, a half dozen rivulets running down the wall. The man moved the funnel a few inches and repeated the process, the new rivulets overlapping those already dry or drying.

"It's the stucco," said Farouk, "like you've seen over at the School of Nursing. It's a painstaking process, but it will look great. Plus, the textured surface casts its own shadow to help keep the building cool."

"Neat," I said, biting back, *That's cool,* which seemed too flip even for me.

"Just so," he said. "We want to get this part done for HH so he can see how it will look."

"It's going to be magnificent," I said, understating my impressions.

I continued my walk through the medical college, poking my head into a few of the classrooms and offices. Before going on to the hospital, I stepped into the school's auditorium. The room's terraced floor, still bare of seats, sloped down to a raised stage. A high ceiling arched overhead. The room was empty and cavernous and smelled of drying plaster, but it was easy to envision medical students leaning forward in their seats, eagerly attending the lesson of the hour.

I walked out of the college building agreeing there was no way the construction team could get the classrooms done in time. I knew Cheves was disappointed but he wasn't about to delay opening, and Shamsh wouldn't let him if he wanted to.

Construction of the hospital was even less advanced. The maze of interconnected buildings was months behind schedule.

As I walked through the building's concrete shell, I tried to see it through the Aga Khan's eyes. Like all big hospitals, it seemed all long corridors and mysterious spaces. There weren't any signs or labels to identify one area from another. Some areas were unlighted, dark and foreboding. I knew the floor plans pretty well or I wouldn't have been able to find my way around.

As I walked, I came to an out-of-the-way corner where interior walls were being framed-in and a crew was busy laying a floor of terrazzo tiles. "So His Highness can see," said a supervisor.

"Good idea," I said.

I wasn't idle while I waited for the construction to advance or for His Highness to visit. I was still recruiting key management staff and I was working on still another version of the beloved Forecast. After our ping-pong match, HH had sent down word he wanted six months cut out of my projected forty-eight month schedule for opening hospital beds. He also said we needed a marketing plan to attract patients. Play continued.

I was also asked by Shamsh to help select hospital furnishings and equipment. I wasn't directly responsible for the task, but a few of us from the hospital commissioning team were asked to advise Farouk, the architect, so orders could be placed well in advance of the buildings being complete. We helped determine what needed to go in each room. Some spaces were quite technical, like radiology and laboratory, and Cheves Smythe and others developed the specifications. Neen and Winnie focused on patient wards and nursing stations. We all collaborated on the outpatient clinics, exam rooms, and administrative offices.

We poured over catalogs from the United States, Europe, and Japan. We were hoping to buy some items from within Pakistan, but local sources for furniture and equipment were few. We did find some local wholesalers, but mostly for pharmaceuticals, linens, and routine supplies.

"Look at this," John Cushing said, holding up an equipment catalog from Great Britain. "They have a patient scale that's on sale." We would need several dozen.

"Let me look at that," said Winnie. "Nice scale," she said, looking over the photograph and list of specifications. "Only one problem."

"Oh, what?" John asked, playing the straight man.

"It doesn't weigh in kilos," she said. "Or even pounds." Winnie paused a moment to deliver the punch line. "It weighs in stone."[34]

We were all tense before His Highness arrived and Shamsh was sharing his anxiety, using what I called the peanut butter approach to stress management: spread it around. He telephoned my office frequently, or stopped by and paced in and out of my door, checking on this concern or that. Cheves was getting the same treatment while he struggled with a paper on commissioning the medical college. We were both sympathetic to Shamsh, but there was little left that wasn't already underway.

When the day arrived, the weather was perfect, clear skies and a soft breeze. A huge *shamiana* had been erected on campus, the sandy ground covered with oriental carpets. In the front row, oversized chairs faced the raised dais, reserved for VIPs, backed up with row after row of precisely aligned folding chairs designated for other guests.

People began to arrive mid-morning. There were several hundred Ismailis in the mix, with a number of diplomats and representatives of the business community. Most of the men were dressed in dark western suits and ties, and many of the women in silk saris. Everybody seemed to know everybody else and the crowd was animated and noisy until a few minutes before the ceremonies were to begin.

After an opening prayer, President Zia-ul-Haq, dressed in an ivory knee-length tunic buttoned to the neck, congratulated His Highness for all he had accomplished, then handed him the charter of the Aga Khan University. It was the first charter granted to a private university in Pakistan's thirty-five year history. Importantly, the charter allowed the University to establish faculties abroad, laying the groundwork for it becoming an international institution.

As Zia and His Highness posed for the cameras, everyone in the crowd stood and applauded enthusiastically.

President Zia also returned to His Highness several Aga Khan Schools that had been nationalized years before. I thought it was a cynical gift since the schools were now run down and neglected, having received no more support from the government over the years than public schools.

Whatever he was thinking, His Highness was predictably gracious. He thanked Zia and smiled warmly.

His Highness went on to reference the contributions Islam had made to western civilization. "It is no exaggeration to say that the original Christian universities of the Latin West, at Paris, Bologna and Oxford, indeed the whole European Renaissance, received a vital influx of new knowledge from Islam: an influx from which the later Western colleges and universities, including those of North America, were to benefit in turn."[35] He looked up at the attentive audience. "It is therefore most fitting that Harvard, McGill and McMaster Universities should today be associated with this Medical College which is the first faculty of the Aga Khan University…Making wisdom available from one country to another is truly in the finest tradition of Islamic learning."

After the charter-granting ceremony, Zia and HH laid the foundation stone of the Aga Khan University Mosque, an event I had been looking forward to since my days living at the Holiday Inn. The AKU mosque was to be built near the campus entrance, right across from the Filter Clinic, the hospital's outpatient service. I had successfully ducked any responsibility for the decision, except to agree that the chosen site was excellent.

The next morning, His Highness toured the construction site, starting with the medical college. HH walked briskly, flanked by Cheves and Shamsh, as Farouk, Neen, and I trailed at their heels and a dozen others stretched out behind. HH gestured and pointed and peppered Cheves with questions about the students accepted for admission.

"We had 1,400 applicants, seventy-six from abroad," said Cheves. "We accepted fifty. Thirty-five are from Sindh, ten from Punjab, three from the Northwest Frontier Provinces, and two from overseas. One third are women."

Earlier, Cheves had told me the students had been selected on merit. "A couple of applications were submitted with checks attached, trying to buy their way in," he had said. "We returned them."

"How many students are Ismaili?" asked His Highness.

"Nine out of fifty," said Cheves.

"Good," His Highness said. I knew HH wanted a balance. The school wasn't intended to serve only his followers.

Occasionally HH asked something about the building, and Farouk moved foreword to respond.

When we headed toward the hospital, Neen and I stepped up to join His Highness as Shamsh and Cheves retreated to the entourage, looking relieved. The pace was quick but HH paused frequently to step into one space or another, several now lighted and labeled with descriptive signs. He asked good questions and I was surprised at how informed and familiar he was with the hospital's layout. Standing in the radiology suite he asked, "Where will the equipment come from?"

"Japan, most likely," I said. "Their quality is good and their prices are right."

"And they will help with financing," added Shamsh.

HH nodded, one of several signs of affirmation I'd seen him offer.

We continued the tour, purposefully steering HH to the corner where a sample of the flooring had been laid. Farouk answered a few questions about the flooring and about wall finishes.

And then we were done.

The next day I asked Shamsh, "How'd it go, do you think?"

"Fine, for the most part," he said, looking drained but more relaxed than I'd seen him in several days. "His Highness seems resigned to the construction delays, as long as the medical college begins classes as planned. He does want us to work harder to keep construction on track."

"The contractors expect to turn over the building next winter," Shamsh continued. "Based on your forecast, we can open in the fall of 1984."

"That's several months beyond my contract," I said.

"Yes, I know. I'd like you to stay on for another year."

"I'll talk it over with Sue. I'll get back to you right way."

# 30

# NO NEIGHBOR IN THE 'HOOD

"We need to talk," I said to Sue when I got home that evening. "Shamsh wants me to stay on for a fourth year, so I'm here for the hospital opening." I wasn't sure how she would respond. She seemed to enjoying living in Pakistan, constraints and all, but she had only signed up for three years. Four years could get long.

"I understand why we should stay," she said. "But if we do, we need to move. I could tolerate one more year out here, but not two. This isn't a neighborhood. There's no place to go and no one to talk to."

She was right. We didn't know the people next door or the folks up the block. We didn't gab with neighbors on the street or hobnob over the backyard fence. One does not hobnob over an eight foot high concrete wall capped with shards of glass. Hardly anyone we knew, expat or local, lived anywhere near us. The few friends who did live nearby we met somewhere else: socially, or through the school, or through work.

"The only person I know out here is our landlord's wife," Sue continued. "And the last time I talked to her was when she told me Peter and Margaret were tossing trash over the wall into the vacant lot next door."

"I remember," I said with a shiver. Peter and Margaret had been doing it for months. There were several garbage collection points scattered throughout the neighborhood, open concrete bunkers where people were supposed to dump their household trash. We drove by one every morning and I couldn't blame Peter and Margaret if they didn't like the place. Trash would sit there for weeks being recycled by rag pickers, water buffalo, goats, dogs, cats, rats and other scavengers before the city garbage collectors claimed the scattered remains. To avoid the problem at the hospital, we were constructing an enclosed, refrigerated room to hold all our trash and medical waste until it could be collected and disposed of properly. I had been appalled that at home we were creating such a health hazard in the lot next door.

"I bet those folks who live in the squatter villages have a stronger sense of neighborhood than we do here in Defence," Sue said.

I was sure it was different out in Pakistan's rural villages. They had to be similar to small towns throughout the world where tribes and families live in isolated conclaves. Everyone knows everyone else, and the constant exchange of favors and gossip binds people together in community. There were neighborhoods in Karachi like that, rural folks from the same village moving to the city for work, settling among friends or relatives, trying to hold on to their identity and sense of community within the amorphous urban crush. But not in Defence.

"Everywhere I want to go," Sue said, "I need to be driven. I spend more time with Sohir than I do with you."

Every morning Sohir drove the kids and me to school and work. Unless I had a specific need for the car that day, which was seldom, Sohir drove back home to shuttle Peter or Margaret to the market, or to take Sue to a meeting of the American Women's Club or to one or another of her obligations or interests. And then, at the end of the day, Sohir had to come back to pick me up, and also the kids, who often had after school activities or just hung around campus with friends, and bring us home.

"And it's much worse for Jennifer and David," I said. "When they're home they're in isolation. David couldn't ride a bike if he had one. Jennifer can't even go for a walk let alone train for sports. They don't have any friends nearby, we don't have a TV, the telephone rarely works, and they have to be driven everywhere. I should have listened to Orville."

I paused to catch my breath. "You've put a lot of effort into this place and moving will be a lot of work. Are you sure you want to go through all that again?"

"If we get a place that's been lived in, and we can move all our things, it won't be so bad."

I liked the house and all Sue had done to it, but she was right, it was only a house. "Our lease is up this summer and we can move if you're willing."

"I think we should, someplace near the school. Jennifer will be gone, so we can do with fewer bedrooms." She looked thoughtful. "If we're here two more years, it will be worth the effort."

"Okay," I said. "I'll talk to Shamsh and tell him I'll stay another year. You can start asking around. Maybe someone's leaving or knows of a place."

A few days later, after dinner, Sue told me, "Margaret and Peter's son wants to go to Saudi for work."

"A lot of Pakistanis are doing it," I said. "I guess there's good money in it. I hate to think how they're treated, though." Thousands of Pakistanis worked abroad—in Saudi, Kuwait, or Oman—and they sent a lot of money back home. It was a real temptation, but I had reservations. A friend back in Minnesota who was involved in a hospital project in Saudi told me that unskilled workers from Pakistan and other countries were everywhere—hospitals, restaurants, hotels, construction—but he thought the working conditions were terrible and they were often treated like slaves. "Does he know what he's getting into?" I asked.

"I don't know," Sue said. "They want a loan to pay an agent, travel papers and such. They said we could deduct money from their pay to repay the loan. I'll talk with them some more in the morning."

A few days later we gave the loan to Margaret and Peter, and their son came by to thank us.

A little over a month later, Sue asked Margaret, "How's your son doing in Saudi?"

"He's back home," Margaret said.

"What happened?"

"He was lonely. He missed us."

Margaret and Peter must have been disappointed and embarrassed but they were uncomplaining over the several months it took to repay the loan.

A few days later, as we pulled out of the driveway on the way to school and work, I told Sohir, "Turn right. Let's go by the Oman Consulate up the block." I had always known the consulate was there, only a few lots away from our house, but we rarely drove that direction and I had never paid it much attention. Even so early in the morning, a dozen men where lolling about the Consulate's driveway smoking cigarettes. The two white columns that bracketed the Consulate's iron gate were stained waist high with red betel nut spittle.

"What's going on?" asked David.

"I think they're waiting for visas," I said. "Like Peter and Margaret's son, only they want to work in Oman, not Saudi. I'm not sure there's much difference."

"They look lost," Jennifer offered. "Sad and lost."

"They may be," I said. "It's got to be hard for them. Going someplace where they will be all alone in a strange country. No family, no friends."

We continued around the block, this alternative street indistinguishable from our usual route. There was nothing to see other than high walls and steel gates; no grass, no flowers, only an occasional unkempt shrub or tree along the roadway or a mangy pi dog sleeping in the shadows.

*Some neighborhood.*

# 31

# ON THE FRITZ

"Jeez it's hot in here," I said, wiping the sweat from my forehead. I tapped my finger on the thermostat hanging on our living room wall. It read fifteen degrees above the setting. "What gives with this damn A/C?" I could hear the low hum of the blower up on the roof but the air coming out the vents felt warm, not cool. The swirling *punka* fans on the ceiling provided scant relief.

It was late May, 1983, and the temperature and humidity were firmly embraced in their hot and steamy summer romance, a sordid tryst worthy of Tennessee Williams. The day before the temperature had hit one hundred seventeen degrees Fahrenheit, hot enough to bake flat bread *chapattis* on our stone patio. It had broken one hundred and ten several days running and now our central air conditioner was acting up. "Very, very modern, my ass," I said, mocking and cursing our landlord.

After nearly two years in Karachi we were learning to dodge and weave the worst of the summer's weather when we could, and to tolerate, in small doses, the sultry heat when we couldn't, as when the city's electric services went out for several hours or days. When it got too hot, we became quite adept at dashing from one air-conditioned venue to the next, avoiding any meaningful interaction with the realities of our environment. In the morning, Sohir would start the car a few minutes before he drove the kids to school and me to work, cooling the car down, the reverse of what we did in Minnesota on frigid winter mornings. Sohir had an art for finding parking spots in the shade, and failing that, he inserted a folding sun visor inside the car's front windshield. To handle the burning steering wheel, he kept a pair of gloves in the glove compartment, such a novel use of that ubiquitous cubby hole.

Our home was supposed to be our retreat from all that discomfort; an air-conditioned sanctuary protecting us from the inconsiderate impositions of nature. But now, just as we needed it most, our modern central air-conditioning unit was on the fritz. Most homes in Karachi, big or small, if they had air conditioning at all, had small units that served individual rooms. If one unit failed you could move to another room until the misbehaving equipment was fixed at one of several local repair shops. Not so with our central air. It was probably the only unit like it in Pakistan. Any fool, like me, ought to have known better.

Maybe our house had overheard our conversations and knew of our plans to move. This A/C thing was its revenge for being abandoned. I went to our landlord to complain. "I'll get a man on it right away," he said, graciously, and he did. He came back to me the next day, looking dejected. "The compressor is not working and it can not be repaired. It is very expensive to replace. I think it will be better to install regular air conditioners. Is that not a good solution?"

"I think that's a better choice," I said. "But you know we're leaving and I can't ask the project for the money you'll need."

"*Thika, thika,*" he said, looking resigned. "I will do what I can until you leave."

"Look! I see it," said David, his outstretched arm pointing to a spot just above the horizon, a pinpoint of light moving steadily through a dense field of stars. All four of us were standing on our roof scanning the night sky. We were escaping the house, waiting for the worst of the day's heat to dissipate. The outside temperature had already dropped several degrees, somewhere in the low nineties; just cool enough to hit the dew point. The humidity was congealing on our skin, slick and shimmering in the starlight.

It was now mid-June, the first few days of Ramazan, and from our roof-top advantage we could hear the murmur of people blocks away talking gaily, breaking the day's fast. There *is* life behind those walls, I said to myself.

We were searching among the stars for the space shuttle Challenger carrying Sally Ride, the first American woman in space. "It's funny, isn't it?" said Sue, a tinge of melancholy in her voice. "Sally Ride's up there, while back in the States the Equal Rights Amendment is dead. And here in Pakistan women are being beaten in the streets."

Sue's physical discomfort over the last several months, exacerbated by our disfunctional airconditioner, had to be adding to her mood. She was scheduled for a hysterectomy in July.

We were both relieved to have found another house that suited our needs, an older place near the Karachi American School that had, as Orville recommended, "The kinks worked out." It also had individual A/C units in each room. My summer job, while Sue was in Minnesota with the kids, was to move us into the new place. Sue would add the finishing touches when she returned.

Up on our roof, the night air cooling, we took our last look at the spark of the Challenger and its courageous passengers—soaring, free, and cool.

I couldn't help singing, "All you want to do is ride around Sally. Ride, Sally, Ride."

My loving family let out a collective groan.

Mid-June, a few days before we were booked to leave for vacation, Sue's brother, Dick, and his fiancé, Mary, arrived for a week, on their way to stay on a houseboat on Lake Srinagar, in Kashmir, the disputed territory between Pakistan and India. We had wanted to make the same trip ourselves but had been unsuccessful. The two countries always seemed to be in the midst of a squabble whenever we were free to travel.

Kashmir had been the focus of dispute since the 1947 partition when the ruler of Kashmir, in spite of a Muslim majority, agreed to join India. The two sides immediately went to war which raged for a year until they reluctantly accepted a United Nations negotiated compromise that divided Kashmir in two, the northern and western areas administered by Pakistan; and the southern, central and north-eastern areas by India. There had been two more bloody wars since and the area was still a focus of contention.[36] You had to pick your time to visit.

We pumped Dick and Mary unmercifully about news from home as we gave them a whirlwind tour of Karachi and included them in a number of social gatherings. We took them bunder-boating where they bought tee-shirts saying "We Caught Crabs in Karachi." We were delighted to have their company but relieved to see them off to Kashmir so we could pack for Switzerland and home.

Late June we were in Lucerne, wallowing in its lush and compulsive orderliness, such a contrast to spare and tousled Karachi. Lucerne's street markets were filled with mounds of fresh salad greens and boxes of red strawberries lined up in neat rows. Flowers adorned every street corner, every blossom perfect, all traces of the dead and dying whisked away by dutiful attendants. Cars drove the streets in orderly rows, obeying lane markers as if they were freshly painted.

I attended the International Health Federation Congress while the others lived it up in Lucerne. At week's end we dropped David off at a computer camp in Leysin, in the mountains above Lake Geneva. I said goodbye to Sue and Jennifer as they flew off to Italy for two weeks, to be followed by a tour of colleges back in the States.

Jennifer wouldn't be coming back to Karachi. As an advanced student at the Karachi American School she had done well academically—plus publishing her book of poetry, *Shards*—and excelled in photography. She had run out of classes and would take her senior year of high school in Minneapolis, living with my mother. She seemed so mature and confident. *How did this happen? How did she become this accomplished woman so quickly?*

I flew back to Karachi and our over-heated house only to learn that the rental of our new place had fallen through. *What fun*, I thought. *I have less than two weeks to find another house before I go pick up David.* I did not want Sue to come back to Karachi and face the strain of a move, not on the heels of her surgery. *Even if I find a place, I'll have to come back early and move all our stuff.*

I went to Orville Landis's office to seek his guidance. "He's gone," I was told. "He retired and moved back to the States."

I was dumbfounded. I had no clue, no advanced warning. *Gone?* I felt abandoned. "What do I do now?" I sputtered. *If we can't move, Sue's going to kill me. With no air-conditioning, we can't stay where we are.* Moving back to the Holiday Inn was out of the question. *She might not come back.*

# 32

# REDEMPTION AT THE GATE

I scurried around looking for another house, losing sleep for several nights. One night I dreamt I was climbing a steep mountain, picking my way along a narrow ledge, my fingers clinging to vertical rock. I couldn't retreat and I didn't dare look down. During the day I felt as listless as my Ramazan abiding associates. But I *had* to find another place. I asked Mohajir to find me an agent. I put out the word at the school and the American Club and talked with every expat I met.

With only days to spare, I found a house immediately outside the American School's back gate. The house was, however, a smaller place and needed some work to make it habitable. "How am I going to get this done?" I anguished. I sent Sohir to find Sadiq, our contractor when we moved into our first house, to help with fixing tiles, painting, and installing a new stove. I ordered a couple of new air conditioners—small wall units, thank you—and told Sadiq to install them while I was away.

Leaving for the airport to fly to Europe, to pick up David and fly on to the States, I told Margaret to nag Sadiq if necessary and set her to work giving the new house a thorough cleaning. "We'll pack and move as soon as I get back."

David and I arrived in Minneapolis several days before the girls were due to finish their tour of colleges. I had been given instructions to shop for a car for Jennifer. She would need one to drive to school, and then next year when she went off at college. It would be a premature high school graduation present.

I visited several used car lots before zeroing in on a small Honda four door with stick-shift, about the same size as our Toyota that Jennifer learned to drive on the flats behind French Beach.

The car salesman asked, "You say you're working in Pakistan?"

"Yes."

"I used to do that kind of work. The Middle East, mostly. But I got sick and almost died. I didn't dare go back. Now I do this. I miss the excitement and I enjoyed my work. And the pay was great." He looked thoughtful. "But it's more dangerous over there now."

He was right. The Middle East was a mess. A few months back, in April, sixty-three people were killed when a suicide bomber in a pickup truck rammed the U.S. Embassy in Beirut.[37] The bombing was not at all like the opportunistic burning of the Embassy in Islamabad. In Beirut, Americans were targeted. It was a planned, purposeful attack. There had been more kidnappings there too.

There *had* been that incident in Karachi, the bombing of the Air France office by outsiders. And recently, there had been riots in the Karachi neighborhoods of Orangi and SITE. But so far I had never felt personally threatened.

*Maybe I need to be paying closer attention.*

When Sue and Jennifer arrived in Minneapolis, Jennifer was almost unrecognizable; mature and fashionable in a miniskirt and tank top. "We bought a few things in Italy," Jennifer said as she did a slow pirouette. "I'm done with my Karachi clothes. I wanted a new look."

"You look fabulous," I said. "You'll drive the boys wild."

In contrast, Sue looked bedraggled. "Italy was great, and touring the schools with Jen was fun. But I am so ready to have this surgery."

"Let's get this done," I said.

The surgery was uneventful. Sue was only in the hospital overnight. "The doctor told me the tumor was the size of a grapefruit," she said when David and I came to pick her up.

David was quiet, trying to hide in the back seat of the car.

"I'm glad it's taken care of," I said. "I've been apprehensive. Getting sick over there is scary. The Aga Khan Hospital isn't ready and the alternatives are dismal. I wouldn't want to see you have even a simple procedure done in any of the hospitals I've visited. People go there to die. And if there was a real emergency, it's a long way to go to get help."

I told Sue and David about the alternative house. In my rush to leave Karachi, I had neglected to take any photos and I had a hard time remembering details. I was having doubts about my choice but I tried to sound positive. "David, you can finally get a bike. There are lots of nearby places to ride, the school grounds included."

"Cool," David said.

"Sounds like a great location," Sue said. "I'm sure it will be a real improvement. I should be able to come home in a few weeks."

"I'll be ready," I said, hoping I could get everything done that needed doing.

David stayed with a friend while Sue and Jennifer moved into my sister's house. Gail and her husband, Stuart, were off traveling and offered their place while Sue recovered.

I flew back to Karachi, relieved that Sue's surgery had gone well, and heartened by her response to the new house.

They say moving is a little less stressful than being thrown in jail or having a spouse in the hospital. I had two out of three going for me. I arrived back in Karachi ready to fight through jetlag to supervise a local moving company as they packed and moved us into our new home.

The house was smaller than I remembered. The living and dining rooms were at the front of the house, toward the street, a small kitchen tucked behind. A long corridor, lined with jalousie windows, led to three bedrooms at the back. The corridor was the perfect spot for a scarred and discordant upright piano I bought from a departing expat. If I could get it tuned, Sue would enjoy playing. I found it relaxing to hear her at the keyboard, especially her rendition of Debussy's *Clair de Lune*. Maybe David would take an interest too.

The front yard was open to the street, surrounded by a high fence rather than a wall. The lot sloped from the street toward the back where there was access to a partial basement under the bedrooms. The backyard, dominated by a mature mango tree, was enclosed with a high wall that marked the perimeter of the American School's property.

I unpacked our clothes and hung as many as I could squeeze into the house's fewer and smaller closets. The rest, mostly things we'd wear when the weather turned cooler, I stored in the basement, along with several boxes of books, art work, and extra linens.

Peter and Margaret and Sohir moved with us, but Abdullah, our *chokidar*, stayed on at the old place. Margaret lined up a new security guard, a young man who was with us less than a week, then just disappeared. Margaret said, "We need to ask the neighbors for someone. We need a man who can get along with the other *chokidars* here." She explained that *chokidar* jobs are divvied out by whichever tribe, all men from the same rural village, controlled the neighborhood. It made sense to me; so much in Pakistan depended on tribe.

The other household positions—*dhobi, mali*, and sweeper—were easily filled by referrals from our neighbors. Knowing I'd be toast if I didn't, I also made sure Sue's transient magician-tailor got our change of address.

Although there was still a lot to do to make the house feel like home, I had things in pretty good shape by the time Sue and David returned in early August. They both declared, with kindness if not enthusiasm, that the new place was fine, not as large, but way more convenient to school and my work.

Peter and Margaret were the most disappointed.

If you drew a graphic picture of Pakistan's economic hierarchy, it would look like a bud vase with a broad base representing the vast majority of poor and a long slender neck reflecting the spare middle class. The well-to-do, those Pakistanis we knew as friends and colleagues, were clustered together at the narrow upper lip.

Peter and Margaret were somewhere along the bud vase's elongated neck and the new house was a direct hit to their status. They viewed themselves as middle class, and rightfully so. They had good jobs, a regular income, and a modest home of their own. We hadn't realized they judged their worth, and were measured by their peers, by the size of the house they managed. From their perspective, our new home was an embarrassing come-down. We gave them a raise to soothe their feelings.

# 33| FUN AND GAMES

*"Allahu Akbar."* The call to Morning Prayer—melodic, haunting and insistent—seeped in through the window of our bedroom with the early light that slowly diluted the dark of night to a soft gray. Morning in our new neighborhood was decided by the call of the *muezzin* in a nearby mosque when the growing light allowed him to distinguish between a black thread and a white thread. A cacophony of house crows, thinking the *muezzin's* alarm went off early, set up a scolding chatter. As the sounds faded, Sue rolled over for another half hour's sleep while I donned my running shoes for a jog around the school's soccer field.

At breakfast, we lingered over our coffee, looking out at the alley that led from the street to the back gate of the Karachi American School. David was getting his backpack together to head off to classes. Unlike our previous house, we could see people who walked past through the alley, mostly teachers and students that lived in the neighborhood. So could Carrie, David's dog. When we first moved in, she snarled and barked at every passer-bye. We relegated her to the back yard so we could exchange a wave or a nod with someone we knew without having to apologize for the dog's inhospitable behavior.

When we moved into KDA, you would have thought we were new in town. Maybe it was our proximity to other expatriates, or because our new telephone worked, at least for local calls.

The paint wasn't dry in our living room, when Tony Horton asked me to serve on the Board of the Karachi American School. I wasn't eager for the extra work but the school had become central to our lives in Karachi. And now, living at the school's back gate, I couldn't say no. The penalty for saying yes was that I was elected Board President.

Islamil Gulgee, the artist, and his wife Zarrin, were our neighbors up the block. Gulgee spotted me coming out of our gate and invited Sue and me to their home. They were one of the sweetest, most gracious couples Sue and I had met. Their house was filled with examples of Gulgee's work: abstract oils, sculpture, and finely executed drawings of camels, similar to the one I'd seen at the Horton's. Gulgee was small and wiry and crackled with energy and enthusiasm. He eagerly gave us a tour of his studio where he was grinding bits of lapis and onyx. He showed us a partially complete mosaic of a Saudi prince, the facial contours and expression expertly captured in subtle shades of blue, a small diamond inserted as a glint in the prince's eye. Sue and I were in awe. "I did a similar portrait of President Reagan as a gift from President Zia," Gulgee said.[38]

It didn't take us long to discover we had a lot in common with our most immediate neighbors, the couple who lived across the alley, Dick and Isabel von Glatz. Unlike us casual Minnesotans, the von Glatzes were quite proper, always tastefully dressed, courteous, and demure. Dick was a career diplomat with the U.S. State Department, currently serving as the cultural attaché. Isabel was wiry, prim, and as smart and engaging as her husband. Both were intellectually curious, infatuated with living in Pakistan, and unfailingly generous. And, to our surprise and delight, they were closet liberals by politics and Unitarian Universalists by religion, just like us. I was surprised we found them out so quickly. Diplomats don't usually express their political leanings in public and UUs usually keep their chalice light under a basket.

We were surprised at the number of UUs among the expatriate community. I liked to think it was a shared openness to cultural diversity, or a desire to do good while we have the chance, or some such high-minded principle of living spiritually in this transient world. A few weeks after we became neighbors, Dick and Isabel threw a party; several of the guests were UUs either by affiliation or spirit. We soon organized ourselves into what we called the "Karachi Unitarian Universalist Fellowship and Garrison Keillor Fan Club." We started meeting every few weeks, usually at the von Glatz's, drinking wine and eating snacks while we listened to recordings of *A Prairie Home Companion* and discussed the implications of Keillor's monologues on the meaning of life and the state of the human condition.

We still enjoyed going to the movies, especially since the venue had been moved from the parking lot into a small theater in the Consulate's air conditioned cultural center. The quality of the setting improved, but not the choice of films. Sometimes David and I, having a higher tolerance for shoot-um-up and adventure films, would leave Sue at home. I did drag David *out* of more than one movie I thought was too violent—too violent for me, at least. David would have happily stayed.

Sue and I were also appointed to serve on the "Fun and Games Committee," that planned the annual Karachi Olympics. The Committee worked all year lining up sponsors, planning events, getting volunteers to organize teams, and making sure there would be plenty of food. We fulfilled our committee obligations by having rotating dinner parties every few weeks where we spent fifteen minutes on business and the rest of the evening eating, drinking, and telling jokes.

We were also invited to an endless number of dinner parties, dance parties, croquet garden parties, and, not my favorite, costume parties. On one occasion, a month or so after we joined the Fun and Games Committee, Sue and I dressed up for a His/Her costume party, sort of an ambiguous gender affair. Sue wore blue jeans with one of my western shirts and snuggled into my cowboy boots with an extra pair of socks. I wore a billowy cotton dress Sue purchased in India, my face dolled up in lipstick and my eyes lined in black. My feet were in flip flops that exposed my painted toenails. I thought I looked like a Pakistani drag queen. Since the host's house was only a half block away, we decided to walk. I tried to stay in the shadows. We had gone only a few doors when we were confronted by a neighbor's *chokidar*. He looked us over with a stern frown that quickly turned to a big smile. He pointed first at me. "Sahib, Memsahib," he said. Then to Sue. "Memsahib, Sahib."

I'm sure we were the talk of the neighborhood *chokidar* community. We may even be legend, an amusing footnote in the verbal history of some village in Pakistan's remote Northwest Frontier territories. The threat of exposure has kept me from running for political office.

Now, with over two years in Pakistan, we were well schooled in the expatriate model of making friends quickly and creating our own entertainment.

A friend with the U. S. State Department, who was being reassigned, offered to sell me his television set and a VCR. Several of his colleagues shared tapes they received from friends and relatives back home. They were kind enough to include us in their tape pool. Even so, the tapes were few and not of great interest to any of us, David included. Over our years in Pakistan we were mostly weaned of television, or at least became more discriminating viewers, a blessing with long term benefits for all of us.

Theater was a good substitute for television. Two Ismaili brothers, the ones who owned the Holiday Inn, built a theater and stage around the corner from the hotel and booked a variety of cultural events, both domestic and international. We attended a mesmerizing performance by a mime troupe out of Germany that puzzled and bedazzled the mixed audience of Pakistanis and expatriates. "Say something," a Pakistani fellow in front of us yelled early in the performance. His neighbor leaned over and whispered in his ear, and he went quiet.

We saw several performances of traditional dance, women and men dressed in elaborate ethnic costumes swirling about and stomping their belled feet to the rhythms of drum and hand organ. We listened to accomplished sitar and tabla musicians, rhythmic sounds familiar to us from a performance by Ravi Shankar we'd attended years before at the Guthrie Theater back in Minneapolis. And whenever we got the opportunity, we attended other performances, by other artists and musicians, at other venues both grand and intimate.

We also brought a bit of theater into our homes. Sue and I were invited to join a dramatic reading club. Like my poker group, it was a mixed bag of folks—Pakistani, European, and American—but with a common bent toward the theater. We brought our own selections from Chekov, Poe, Shakespeare, Mark Twain, Ogden Nash, or whoever caught our fancy, and took turns reading aloud. We also did play readings, assigning roles when we had multiple copies of a script, or simply passing one copy round the room, each person reading the dialogue for whatever character came up when it was their turn. On occasion, some brave soul would memorize a part and act it out for us, always with gusto and sometimes with real skill.

Months before our move, Sue looked around at her growing circle of friends in the American Women's Club—women from all corners of the globe who had met their American husbands on postings in Asia, the Philippines, India, and the Middle East. "We should have cooking classes," she said. "We can learn from each other." They started small, sharing favorite recipes and techniques among themselves. When the owner of the new Sheraton Hotel learned what they were doing, he invited the group to lunch and had his chef put on a cooking demonstration. By the time we moved, they were meeting monthly, with chefs sharing dishes from their home countries.

Sue was constantly bringing home recipes. Sometimes she would co-opt the kitchen from Peter and assemble some new and delectable dish. Or she would give the recipe to Peter, suggesting he try it when he had the ingredients. At first, Peter seemed reticent and Sue was puzzled until she was struck with an insight. "Peter can't read English," she said to me one evening. "Margaret reads the recipe to him if he doesn't know it by heart."

With a little encouragement, though, Peter seemed happy to expand his repertoire.

# 34

# STREET FIGHTS

I subscribed that fall to a service out of Europe that recorded every National and American Football League game in the States. They sent me a VCR tape of the game-of-the-week which was selected by the intensity of the battle rather than the ranking of the teams. I usually got the cassette by the next weekend. It didn't matter that it was late, I rarely knew the score. I invited a few buddies over to watch the game, which was always a hard fought and down-to-the-last minute contest. The tapes continued through the playoffs and even the Super Bowl. We were spared the hype because of our isolation and every game was a heart stopper—except the Super Bowl, a 38-9 romp of the Los Angeles Raiders over the highly favored Washington Redskins. It was the best season of football I've ever experienced.

John Cushing was a football fan, so he was included. I also invited him to join our poker group. John didn't know squat about poker and kept a crib sheet next to his beer can. He asked questions such as, "Is a straight all cards in a row or all the same suite?" Then he'd take a peek at his crib sheet as we'd all fold, leaving him the pot. After a few hands, though, I began to suspect he had caught on and was bluffing. But I felt ashamed distrusting my sweet and gentlemanly friend, so he continued to steal my money.

Meanwhile, President Zia called for an election. Even with football and poker and the demands of the Forecast—and Cheves all atwitter dealing with the first class of students at the Medical College—the political drama was too much for me to ignore. Zia wanted to serve another five years in office. No one had the guts to run against him even though not everyone was happy with his candidacy.

People from Sindh, the province that included Karachi, had no love for Zia. Zulfikar Bhutto, the Prime Minister whom Zia overthrew and hanged, had been from Sindh. Because tribe is paramount, and because he could, Zia had given the bulk of military, political, and economic power to his fellow Punjabis, leaving Sindh on the fringes. The people in Sindh, especially in the rural areas, where unhappy and showed it by demonstrating loudly and violently. There was some violence in Karachi, too, although we wouldn't have known if we had relied exclusively on local papers. We learned more from the BBC and the international press.

Reactions to the elections were more mixed in Karachi than in Sindh proper. The city was an amalgam of folks from all corners of Pakistan. Still, most of our contacts were well-to-do Pakistanis with an economic stake in the status quo. Several said they weren't fans of Zia but they thought he was doing okay. What they liked least was his playing to the reactionary Islamic fringe.

If any of us had been reading the clues more accurately, Zia wasn't pacifying the conservatives, he was leading the pack. One of his first acts as president was to overturn parliamentary law in favor of Sharia law. He introduced blasphemy laws, and the restrictive Hudood Ordinances that so marginalized the rights of women. A Pakistani friend said, "It's better being here in Karachi. The closer you get to Islamabad and Zia, the more restrictive things get."

The constraints coming from Islamabad didn't impact our expat lives much. We could still party freely in private venues. I could still watch football games and play poker with my friends.

# 35

# SHOULDER TO SHOULDER

John Cushing looked distraught. "Sheikh's been shot," he said. "He's dead."

"What?" I said. "How? What happened?"

"A couple of days ago he was in his jewelry shop and some guy came in to rob the store. Sheikh stood up to him but the guy had a gun. He was in the hospital but didn't make it. The funeral's this afternoon."

"Jesus. We were supposed to play poker with him next week." I was staggered. "Let's drive out to the funeral together."

The death of a thousand in another country, even the death of a dozen on the other side of town, seemed distant, unreal, and incomprehensible. But Sheikh's murder, a friend gunned down in an act of violence, was immediate and inescapable, an in-your-face shock. It turned my stomach.

Sheikh had been right. Violence wasn't uncommon in Karachi but its nature was changing.

A year before, Sue and I and several of our friends had gone to a sports stadium to watch a big-deal soccer match, Karachi playing some hated rival. Karachi lost and the local fans weren't happy about it. After the game, as we were leaving the stadium, we could hear yelling and could see stones arching through the air. Policemen in riot gear were shooting teargas into the crowd and we could smell its sweet sting. A Pakistani friend steered us toward a back exit. "You don't want to get into that mess," he said. "You've heard crowds can get violent? That's what we mean."

A yelling crowd, teargas, and stones in the air—all were upsetting but common and of no great consequence in the long run. More unnerving were the recent bloody demonstrations around the elections, the ethnic riots in the Orangi shantytowns, and now Sheikh's murder.

The Orangi neighborhood was burgeoning with immigrants who moved to the city from rural villages to find work in the nearby Sindh Industrial Trading Estates, or SITE, the city's industrial quarter. Tensions were mounting between the Pathans, from Pakistan's Northwest Frontier Province, and the Mohajirs, people who migrated from India after partition. The conflicts were becoming more common, and now, with firearms coming in with refugees from the fighting in Afghanistan, more deadly. Neighborhood civil war was being fed by ethnic mistrust, killings, and escalating demands for revenge.

Our friends, expatriate and Pakistani alike, usually rationalized away such incidents. "That neighborhood's always trouble," they said. "That's just among them. It's on the other side of town. It doesn't concern us."

Still, the frequency and seriousness of incidents was beginning to wear on Sue and me and others we knew. A Pakistani acquaintance said, "We're cautious about investing our money here, even too much in our house. We keep a nest egg somewhere abroad. If you've got the means, you keep one foot in another country just in case things get bad here." He also said it wasn't just the violence it was also the government. "Zia's trying to take us back, not forward. All this talk about 'true' Islam. It's a dangerous path. You, though, you can leave anytime you want."

My Pakistani friend had a point. We could leave if we wanted. Sue and I were feeling increasingly disturbed by the growing violence. Moving to a more friendly neighborhood and Sue finding work had helped. And I had made a commitment to Shamsh that I'd continue an additional year. I really wanted to be around when the hospital opened. In balance, Sue and I were willing to stay on, at least through the fourth year of my contract.

Sheikh's funeral was held at a small mosque on the edge of town. John guessed it might be Sheikh's old neighborhood, the place where he grew up, maybe a village now swallowed up by the city. Sohir dropped us off and found a spot in the parking lot already crowded with cars and motorbikes. "Sheikh had a lot of friends," John observed, as we joined others gathered in an outside courtyard, talking quietly beneath an ancient acacia. Like other public gatherings, there were no women present. Most of the men wore white *topis*, skull caps, and white *shalwar kameez* that appeared smudged by the dappled shadows. John and I both wore dark suits. Several people nodded in our direction as we approached. We knew a couple of men and joined their group, greeting each other with a nod and a hand over the heart.

After several minutes Sheikh's family arrived and entered a small side building adjacent to the mosque. Half an hour later the family emerged and the crowd of men began to file into the same small building, two or three at a time. John and I fell in line behind a man we knew. "We are going to view the body," he said. "It is our chance to forgive him, and to ask for his forgiveness."

It took a moment for my eyes to adjust to the dark room. Sheikh's body was tightly wrapped in white cotton, lying on a litter made of wood and cane, only his pale face exposed. "The women have washed his body and prepared him as you can see," said our friend.

We stood quietly for a moment, our hands folded. "Sheikh, I wish I'd known you better," I whispered.

We filed out and again joined the rest of the men. Other than the family, there were still no women anywhere in sight. After everyone had visited Sheikh's body, a *maolvi*, a holy man, appeared from within the mosque and called the men in for prayers. John and I were invited to sit near the back. We watched as each man completed his ablutions, took a prayer rug, and found a spot to kneel on the floor of the small hall. We sat quietly while the *maolvi* led those attending in prayer, each man repeatedly pressing his forehead to the floor.

After prayers several men went into the small side building and re-emerged carrying Sheikh's body on its pallet, now covered in black and adorned with flowers. We gathered around as the men lifted the litter to their shoulders. As they slowly walked toward the grave site, John and I joined them, falling in line with the procession, passing the litter from shoulder to shoulder.

The graveyard was surrounded by concrete walls. Mature trees shaded barren ground and scattered family burial plots. The plots were ten feet wide and twelve feet long, bordered with rows of stones and separated by narrow walkways. Some of the individual graves were covered with carved concrete blocks, some four feet high and six feet long, the ground around each was strewn with rocks and pebbles.

We waited quietly under a tree while the grave site was covered with a plain black linen sheet. Under another tree, the *maolvi* sat on a carpet covering the pebbled ground, a round prayer callus in the middle of his forehead proclaiming his piety. In his right hand, he was thumbing a ring of prayer beads. Several men held the ends of another black cloth tied around the pallet's mid-section as they slowly lowered Sheikh into the shallow grave. I could smell the faint aroma of flowers and fresh turned earth.

John and I joined the others as we threw handfuls of dirt into Sheikh's grave, slowly covering the black cloth that shrouded his body.

# 36

# WOMEN'S WORK

I told Sue about Sheikh's funeral and how helpless it made me feel. "Things can go from good to bad in an instant," I said.

"It makes my problems at work seem insignificant," she said.

"Still haven't been paid for the stuff you did for Janmohammed?" I asked.

"No. And I've given up trying."

Sue's work for Zahir Janmohammed had been productive. She developed a slide show for recruitment using many of her own photos to illustrate her script, a well-rounded portrait of Karachi's contrasts. She designed a plan for helping newly hired expats settle in Karachi. She interviewed a number of people at the Project and a cross section of expatriates, gathering hints on how to ease the logistics and stress of moving.

Sue enjoyed working for Janmohammed, and the materials she produced were used extensively. But she was snubbed by the higher ups—Shamsh and others—who seemed less than happy to have her around. "They said they'd find me something," she said. "And now they seem put out that I've made a contribution."

Whatever clearance Janmohammed might have gotten, my boss must have felt uncomfortable having my spouse employed at the Project. But I don't know for sure; I never talked to Janmohammed or Shamsh about it. Maybe I was chicken, but I thought it inappropriate.

A few months after completing the job, Sue was still unpaid. Her resentment was exacerbated when Martha Cushing, John's wife, was hired by the Project. Sue and a number of other expatriate women were jealous.

Until Martha's marriage to John started to unravel.

Martha was in town less than a month when people began to talk. A successful manager in her own right, Martha nevertheless arrived in town on John's coattails, like so many other expatriate spouses, Sue included. Back in Minneapolis, like Sue, Martha had been stretched thin balancing a challenging career with the demands of a growing family.

I heard whispers from my expatriate friends. "Martha has the same problem being chauffeured around that you did," I told Sue. "But she decided to ride in the front seat with the driver. Women's liberation, and all that, but you don't do that here. It's all the talk."

Martha said she had started studying Urdu while she was still back in the States and sat up front so she could practice her language skills with her driver. Whatever the reason, her driver must have felt uncomfortable; such male/female proximity was rare in Pakistan except among family members. The awkwardness didn't last long. Within a few months, Martha bought her own car.

I'm sure many women in Pakistan, both foreign and domestic, shared Sue and Martha's frustrations. But there were always consequences for those who dared to ignore society's constraints.

Sometimes the consequences were small, occasioned by an act of ignorance or disrespect. Now and then, for example, a woman tourist would visit the bazaar wearing a tank top and shorts, ignoring warnings to "cover your arms when you're out in public," and then be incredulous when an elderly man threw a stone or spit in her direction. John and Martha's teenage daughter and her boyfriend were held by the police for a couple of hours when they were caught holding hands in public.

A friend who had worked in Saudi said Pakistan was easy. "In Riyadh women aren't permitted out on the streets without a male escort," he said. "The religious police—sour little men with sticks and bare ankles showing beneath their smocks—would scold the woman if she didn't have her head covered. Or they would berate her escort. Local or foreigner, it didn't make any difference. The religious police didn't have any official authority but they could call in a real police-man and have your passport pulled. Then you were in trouble."

It wasn't so draconian in Pakistan, although it seemed so to those who hadn't served in more restrictive postings. Sue said many of her expatriate friends felt intimidated just being in the bazaar. "When they're in the market," she told me, "even when they're properly dressed, they can still get groped, pinched and patted."

It didn't help that many Pakistani men felt it was perfectly okay to stare at a foreign woman however modest her dress. In a harsh coun-try like Pakistan, where feminine pulchritude was hidden behind veil and burqa, what was a fellow to do?

One morning, when I arrived at the office, I found Nazia all atwit-ter. "What's up? I asked.

"One of the girls in Neen's office had a male visitor," she whis-pered. "She thinks he is the fellow her parents are trying to line up for marriage. She thinks he wanted to get a peak at her before his parents made a request,"

"I can't blame him," I said, as Nazia giggled and covered her mouth with her hand.

Men are curious beasts. Not infrequently, *Dawn* reported that an "Eveteaser" had been arrested, some guy that hung around outside a girl's school gawking at the students.

I can attest that even President Zia succumbed to the tempta-tion to gawk. Sue and I were at the recently opened Sheraton Hotel, the concluding program of a three-day trade exposition sponsored by the Turkish Consulate. We were the guests of our Turkish friends, the Kosals. We were sitting in the second row just behind President Zia and his entourage, an arm's length from the low stage. It was an up-scale event featuring a fashion show with willowy Turkish models parading the latest western-style, form fitting, and titillating fashions, prancing boldly in high heels to thumping disco music.

"This is the hottest thing I've seen since we've moved here," I whispered to Sue. But it was just a warm up. The main event was a popular Turkish singer dressed in a gold lame' jumpsuit, beltless and loose fitting overall, but cinched at her neck, wrists, and ankles. Technically her outfit met local standards, except when she moved, which she did with knowing skill. The glistening material tantalizingly brushed and clung to her voluptuous and unencumbered body. Sue and I agreed it was the sexiest costume either of us had ever seen anywhere, custom made to invite appreciative admiration. If we'd asked him, I think President Zia would have agreed. Zia applauded her songs enthusiastically and his shoulder blades didn't touch the back of his chair during her entire performance. Neither did mine.

Martha Cushing's skills were in short supply and she was quickly hired by the Project to work in the finance office, an enviable accomplishment.

Martha shared an office with a tall and handsome young man. He had an MBA, soft eyes, and a charming boyishness about him. In all innocence and with the best of intentions, I'm sure, their relationship progressed over a few months from professional, to friendly, and then intimate.

In Karachi less than a year, Martha left John, filed for divorce, and moved into her own house not far from John and the kids. She started wearing *shalwar kameez* and studied to become a Muslim. When she and her boyfriend got engaged, he moved in with her. Whatever the new couple's true feelings and intentions, they got little sympathy. Her friends warned her, "He just wants a U.S. passport." Eventually, she left her job at the Project and was hired by USAID. "She's ruined it for the rest of us," lamented more than one unemployed expatriate spouse.

Whatever impositions felt by expatriates, the constraints of Pakistani society fell most heavily on local women. I didn't know how it felt to have lived one's whole life in purdah, but I did know several Pakistani women who had been educated abroad, or who had lived and worked several years in the west, who bridled at Pakistani mores. That stunning woman we met when we first arrived, the dress and furniture designer, was all but estranged from her middleclass Pakistani family. She was just too assertive and independent and too *unmarried* to conform.

Those women who did pursue a profession, like the young women attending our School of Nursing, or those female barristers up in Lahore, the ones who were beaten in the streets, didn't find their path to respect and recognition easy.

One of John Cushing's prized recruits was a sad example. He hired a Pakistani woman with years of professional success as a lab technologist in Canada, the wife of a repatriated doctor. When she returned to Karachi she was told by her in-laws and family to quit her job. She didn't, but the pressure got worse when she got pregnant, and unbearable when she lost the baby. She and her husband gave up and returned to Canada.

Foreign women married to Pakistani men didn't have it much easier. Wooed in the west with charm and consideration, a foreign-born woman who moved to Pakistan could be isolated by her husband's family, unless her husband was liberated and wealthy and able to set up his own separate household. Our American friend from Bemidji, the one married to a Pakistani business man, said, "Even in my own house, the in-laws can drop by anytime, unannounced, at late hours, and expect me to get the kids out of bed for a visit. It really disrupts their routine."

On the up side, sometimes a woman could have her in-laws move into *her* household and have someone to share responsibilty for the kids.

But even with help at home, it was tough to find meaningful work for those Pakistani women who wanted it. For couples with the means, moving away, or staying away, was one way to cope—living in Canada, or the United States, or Great Britain.

For most foreign women, the restrictions of Pakistani society were mostly annoying, but sometimes of consequence—the difficulty of finding work being near the top. Even small constraints, repeated often enough, can try one's patience. Sue occasionally complained that Sohir, our driver, would always take the same route—frustrating for someone with an explorer's heart—and would ignore her requests to stop along the way. Expatriate women learned to live with situations like that. They learned to conform, to not draw too much attention to themselves.

Our American friends would sometimes deride the sexual suppression in Pakistan, but it hasn't been *that* long since women have had the vote in the States. Too many men still try to make decisions for their women. We are not that far removed from our past.

After finishing her work for Janmohammed, Sue was offered some challenging volunteer positions. She was already the writer/editor of the American Women's Club newsletter, and recently she had been elected the first female Chair of the Fun and Games Committee, the group that planned the Karachi Olympics.

She was offered the chance to be the director of the Karachi American Cultural Center, where she had chaired the photo club. The position had been held for years by a dynamic friend of ours who was finishing her tour. The job was extremely demanding; the Cultural Center put on several plays each year, some in English and some in Urdu. "I might have taken the job if it had come up earlier," Sue said. "But it's just too much and too late. We have less than eighteen months left. I couldn't get much done and I want *some* time for travel before we go."

In early 1984, Sue got part of her wish, the travel part. My sister, Gail, and her husband, Stuart, arrived in Karachi and were eager to see the territory. Sue worked out an itinerary for the three of them to visit the sites of Karachi, then up to the frontier town of Peshawar on the border with Afghanistan, then on to Nepal where David and I joined them.

We walked Durbar Square in Katmandu and stayed at the famed Fish Tail Lodge in Pokhara, so reminiscent of a cozy cottage in Minnesota's north woods, but surrounded by towering mountains. We hiked the foothills of Nepal's Machhapunchare range with the 26,000 foot peak of Annapurna hovering above the clouds. David and I gawked—yes, gawked—at the erotic *Kama Sutra* carvings in Khajuraho, in northern India. In Varanasi we were all in wonder watching the smiling throngs bathing in the caramel waters of the Ganges River under a soft lavender sky, the pilgrims serenely oblivious to the carcass of a sacred cow drifting in the current.

# 37

## OTHER SKIES AS BLUE AS MINE

"If I don't start looking for a successor," I told Sue, "we'll be here forever."

It was the spring of 1984 and the hospital was due to open in twelve months. I was scheduled to leave Pakistan a few months later. I knew the recruitment process was going to take time. I wanted someone who could overlap with me by several weeks to assure a smooth transition. If I didn't take the initiative to recruit, I knew nothing was going to happen.

Shamsh was reluctant, but agreed to let me start looking.

I telexed Merlin Olson to get things moving. "Can you line up a few candidates I can interview this summer?" I asked. I also put the word out to some friends who had worked internationally, in Saudi Arabia and elsewhere. A few weeks later I learned that prospects had been lined up in Toronto and Houston.

Before we got on the airplane to fly to Minnesota, Sue's other wish came true. She was asked by the high school principal at KAS if she would teach photography during the fall semester. The teacher who had handled the job, an add-on to his science classes, moved to another school in another country. Sue eagerly agreed. "I'm really looking forward to it," she told me. "And I get to use the darkroom. Some of my photographer friends are going to be *so* jealous."

In Minneapolis, the event of the summer was Jennifer's high school graduation. She looked so mature and composed in her cap and gown. I asked her how the year had gone.

She said she reintegrated into her old school pretty easily. "But it was funny, Dad," she said. "When I first got back a friend asked me how it was to live in Pakistan. I started to tell her about my friends and the school, but her eyes glazed over. I learned most people want a simple answer like 'fine' or 'it was interesting.' Only if they ask me a pointed question do I give them more. There are a few others here who have lived abroad, but you have to ask. They don't wear it on their sleeve."

"How was it living with my mom?" I asked. We had talked only a few times over the year, mostly abbreviated conversations on our unreliable telephone.

"Grandma's great. In the winter I'd light the fireplace and she'd read while I studied. We took turns cooking and cleaning. She's easy to live with." Jennifer paused before adding, "Do you know I'm like the fourth or fifth grandchild to live with her? She gets along with everybody."

"Yes she does," I said. "But she loves me best."

"No, I'm sure she loves me best," she said, and gave me a hug.

"You are such a charmingly delusional child," I said as I gave her an extra squeeze.

Jennifer selected Wesleyan University, in Connecticut, as her college of choice, surprising us by turning down an invitation from Brown where her cousin was attending. "Wesleyan's a better fit for me," she said. "They're good in math and science and they're also strong in film, and theater, and the arts. Besides, I like the feel of the place."

Before Jennifer took off for Connecticut, Sue and I flew to Toronto and then to Houston to interview candidates to replace me. As well as helping evaluate candidates, Sue had two additional responsibilities: answering questions about life in Pakistan and getting a take on the spouses' abilities to cope and adapt.

We showed Sue's slide show repeatedly, Sue reciting the script. I was already a fan of how well she'd captured Karachi life and culture, but there was a second, deeper message that crept into my consciousness as I looked at her photographs. Maybe it was pictures of all the flowers, or the clear blue skies, or the wise looking old men in turbans and beards that hunkered on the streets of Peshawar—images I hadn't seen clearly in those first months in Pakistan. I was reminded of lines from a hymn we sang in church:[39]

> My country's skies are bluer than the ocean,
> And sunlight beams on cloverleaf and pine,
> But other lands have sunlight too, and clover,
> And skies are everywhere as blue as mine.
> O hear my song, thou God of all the nations,
> A song of peace for their land and for mine.

Sue had come to cherish Pakistan and its people, in spite of all the downside cultural constraints. I had too. A lot of the backwardness we saw was a reflection of governmental failures: corruption at every level, chronic neglect of schools and health care, the disenfranchisement of those out of power, and kowtowing too much to religious conservatives. Beyond that, the country was rich in cultural heritage and the arts. The people valued family and wanted what most of us want: food, shelter, respect, and the opportunity for gainful work. Without much help, they had survived countless hardships and challenges. You had to admire that.

All the candidates asked about the dangers of living in Pakistan. I was being honest when I said there had been increased violence but I thought most of it was political and not targeted at foreigners. I repeated the caution of staying out of certain neighborhoods and avoiding crowds. Even as I put a positive face to it, I couldn't escape my own growing sense of ambivalence.

In Houston, I gave Merlin a hooded ship's compass I'd bought from a brass *wallah* in Karachi. It had been salvaged from one of the ships driven up on Ghadani Beach. "Thanks for making me take the job," I told him. "It has been a great experience and the opportunity of a lifetime." He looked genuinely pleased. "But," I jabbed, "If you don't find me a replacement, I'm taking this back."

Over a couple of days we interviewed a handful of candidates, using the same conference room where I'd been interviewed by Aziz and Cheves years before. We finally zeroed in on two prospects. "Let me see who else turns up," I told Merlin. "You know I need to check with others but I think we may want to invite one or both of these men to Karachi."

I was pleased and optimistic as Sue and I flew back to Minneapolis.

After another week with family and seeing Jennifer off to college, I flew back to Karachi to spend several weeks alone. Before I left Minneapolis I bought a machine that was new on the market, a Macintosh personal computer recently introduced by the Apple Computer company. I also bought a dot matrix printer to go with it. I checked the two unopened cartons along with my luggage.

On my way through Europe I stopped off in Switzerland to interview another candidate and his wife. An American, he had worked for several years as a hospital administrator in Saudi Arabia. They picked me up at the Geneva airport and we drove up into the mountains to St. Cergue, a small ski town where they had a retreat. It was a day of good conversation followed by an evening at a local winery eating *morgalana*, a melted cheese, on pieces of French bread torn from the loaf, and sipping a delicate estate bottled wine.

"Nice wine," I said.

"You'll never find it in the States," my host said. "It doesn't travel well."

I was very excited when they dropped me at the airport for my flight to Karachi. I now had three strong candidates. This recruitment effort was going better than I had hoped. In celebration, at the duty-free shop at the Geneva airport, I bought myself a bottle of bourbon, a beverage I knew would travel well.

# 38

# DECLARATION

I knew the drill. I had gone through customs at the Karachi airport dozens of times. You walk straight ahead, nose in the air, and look as much like an arrogant British colonialist as you can pull off. I was confident I wouldn't have any problems. As I checked through, the agent asked, "Anything to declare?"

"Yes," I replied. "I have one bottle of liquor for my personal consumption."

"It is forbidden," he said, in a more officious voice than I'd heard from agents before. "You will be so kind as to be giving it to me."

I pulled the bottle out of my carryon and handed it to him.

"Come with me," he said, and led me to a closet near the passport security desk. He unlocked and opened the door. Inside, there were dozens of bottles of wine and liquor standing on the shelves, a waypoint I guessed to the liquor *wallah* and a moldering box in that go-down by the seaport. "Write your name on the bottle," he said. "And put it in a place you will remember."

"But I live here," I protested weakly.

"No problem," he said. "We will keep it six months. You can retrieve it when you leave the country." He said it like he knew I wouldn't be staying long.

As conspicuous as they were, the agent never asked me about the two boxes I had with me, and I didn't bring them to his attention. I may have brought the first personal computer into Pakistan.

The electricity was off when I arrived home and the house was hot and stuffy. After a restless night, I awoke to the call for morning prayers and made myself a pot of strong coffee. After the crows quit scolding the *muezzin,* I sat for an hour gathering my thoughts and listening to the fluty call of a cuckoo who had claimed a perch in the papaya tree in our side-yard next to the alley.

I went to the office mid-morning. It was the Eid-al-Fitr holiday, the end of Ramazan, and the office was deserted. It was a good opportunity for me to tackle my in-box back log, and a chance to get a start on my reports without too many disturbances.

Before I sat down at my desk, I took a moment to look at the photos and art work I'd hung on the walls of my office. I spent a little time studying the most recent addition, a blow up of a snapshot Sue had taken from the lot we'd purchased in Colorado. It was a view of the lower Vail Valley, the Eagle River in the foreground and mountains in the distance.

I shook off my daydreams and turned my attention to the most recent revisions of the Forecast. I was making progress. Working with the commissioning team, we had found a way to cut six months out of the schedule for reaching full occupancy, meeting at least one of the Aga Khan's expectations. We gained three months by reducing the time between when the contractor turned over the buildings to the commissioning team, and when we could admit our first patient. Part of the reason we could open more quickly was because of our success in hiring and training staff and the extra time we had to prepare, the up side of construction delays. I hoped we'd get the building in early December so we could be open by April, 1985; two months before my scheduled departure.

Now I had to update the report which I expected to present to my boss, and His Highness, in the next few weeks. Before then I also had to write a paper ranking the candidates I'd interviewed, help prepare for a trip to Sardinia for an ORB meeting with HH, compose two presentations for a gathering of Aga Khan Health Service managers in Nairobi, and draft an outline for another presentation that some unknown somebody, probably my successor, would deliver at the International Health Federation Congress in Puerto Rico the next May. I figured the last one could slide a bit.

It never occurred to me that I could use my new computer to help me with those work projects. That was all business, and the computer was for personal use at home. I unpacked the cartons and set up the computer and printer in a corner of our bedroom.

That weekend, Friday, July 6, the American Consulate sponsored a belated Fourth of July picnic on the Consulate grounds. I was told to bring beans or a salad. I had Peter make a fruit salad but everybody else who attended brought beans. We had Boston style beans, Van Camp baked beans, beans in chili sauce, big beans, little beans, brown beans and white—a meager few cupcakes—and my lonely fruit salad. Fortunately, there were enough hotdogs and beer to fuel a volleyball challenge between those of us over forty and those under. We elders beat the youngsters every game. I think it was the beans that helped me levitate, finally, for those killer spike shots.

I discovered when I got home that at some unknown point in the volleyball contest I had twisted my knee and split my pants. "What's with this?" I said to the empty room. "My arms aren't long enough to read anymore. I've had two teeth capped since we moved here. My daughter's already in college." I noticed I was tiring more easily, feeling weary from the stress of long hours and unrelenting expectations at work. "You old fart," I sighed, as I dropped my torn pants into a basket to await our tailor's next visit.

"Sometimes I feel the same way," John Cushing said when he returned the next weekend. We were having a catch-up conversation over lime shrimp and chicken with cashews at our favorite Chinese restaurant. John had taken his boys to Korea over the summer, the first time they'd visited their native country since their adoption. "What with the divorce and all, this has not been my best year. Right now I'm feeling old and exhausted."

I knew that as soon as the divorce was finalized Martha had married her fiancée. As was the custom in Pakistan, the new couple moved into his parent's home. "It didn't work out too well," John told me, with no tone of glee or vindictiveness in his voice.

John said Martha's new mother-in-law ran the household with a firm hand, issuing directives to servants and family members without favor. I had an image of the new bride clinging precariously to the bottom rung of the household ladder, the sweeper the only person beneath her. John said she had implored her new husband to intervene, but he had sided with his mother, his family.

Martha's new marriage lasted only a few months. She must have been heartbroken and disillusioned. She moved out of her new husband's house and into her own apartment and saw her children often. Sue and I didn't see much of her after that. Martha had her own circle of friends and we had ours.

"You know," John continued, "Martha and I were having some troubles before we came here. I knew you and Sue were separated but I didn't tell you about our problems. I'm sorry."

"Don't be," I said. "Moving here might have helped. Karachi's brought Sue and me closer, but it could have gone the other way for us too."

"One thing's for sure, being a single man over here is tough," John said. "There are very few unattached foreign women and dating local women is a definite no-no. Speaking of women, I don't think I've told you about my trip to Thailand."

"I'm eager to hear." I was apprehensive when he told me he was going, but a number of guys, mostly from the British construction crew, went with some regularity.

"It was not my thing," John said. "One of the Brits I went with had met a girl he wanted to marry. He planned to propose when he got to Bangkok. It was kind of scary and sad, and funny too. I told him to be careful but he was sure it was true love. When we got there, all the girls in the bar lined up so we could take our pick. He scanned the lineup but his girlfriend was gone. Her friend said she married some other guy. The fellow was heartbroken for all of five minutes before he took up with another girl."

We each ordered an ice cream bar for dessert. "I think I'll find other ways to get by," John said between bites.

"Maybe you should become an Eveteaser."

"Yeah, right. A white guy hanging around a girl's school. You'd need to bail me out of jail. Seriously, I still like being here. I'm really glad I got the chance. Thanks."

"You're welcome."

I told John about Jennifer's graduation and about Sue's job teaching photography at the school.

"I'm jealous. I'd love to be able to use the darkroom," John said.

"Sue said you'd feel that way."

John and I planned our next poker party. And, dutifully, we reviewed the agenda of things to do at the office. I also gave him a rundown on the candidates I'd interviewed.

"Great," he said. "You know I'm planning to stay on after you leave. That will be four years and that's probably enough."

"I heard. And Neen's staying on too. I'm leaving the hospital in good hands no matter who replaces me."

That evening, home in our empty house, I wrote Sue a letter, the first I had composed on our new computer. It took several tries before I could get the printer to work. I noted the short time we had left in Karachi, less than a year. "I really enjoyed our month working and playing together," I wrote. "With my clever wit and your organizational abilities, brains, energy, personality, and good looks, we could do pretty well on some fantastically successful and rewarding enterprise. Being free of institutional support and constraints is both frightenly insecure and liberating, but I'd love to have the flexibility to catch the changing seasons, and our work should permit, if not outright support, travel to interesting places."

I knew I didn't want to go back to a conventional job being an institution-based hospital administrator. I also feared going back to a predictable life might put Sue and me back into a state of normalcy, eventually eroding the relationship we had rebuilt living in Pakistan.

Back to earth, I ended the letter with, "Bring some slide mounts. The ones I have jam in the projector."

After a few blissfully quiet and productive days at work, activity around the office ratcheted up when Shamsh returned from his summer travels. He had gotten word from Aiglemont that a paper Cheves had prepared on organizational issues badly needed editing. Cheves had been asked to suggest how the University might relate to the Aga Khan's Health System. Cheves and I talked about it.

"HH sits on top of what has become a very complex, multifarious conglomerate, with all the problems facing any modern holding company," I said. "I think Aiglemont ought to get somebody outside to help them develop some recommendations for *their* organization."

"Damn right," said Cheves. "How are we supposed to recommend a way to relate to that kind of amorphous structure?"

I was sympathetic to Cheves' frustration but figured it was part of a pattern. It didn't matter how good his first ping-pong serve might be, the ball was going to get hit back hard. We were caught up in an organizational culture that unrelentingly strove for perfection. I had my "Forecast" and now Cheves had his "Organization Plan."

Two weeks before my departure to Sardinia, Aziz telephoned me at home. "Are you free to come to the office?" he asked. "Shamsh and I need your help to revise an ORB paper."

"Of course," I replied. "I'll be there in fifteen minutes," and set aside the slides I was sorting for my Nairobi presentation.

"This report is poorly organized," said Aziz. "Can you help straighten it out for us?"

I panicked for a moment, thinking they wanted me to tackle Cheves' paper, a task I would have to refuse unless I was asked personally by Cheves. I was relieved when it turned out to be another paper someone had drafted for Shamsh. It had some good content but was an organizational mess. I spent a couple of hours doing a cut-and-paste exercise, clarifying a few points and adding several transitional phrases.

When I finished, I waited for Aziz to read my rewrite. "This is very good," he said. "Very clear, very well organized. I am surprised you could do this in such a short time. Thank you."

Such praise was so rare I wasn't quite sure how to take it. "Glad to help," I said.

That evening I wrote Sue and described the incident. "Am I being too proud?" I asked.

My social life was also busy. I was invited by Dick von Glatz to attend a bachelor dinner to meet a prominent professor visiting from Yale. Another evening I went to see a concert by the Long Island Youth Orchestra, and I was invited to the reception afterward. In late July, I had to fly off to Sardinia, so I missed the reception for the new United States Counsel General. Richard and Anne Post had been reassigned.

During my month home alone I didn't have time to be lonely, what with the demands of work and living in such a cosmopolitan city. I was eager to leave, though, knowing my busy schedule would make the time fly. I'd be back to Karachi just before Sue and David returned from the States.

Before getting on the airplane for Sardinia, I freed my bottle of bourbon from its confinement at the airport and took it with me. Cheves and I were on the same flight. We made a stop in Dubai where several women in black burqa boarded the airplane. We watched in wonder as one by one they disappeared into the head, to emerge several minutes later in makeup, high heals and fashionable clothes. There wasn't a burqa to be seen by the time we disembarked in Rome.

From Rome, we took an air shuttle to Sardinia. Cheves and I weren't the most compatible of travel companions. Cheves liked to walk, as did I, but he had no tolerance for the pool or the beach, or the street scene, or the bustle of sidewalk cafes. We agreed to march to our own drummers.

We checked into the Hotel Luci Di La Muntagna in Porto Cervo, Costa Smeralda—I loved just the sound of it. The island of Sardinia was much like Greece with scrub pine, rolling hills, and earth tones of burnt grass, red sandstone and mixed greens. Porto Cervo was a resort town, created by the Aga Khan and other investors in the 1960s to appeal to the jet set. It had narrow streets, charming tavernas, and up-market shops. The buildings were mostly adobe or white, with tiled roofs, balconies, terraces, and small gardens, all with views of the strikingly blue Mediterranean. The Costa Smeralda harbor shimmered in the distance, where the twelve meter sailboat *Azzurra* was moored, the Italian entry in the previous year's America's Cup, sponsored in part by His Highness. A stunning array of other boats filled the harbor, ranging from grand to magnificent.

My room had a small terrace overlooking a swimming pool where long-limbed women sunbathed topless. Not a bad life for a boy from Minnesota. I was sorry Sue wasn't with me. Really.

We met with His Highness several times. I didn't have much of a role in any of the sessions. I had sent in the latest draft of the Forecast, expecting another round of ping-pong. I didn't know if I was disappointed or relieved when Shamsh told me that HH had accepted my report.

Unlike most ORB meetings, where everything was quite formal, one session in Sardinia was called hastily to follow up on some issue of importance, and was remarkably casual. His Highness showed up in a short sleeved shirt, white shorts, and sock-less deck shoes. Rather than sitting, he stood at the end of the table, one foot on a chair, as if he might bolt the room at any moment. Through the window behind him, out in the harbor, I saw the blue hulled *Azzurra* pass by being towed by a tender. Then, to my surprise, another sailboat, identical to the *Azzurra*, glided past the window.

I was mesmerized. I'd seen His Highness in several roles: humble religious leader, philanthropist, statesman, visionary, and disciplined task master—but never the international bon vivant. He was full of surprises.

Reluctantly, I left Sardinia for Nairobi. Managers from health facilities throughout the Aga Khan Health System were gathered for a conference at the Serena Hotel, part of His Highness's chain of hotels. I gave a presentation on the Project in Karachi, an abbreviated version of the slide show Sue created for recruitment. I also led a session on organizing and managing for quality. It all went well and I managed to sneak away for a two-hour tour of a game park on the edge of the city.

After the conference, I took my well traveled bottle of bourbon, still unopened, and flew back to Karachi. This time when the customs agent asked if I had anything to declare, I said, "No."

# 39

## KNEE DEEP

Sue was eager to begin teaching photography at KAS as soon as she returned with David from summer break. She was barely off the airplane when she was approached by the high school principal. "Can you also teach English for us this semester?" he asked. "Our regular teacher is pregnant and has decided to have her baby in the States. She won't be back until after Christmas."

"I'm not an English teacher," Sue protested.

"No, but you speak good English," said the principal. Before Sue could ponder the full implications of that sales pitch, the principal continued, "You get paid and we'll give you some help on lesson plans."

"I'll give it a try," Sue said, launching herself into an overwhelming learning experience. She had four classes, tenth through twelfth grade, each a mix of students from more than a dozen countries. For many, English was their second language. From Shakespeare to Nathaniel Hawthorne, she was just one day's prep ahead of her bright students. In a spark of what she thought was a creative twist, she told the students she was going to introduce humor by playing some Garrison Keillor tapes. "He's a writer and radio personality back in America," she said, and was surprised when the eyes of several students lit up.

"Oh, good," one student said. "We know him. We had him last year."

"I should'a guessed," Sue told me. The head of the English Department *was* from Lake Wobegone country.

Not quite understanding the consequences, Sue gave all four classes a writing assignment. The next week she was flooded under a pile of blue books, each paper needing to be graded. She knew she was in deep trouble when she looked at the first paper. It was written by a student from Turkey. Although the ideas were cogent, it was filled with misspellings, poor grammar, and indecipherable punctuation errors.

Sue went to her friend who headed the high school English Department. "Help!" she pleaded. "How do I deal with so many issues and not discourage my students? I have others like this."

"Just pick one issue in each paper, and don't mark up every mistake," she suggested. "Forget spelling. It's not important. Just concentrate on matching subject and verb, or tense. Help them learn one thing and then move on to another lesson in the next paper."

"I am *not* assigning another paper anytime soon," said Sue.

Weeks into the semester Sue told me, "I wanted work and I got it. But, boy, do I ever appreciate what teachers do. I've lost nine pounds in the last eight weeks just trying to keep up with these great kids."

"Well, you look terrific," I said. It was probably not the kind of sympathy and understanding she was looking for.

In early September it rained and rained, a late summer deluge that knew no end. Our roof leaked and the sewer backed up into our basement. In the midst of the downpour, Sue was on the roof sweeping water into the scuppers. I was in the basement with Peter frantically hefting boxes of books and clothing to the top of makeshift tables and benches. Mohajir sent over two young men who stood in the basement muck in their bare feet and shoveled the black smelly mess out into the yard. They flushed the floor with a hose and washed it down with bleach. Carrie retreated to a dry corner of the yard under an overhanging roof, sad-eyed and whimpering.

The washing machine that came with the house was ruined and our *dhobi* offered to do our laundry in the bathtub. While we were happy not to invest in another machine, Sue felt we were taking advantage of his good nature as he sloshed wet sheets and towels in the tub. He seemed to prefer doing the laundry by hand.

The entire city was drowning in water, a quagmire of mud and sludge. I wrote my mother. "When Sohir drove me to work the hospital parking lot had a muck factor of 3, slick and slippery. By noon, after continuing rain and the tread of several dozen automobile tires, the muck factor had escalated to a solid 5, easily able to swallow those offending tires up to their hubs. By mid-afternoon there were corners where the muck factor hovered in the 7-8 range, a bubbling quagmire waiting to suck in an unwary motor-rickshaw or an inattentive Pathan. In fact, there was a small Suzuki truck reported missing, over-loaded as usual with three *malis* from Mahmudabad, 200 kilos of planting soil, two shovels, and a wheelbarrow, transporting a half dozen small palm trees to the back of the construction site for a landscaping job. The only clues to its whereabouts were a broken plastic sandal, a badly soiled turban, and a palm frond found floating on the oil-glistening surface of a belching pot-hole. I fear for the worst."

The next day, I felt my letter had been too flippant when I rode by one of the squatter villages that had sprung up along a deep wadi. Flooding had undercut the bank and several shanties had collapsed. I wanted to know more about the rain and flooding, and the resultant damage, but the newspaper *Dawn* was silent on the topic.

The water in our basement was barely dry when Sue and I hosted the two most promising candidates for my job, one after the other, introducing them to the Project and the city with our usual razzmatazz. Ultimately we settled on Bill Borton, a fellow from the States with experience working in big hospitals. Shamsh agreed to take his name to the Owner's Representative Board and extend an offer.

I was greatly relieved and looked forward to having my successor start by December or January so he could be around for the construction turn-over and shadow me until we admitted our first patient, *Insha'lah*.

# 40

# DAVID BUYS A CARPET

The shop owner looked at me expectantly as his young assistant rolled out another carpet at my feet. "No," I said. "Please show the carpets to my son here." I repeated my instructions a couple of times, but the shop owner seemed puzzled by my request.

It was September, 1984, and David and I were sitting on low stools in the carpet shop of the Intercontinental Hotel in Peshawar. The hotel was the best in the city and rich in tradition, but it looked threadbare at the edges, much like the tribal rugs Sue and I favored after four years of visiting numerous shops and seeing hundreds of carpets. I wasn't sure what kind of carpet David might prefer.

We were in Peshawar more by accident than by intent. Sue, David and I, along with Tony and Nana Horton and their two-year-old son, Michael, had decided to go "up north" for the Eid-al-Adha holidays, the Festival of Sacrifice. Our target was the hill town of Gilgit, deep in the inaccessible Hunza Valley, surrounded by the Karakoram Mountains, and only miles from the border with China. Gilgit is not far from the Great Trango Tower—its east face a sheer rock precipice that plummets 4,396 feet, the largest near vertical drop in the world. The massive K2, at 28,251 feet the second highest mountain on earth, hovered nearby.

Along with its spectacular scenery, I wanted to visit Gilgit because it was heavily populated by Ismailis and had several health clinics sponsored by the Aga Khan. My earlier plans to visit the valley had been thwarted by business or weather. This was my last chance.

The region was also known for the longevity of its people. It was told that one centenarian, still fit and mentally alert, was asked to what he attributed his long life and good health. "Hunza water," he replied. It was a potent fermented drink home-brewed from mulberries, euphemistically named to skirt the Islamic taboo against alcohol. When asked where he got the Hunza water, he pointed across the valley to a spot on the opposing hill, a trip that required a two mile walk, first following a switch-backed trail down-valley several hundred feet, then an equally steep climb up to his source of the valued brew, and then return. "I walk there every two or three days," he said.

Healthful hiking and Hunza water sounded appealing.

The six of us flew into Islamabad for an overnight, hoping to catch the early morning shuttle to Gilgit that flew out of nearby Rawalpindi. When it went, the flight into Gilgit was one of the most dangerous and harrowing on the planet, squeezing between steep rock walls and skimming over high mountain passes. It was an adventure we anticipated with a combination of excitement and foreboding.

Shortly after checking into our hotel, I got a telephone call from Tony. "Come up here. You've got to see our room."

The Hortons had been upgraded to the Presidential Suite by the hotel's manager, the same suite used by our own Vice President George Herbert Walker Bush. The space was enormous with richly carved woodwork and elegantly upholstered furniture. There was a well stocked bar and the dining room table was set for a formal dinner for six. Tony looked embarrassed. "The hotel's owner back in Karachi has a son he wants admitted to the American School. The boy's qualified and can make it on his own. How can I say no to all this?" he said, as he swept his hand around the room.

"You can't," I said. "As my mother would say, 'it's our obligation to enjoy it.'"

When we awoke in the morning, bolts of lightning flashed in the still black sky. "Maybe it's just a local squall," said Nana, always the optimist, so we headed to the airport. When we arrived at the terminal there were already more people in the lobby than the small plane could hold, including a few teachers from the Karachi American School with plans like our own. "Don't worry, we have reservations," said Nana.

"Yes, you most certainly have reservations," said the attendant. "But see here, you are not on the list of those certified to go." Before we could protest, he added, "But, no problem. Today's flight is cancelled due to rain, isn't it."

Tony said, "I don't like the prospects, We can spend half a day getting registered with the local authorities and then risk that tomorrow's flight will be cancelled anyway." We had already agreed that traveling to Gilgit by jeep was not an option. It was a sixteen-hour trip each way over narrow, muddy and treacherous roads. We had too little time and a two-year-old in tow.

"Sounds like it's our back-up plan," I said. "Let's go to Swat."

Tony rented a nine passenger van from the International School, big enough for the six of us and all our clothing, sleeping bags, extra food, and a case of beer. With Tony at the wheel, we drove up-valley, following the Swat River. We stopped at a promontory overlooking the Tarbela Dam, the largest earth dam in the world. Roaring columns of water rushed down its face, then plumed thunderously into the air. We all gaped in wonder as Michael yelled above the din, "For walks."

"Yes," said Nana. "We'll go for a walk."

"No, for walks," said Michael, as he picked up a stone.

"Oh, throw rocks," said Tony, as Michael pitched the stone into the roaring abyss, then bent down to pick up another. We all joined in the fun, throwing rocks to Michael's gleeful giggles.

We continued on, up and over Malakand Pass into the lower Swat Valley[40]—a lush expanse of fruit orchards, rice paddies, and corn fields. We reached the hill station of Saidu Sharif and registered in the famed Swat Hotel in time for afternoon tea. The hotel was very British, with rooms facing onto wide verandas where we sat admiring the English gardens full of roses and manicured hedges. The hotel's glory was diminished by time and a lack of money, with peeling paint and an uninspiring menu, but it was still charming, clean, and the best in the region. We even had hot water—once a day when they fired up the wood-burning water heaters at the back of the building.

Still eager to see the high country, we planned to drive the next day up to Kalam Valley beneath the nearly 20,000-foot Mount Falaksir. Tony said there was a place to ski up there somewhere. "It's not really a ski resort," he warned. "It's just a place where some people ski. It's the best around, but it's no Vail."

I was glad to know it was there even if I didn't plan to ski.

No such luck. Again, we were frustrated by heavy rains that washed out the roads and we had to retreat to Madyan, getting the last two rooms in the local hotel. Later that afternoon our teacher friends from KAS drove into town, looking tired and strained. They had driven ten hours toward Gilgit only to find the roads blocked by avalanches. They were diverted another ten hours over hair-raising passes to reach Swat. They arrived in Madyan too late to find a room and had to settle for a place down the road with no running water and no food service. We shared some of our snacks and beer to tide them over.

Feeling fortunate and a bit smug with the wisdom of our decision-making, we spent the next two days poking around those parts of the rich valley we could access. As we hiked through one village, a gaggle of children fell in behind us. We were good entertainment just by our presence. The village elders were curious too, and invariably hospitable, nodding and smiling as we walked by. We thought our welcome was warmer because we had our own children in tow. We picnicked by a rushing stream and carefully picked our way across a rope suspension bridge, Michael riding on his dad's back.

In one village we were invited to watch the ritual sacrifice of goats for the Eid holiday feast. The week before, back in Karachi, I had again seen goats and lambs for sale on the street corners, small corrals of animals, each with its fleece branded with a slash of irides-cent paint. Here in Swat, half a dozen villagers lined up, each with a small goat cradled in his arms. The man at the head of the line helped another man in a white turban and robe, possibly a mullah, hold the goat on the ground next to a shallow, stone encircled cistern. Nana distracted Michael as the rest of us watched in fascination as the ani-mal was dispatched with a curious combination of respectful incanta-tion and surgical efficiency.

Too quickly, we left the cool, verdant, and hospitable mountains and worked our way to the dust, heat, intrigue, and vibrancy of Peshawar.

Peshawar is strategically located at the eastern end of the Khyber Pass, the main road going in and out of Afghanistan, and was serving as a major staging center for arms and materials headed to the war zone. For much of its history, the city had a habit of being embroiled in one war or another. It had been a major frontier in Britain's Great Game with Russia for dominance over Central Asia, and the site of fierce battles with Pathan warrior tribes. The British had considered the region ungovernable.[41]

It seemed as unruly as ever when we visited, although Sue said the city felt tamer than when she was there earlier, with my sister and brother-in-law. "There are more tourists," she said. "And the locals are less mysterious and threatening in plain *shalwar kameez*. Last time it was winter and they were wrapped up in dark turbans and Pathan shawls. Many carried guns and wore bandoleers."

As we drove the busy city streets toward our hotel, Nana said to Sue, "This town is so exciting. It's a little scary and so colorful and there's so much going on. I can't wait to go to the bazaar, where they have the Afghan jewelry. And the Afghan Metal Works where I bought those copper chafing dishes you like."

We did all that and more, eager to see all we could in two short days before heading back home. That first evening after dinner we played dominos until the adrenaline of the day wore off.

The next morning we were all moving slowly, easing into the day, enjoying a leisurely breakfast in the hotel coffee shop. Mid-morning, across the lobby, the carpet merchant clattered open the sliding metal door to his shop. "Come on," I said to David. "It's time for you to buy that carpet we promised. If we're the first ones into his shop, the owner won't let us leave without buying something."

"I'm ready," said David. "Let's go."

I greeted the owner as we entered the shop. "*A Salam A Lakum.*"

"*Va Lakum A Salam,*" he replied.

"Good morning and welcome." He gave us a couple of minutes to walk around before saying, "May I offer chai to your good self, or a Fanta for the young Sahib?"

David smiled. I think it was the first time he'd been called Sahib. "A Fanta, please," he said. "*Shukria.*"

"I'll have a Fanta as well," I said.

"While we wait, please let me show you my shop." But first he handed me a stack of business cards. "I sell to many foreigners," he said, as I riffled through the stack.

"Here's mine," I said, as I picked out a card and showed it to him. Even though it was my first visit to Peshawar, I wasn't too surprised to see my card in his collection, given to him no doubt by Sue when she'd visited a year ago escorting Gail and Stuart.

The merchant looked at the card and then at me. "He was tall, with two women."

"My wife, my sister, and her husband," I said, impressed at his memory.

He looked at the card again. "Then you are Mister Robert?" he asked, as I nodded. "Then only the best price for an old friend. Please let me show you my shop."

He led us to a wall draped with several Iranian carpets with exquisite floral designs executed in glistening silk. Similar carpets, tightly rolled in colorful columns sorted by size, leaned against the wall. "Persian," he said. "Only the finest silk." He pulled up the corner of one carpet to show us its underside. "See how fine the knots."

I turned to David. "Remember our bargain. You pick the carpet and I'll pay. But there's a limit. You can have one of these but they're expensive, so it will need to be small."

"I *know*," he said, exasperated that I felt the need to explain the rules yet again.

The merchant showed us his assortment of new "manufactured" carpets, commercial pieces made in Pakistan in traditional designs. Sue had told me that many of these carpets were made in orphanages. Earlier, she had visited a Christian orphanage just outside Karachi. The workshop was lined with looms attended by children, some as young as five or six, their small fingers selecting short lengths of colored yarns and nimbly tying knots; working between school classes and play time. She was told the carpets were sold to help cover the expenses of housing and meals.

David looked again at the Persians and once more at the new carpets. "I think I like tribal rugs," he said, a boy after my own heart.

Our drinks arrived and the shop owner invited us to sit at two low stools. David nodded at the young man carrying the tray, a boy about David's age, and said, "*Shukria.*"

The shop assistant rolled out a carpet at my feet. I held out my hand and gestured toward David. "My son is choosing a rug for his thirteenth birthday," I said to the shop owner as I sat back on my stool. "He will decide."

"*Accha*, good, good," the shopkeeper said, finally getting my drift as he gave brief instructions to his assistant.

We spent the next half hour looking at dozens of tribal carpets as the shop owner detailed each carpet's origin and the characteristics of its design. I knew that the tribes of Pakistan and Afghanistan had long traditions of making knotted and woven carpets for both personal use and sale. Although influenced by centuries of wandering and trading along the Silk Road, many tribal styles were unique to specific geographic regions, some to individual villages, even families. Their common characteristics were that they were made of hand spun wools, using natural vegetable dyes, usually with a preponderance of mellow reds and indigo blue/blacks accented with lighter tans.

"Now, because of the war," explained the merchant, "carpets are coming from Afghanistan by the camel load. I sell many carpets to other shops in Islamabad and Karachi, some even to Europe. But the best price is here in my shop."

He showed David several rugs that were charmingly uneven in design and color, the intricate knotting done from memory rather than a pattern. It was easy to imagine a woman, although in some regions men did most of the rug making, teaching her children to tie knots, the youngsters working the loom in shifts in the shade of a knobby tree, running short of wool from one dye lot and substituting another, creating a prayer rug for the patriarch of the family.

He showed us other rugs that looked dirty and worn, as if they had spent their life underfoot as the floor of an earthbound tent.

I was concerned, but kept my mouth shut, when he showed David a couple of new tribals with their traditional designs enhanced by knotted airplanes and tanks, an obvious and disturbing reflection of the influence of the Soviet war on Afghan village life.

With limited international news, local censorship, and a thousand miles of distance from the action, we weren't very well informed on the dynamics of the messy war playing out across Pakistan's Northwest border. We knew the United States was a not-too-silent partner with Pakistan, funneling weapons and financial assistance to the mujahideen freedom fighters in Afghanistan. We'd also heard that border towns inside Pakistan were being used as staging areas for supplies and as safe havens for Afghan fighters who could escape the pursuing Soviets. Looking at those war-hewn carpets, it all became more real.

David sorted the carpets he liked into one pile, then narrowed his choices to his favorites. The shop owner and I politely haggled before settling on a fair price for the rug David most coveted, a handsome tribal in deep red, gold and blue.

"Thanks, Dad," David said, then added as he turned to the shop owner, "*Khuda hafiz.*"

As we were leaving the shop I was approached by the hotel's manager. "I've been watching you," he said, "and I must say that would not happen here in my country."

"What do you mean?" I asked.

"You allowed your son to make a big decision, and he is so young. We think it is the father's responsibility to make such decisions." He reached out to shake my hand. "Thank you for shopping here," he said. "I can see why democracy works in your country."

He had a point. In the States we let our children practice democracy when they're in pre-school, voting on limited choices no doubt—Would you like me to read Goldilocks or Dr. Seuss?—but we do give them a choice nevertheless. We encourage them to raise their hands in the classroom and to ask questions. We ask them for their opinions. We do it imperfectly, but when we get it right, we teach them the winning majority needs to respect the needs of the minority.

"We're giving democracy a test right now," I said to the hotel manager. "Our elections are only a few weeks away."

"Yes, I know," he said. "I like to follow the presidential campaigns, as best I can. Who you elect is important to us."

With the frenetic pace of our life in Karachi, and with no television and few newspaper reports, Sue and I felt interested but detached from the whole campaign process, a drama playing out in a distant land. Our world had flipped. We got news in headlines and snippets from the States with little analysis. Walter Mondale, our Minnesota native son, was challenging Ronald Reagan, who was seeking a second term. At one point Mondale, in an ill-advised but very Midwestern thing to do, said he would raise taxes. We were proud of him when he selected Geraldine Ferrero as his running mate, the first female Vice Presidential candidate ever. It was a bonus when a stranger at an airport asked Sue if she was Ferrero, they did wear their hair in a similar bob.

We were so out of touch we thought Mondale would win. Sue and I were long-time Democrats of the Minnesota Hubert Humphrey tradition, and we were encouraged by our small community of fellow American expatriate friends, so many of whom shared our liberal political leanings. Our daughter Jennifer also gave us hope. "Here at Wesleyan," she wrote, "all my friends are Democrats."

"We've already filed our absentee ballots at the American Consulate," I told the hotel manager.

"Good," he said. "It is important to participate, isn't it."

There was a note of wistfulness in the manager's statement. I wasn't sure our form of democracy would work so well in Pakistan where family and tribal loyalty were paramount and trumped any sense of national unity. If President Zia was any example, I thought, the group in power put its energies into improving its own lot and the lot of its loyal followers, and discounted or disregarded the needs of those who were out of power.

Still, the manager echoed what I'd heard from other Pakistanis. We all yearn for a voice in our government. President Zia made noises about democracy and elections, and serving the people, but he acted to suppress the institutions of democracy: education, a free press, and an independent judicial system. And it wasn't about religion, whatever the political rhetoric. It was all about power and control and suppressing the opposition.

# 41

# PERNICIOUS PARASITES

John Cushing's driver handed me a note when I arrived at the office. "I'm not feeling well and won't be at work today," it said. It was signed by John.

*Another bout of Karachi Crud,* I thought.

At lunch the next day, Neen Lillquist watched as I carefully picked the fine white strands of pith off each section of a tangerine. "Why do you do that?" she asked. "I didn't know you were so fastidious."

I looked down at the neat circle of citrus slices I'd laid out on my napkin like the petals of a flower. "Sorry," I said. "I'm a bit distracted. My mother used to do this for me when I was a kid. She'd put a dab of powdered sugar in the middle, just like a daisy." I paused to reconnect with my thoughts.

"I was thinking of my son David," I said. "Yesterday, he was biking back from a friend's house just at curfew and saw an army truck racing up the street with a soldier manning a machine gun. You've seen them. He was frightened. He thought the guy was going to shoot him."

Several days before, President Zia had called in troops to restore order in the streets. The disturbances started a few days after the beginning of Muharram. As usual, some Shias did their ritual public flagellation, mourning a long lost martyr. As usual, some Sunnis mocked them. The results were inevitable, fights and skirmishes that went on for days. Except this year the unsettledness was more severe and continued on after the celebrations were over. The military had been making a show of their presence throughout Karachi, even in our neighborhood.

"I think things are calmer now," said Neen. "But how would we know?" She too was frustrated with the local news blackout.

"Yeah, I think they are. But it's not just that. A couple of weeks ago it was that illness, when David was so sick." Right after we returned from Swat, both the Horton's son, two-year-old Michael, and David came down with some mysterious disease with vomiting, diarrhea, and profound listlessness. The Hortons put Michael in a local hospital so he could get an IV to counteract dehydration.

Sue and I wanted to do the same with David, but he was terrified. "Don't send me to the hospital," he had pleaded. "I don't want to die. I'll do anything you want." He had heard me complain too often about the horrible conditions in local hospitals. We talked with a local doctor we trusted and got a prescription. Sue and I took turns watching over David at home, encouraging him to sip liquids every few minutes and holding our breath until he recovered.

"We are all so vulnerable," I said to Neen. "Like John. He's not back to work. I haven't heard from him."

"I'll stop by to see him after work today," Neen offered. "With Martha out of his life, I'm not sure anyone is watching over him."

"Good idea. Thanks."

Early the next morning Neen was in my office. "John's sick. So is his daughter, Jordan. They're both running a fever and look terrible. I called Martha to let her know. I'm going back to check on them right now."

Neen was back before lunch. "They're really sick. I don't know what it is. It could be food poisoning, or the flu, but the other kids don't have anything. I just don't know. I'm going to ask Dr. Vellani to see them right away."

Camer Vellani was the Associate Dean of the Medical College, a native of Karachi, an able physician with a calm demeanor. "It could be malaria or something contagious," he said.

"I'm sure they've been taking their malaria medication," I said.

"What kind? Do you know?"

"Fansidar, I'm sure. One pill a week, like the rest of us."

Dr. Vellani looked at Neen and me with an expressionless face. "I'm going to have someone stop by to take some blood. We'll run a couple of tests."

The next day Dr. Vellani and Neen stopped by my office. I offered them chairs but they remained standing.

"I'm going to put John in Civil Hospital, downtown," Camer said. "The blood samples have come back negative but I'm still suspicious. I need to watch him closely while I do some more tests. Jordan is somewhat better. She can stay home if there's someone to watch her." He paused, and looked at me. "Just in case it's malaria I'll have Mohajir check local pharmacies for quinine. It's not easily available here because it can be used as an abortive."

"Let me know if he has trouble," I said. "There may be other sources." If anyone could find the drug it was Mohajir. But if not, I was thinking maybe the American Consulate.

"Whatever it is," Camer continued, "we may not be able to treat them here. I think you should arrange to have them evacuated."

"Martha will stay with Jordan," said Neen. "I'll go over right now to get John ready to move."

"Take Steve Rasmussen with you in case you need a strong back," I said.

Dr. Vellani nodded. "I'll call the hospital and then stop by the house to draw Jordan's blood."

"I'll work on the evacuation," I said, "Call me when you know more, or send a driver if you can't get through."

Late that afternoon John lay on a gurney in the old hospital's intensive care unit, an austere room with peeling paint and several bare bed frames pushed up against one wall. A couple of outdated cardiac monitors sat idle on a side table, dulled with dust. John was the only patient in the unit, attended by a single nurse I recognized from the Project office.

I was standing next to Dr. Vellani in an adjacent room as he adjusted a slide into a microscope on the counter of a makeshift laboratory. "I've been checking John's blood every half hour," he said. "Jordan's got malaria and I'm quite sure John does too, but the parasites hide in the liver and they aren't always visible."

He bent over and peered into the eye piece. "There," he said with a sigh, so quietly I almost missed it. "Yes, it's malaria." He stood up and turned toward me, a look of satisfaction on his face. "I've already got Jordan started on quinine and I'll start John right away." Mohajir had found some vials of quinine in a pharmacy across from the hospital.

Dr. Vellani paused for a moment, his wheels turning. "John's in and out of consciousness and this has been going on too long. We need to get him out of here now."

"I've arranged with Pan Am to fly them to London on tonight's flight," I said. "The airline wanted to know if they're contagious and I said no, hoping I was right."

Dr. Vellani looked relieved. "You are. Jordan can sit but John will need to be flat, with an IV," he said. "Can the airplane accommodate that?"

"I hope so," I said. "Pan Am is taking out a block of seats and they think they can pick up a gurney in New Delhi, one they can strap down during the flight. We won't know until the flight gets here. Gurney or not, we *will* get both of them on that flight. The plane leaves in a few hours. We just need to get them there. We couldn't find an ambulance so Steve arranged with the American Consulate to borrow their Chevy Suburban."

"Good, good," he said. "I've talked to the staff at the Hospital for Tropical Diseases in London. They're ready for them."

Near midnight Sue, David and I were at the airport standing on the tarmac among two dozen of John's friends and colleagues. By now, the entire expatriate community knew John was gravely ill. Sue was holding my arm in a two-fisted grip, unsure we'd ever see John again. Martha Cushing was there to accompany Jordan on the flight. Neen and Steve Rasmussen would watch over John.

We all stood silently watching John's quiet form, strapped onto the bed of Pan Am's special metal gurney. Neen was at his side holding an IV in the air. Together they were hoisted up on a mechanical lift usually used for food service. As they disappeared into the airplane's gaping hatchway, I said to Sue, "I didn't do him any favors bringing him over here. His wife left him and now he might die."

"Don't be too hard on yourself," she said. "He wanted to come, just like us."

I nodded my head and whispered at the closing hatch door, "I hope he gets there in time."

As best I could, I turned my attention back to work. To my consternation, an offer still had not gone out to my successor. I went to Shamsh. "Why the delay?" I asked.

Shamsh looked perplexed. "I don't think we're going to get the hospital buildings in December when we planned. It won't be until next spring."

"Ouch," I said. "That means the opening won't be in April. It's going to be delayed until after I leave."

"I'm afraid so." Shamsh paused before adding, "I'd like you to stay on."

I had expected the possibility of more delays, and Sue and I had discussed prolonging our stay. "We're already late getting back to the candidates for my position," I told her. "If Shamsh doesn't act soon, we'll lose them all and we'll have to start recruiting all over again. When word gets out, we might have problems attracting other candidates. We could be here for years."

"We could stay a few extra months if we have to," Sue said. "But, I'm getting excited about moving back to Colorado. We have good friends there. We can start a business. And I think David needs to be in school in the States for a while and I want to be able to see my folks more easily. I don't want to be under foot or thumb in Minneapolis, but I need to be closer. I'm ready to move on."

"I'm not going to tell Shamsh we might stay a little while longer," I said. "I'm going to keep that to myself. If there are a few more months of overlap with the new guy, all the better."

We agreed I would stick with my announced departure date of June 1, 1985. It was the only way to force the issue.

I told Shamsh, "I'm sorry, but I can't. I'm sorry if I won't be here for the opening, but I am confident the commissioning team can handle the job. It's all the more reason to get my successor here as soon as possible."

"I'm disappointed," Shamsh said. I think he felt I had abandoned him. To some extent, I felt so too.

Shamsh extended an offer to Bill Borton within the week.

A day or so after sending John Cushing off on a litter, I got a call from Steve Rasmussen in London. "Jordan will be fine, but John's critical. He's still in a coma and he's got tubes everywhere. His organs are failing and they're not sure they can save him. We won't know for a couple of days or more."

"Anything else?" I asked. The weight in my chest made it hard to breathe.

"Yes, funny thing, it's malaria for sure, cerebral malaria, falciparum, the worst kind. It's not a strain they expect to find in Pakistan. They think somebody came back with it from Hajj, in Saudi, got bit again in Karachi, and the mosquito gave it to John and Jordan. They also said that middle-aged white men, who weren't raised in a malaria zone, are the most vulnerable to malaria's worst effects. With John it's really touch and go."

"Let's keep hope," I choked. "Do you and Neen have what you need?"

"We're going to be here for awhile and we'll need some money for hotels and meals."

"I'll wire you the cash right away. Tell me which bank."

Two days later Steve called again. "John's still critical, but I have some other bad news."

"Oh god, what?" I said, fearing the worst.

"I was mugged."

"How? Are you all right? Where were you?"

"I went to the bank to get the cash. When I came out a fellow came up behind me and grabbed my elbows. At the same time another guy grabbed the envelop with the money and ran away. The fellow in back held me for a moment, then pushed me down and ran the other direction. Two thousand dollars gone."

"Were you hurt?"

"No, no, just embarrassed. I should have stuck it inside my shirt." I could hear him clear his throat. "We still need money. I'll be more careful, I promise."

"I'll arrange it."

Ten days after John and Jordan had been evacuated to London, Steve called again. "John's stable. He's still out of it, but the doctors are hopeful. His doctor told me that he's had seven patients like John over the years. The other six all died."

"I'm glad he didn't tell us that earlier," I said.

"Me too. On the plus side, the doctor said John shouldn't have any recurrence, like with some strains of malaria." He paused before continuing. "Neen wants to talk to you."

"Put her on."

"I know you're as relieved as I am," she said. "We've been staying at a rooming house next to the hospital and several times, in the middle of the night, I went to the ICU and stood by John's bed, willing him to live. I don't think the staff even noticed me. It was eerie. Kind of an out-of-body experience."

I let the image seep into me. I was too choked up to respond.

"We're coming home. John's dad is coming from the States in ten days or so to take both of them back to Minnesota to recoup. Martha will stay until then."

"Thank you both for all you have done," I said. "I'll see you back here. I'm coming to London next week. Will John still be there?"

"Yes, he won't be ready to travel just yet."

"I'll see him then," I said, and hung up.

When I arrived in London I went straight to the hospital. John was sitting up in bed but looked thin, worn out. "This whole thing was very selfish of you," I said. "Don't you get enough attention?"

John chuckled and grabbed his side. "Please," he whimpered, "don't make me laugh."

"How you doing, old friend," I said, trying to keep my voice from cracking. "Can I get you something?"

"I want a pin-up calendar," he said, in a weak voice. "I want it where I can see it, right there," and pointed to the wall closest to his bed.

"You *must* be better. I'll get you a calendar today. It may take me awhile to sort through them all to find the best one. Anything else?"

"Yes. I want a newspaper, I want to go to *Cats,* and I want a Big Mac."

"*Cats?* Will they let you out of here to go to the theater?"

"Let's find out."

The next afternoon I wheeled John down to the hospital's entrance where we were picked up by a taxi. At the theater, he leaned on me as we walked slowly to our seats. The matinee performance was animated, funny, and poignant. In the second act, we were both teary-eyed as Grizabella sang the nostalgic "Memory."

In the taxi on the ride back to the hospital, the music still ringing in our heads, John said, "I don't have any memory of getting sick, or the airplane ride, or anything." He squeezed my arm and turned his head to look out the taxi window at the boisterous London traffic. "But I do know it's good to be alive. Thank you."

He paused, thoughtful. I knew his next words would be a telling comment on the meaning of life. He didn't disappoint.

"Let's find a McDonalds," he said.

When I got back to Karachi, I had a beer with Cheves. "Reagan won," I said. "Four more years." I had been surprised and it made me feel out-of-touch.

---

"Yup," Cheves said. I couldn't tell how he felt about the outcome and he didn't volunteer.

"Art Lillquist poured a bottle of bleach in that fountain back of John Cushing's place," I said. "It's right under their bedroom window and was full of mosquitoes. He also found standing water in a few other spots in the garden."

"The Brits had the right idea," Cheves said, as he examined his can of moderately cold Heinekens. "They took their quinine every evening, with Gin and a wedge of lime. Gin and tonic, a grand old recipe, when you can get the Gin...and the tonic."

"I'll drink to that," I said, as I tipped my beer in his direction.

He smiled and leaned his lanky frame back in his chair. "But these days, that dog won't hunt," he drawled. "Same's true of Fansidar. It's not the right protection for here. Camer, Neen, and I have written up some guidelines for our staff. What medicines to take, how often, symptoms to look for, that kind of thing. Also cautions on standing water in the yard. We should have done it long ago."

"I'll drink to that, too," I said, and took another swig.

# 42

# LIVING ON THE EDGE

Shortly after we knew John would survive, Kuwait Airways Flight 221, bound for Karachi, was hijacked. Sue and I heard the news the next day, late in the morning on December 4, 1984.

It took days for us to piece together what happened from snippets of news. It was reported that on Monday, December 3, fifteen minutes after the airplane took off from Dubai International airport, a stopover on its way from Kuwait City to Karachi, two men forced their way into the cockpit while two others held guns on the flight attendants and passengers. One of the hijackers held a live grenade next to the pilot's head and forced him to divert the airplane to Tehran, the capital of the still young Islamic Republic of Iran.[42]

It was after midnight, the early hours of Tuesday, when the besieged jet touched down at Mehrabad Airport. *Newsweek* said there was a light blowing snow and the aircraft's running lights cast ghostly shadows as it slowly taxied to an unused runway, a dark and forlorn strip of tarmac well away from the terminal and control tower. Before the whine of its engines died, the aircraft had been encircled by heavily armed soldiers, police, and emergency vehicles.[43]

Inside the airplane, the hijackers riffled through a stack of passports collected from the terrified passengers, the bulk of whom were Pakistanis who had boarded in Kuwait City, eager to return home after long months working as expatriates in Kuwait. The manifest also included: ten Kuwaitis, an American businessman, and three officers of the United States Agency for International Development, USAID, stationed in Karachi.[44] The hijackers forced the Kuwaiti and American men into the forward cabin where they tied them to their seats.

That first morning, the tense quiet was shattered by the sound of screams and shots being fired inside the airplane. A few moments later the cabin door was opened and Charles Hegna, an American USAID officer living and working in Karachi, was dumped onto the pavement. He was shot again as he lay on the snow-swept tarmac as the surrounding soldiers and police watched impotently.[45] He was still alive three hours later when an ambulance was allowed to pick him up. He died at the hospital a few days later.

The hijackers demanded the release of seventeen members of the Islamic Jihad Organization and the Iraqi Islamic Dawa Party, the Kuwait 17, who had been arrested a year earlier for a bombing in Kuwait City. The seventeen had been assisted by the Islamic Republic of Iran.[46] Six people had been killed during a coordinated attack on the American and French embassies in Kuwait City, the Kuwait airport, and a key petro-chemical and water desalination plant. If it hadn't been for the failure of the bombs to fully explode, many more would have been killed and far more property would have been destroyed.

On day four of the week-long ordeal aboard Flight 221, when their demands had not been met, the hijackers tortured and shot a second USAID officer, William Stanford. They also threw his body out of the airplane.[47] In the days that followed, two other Americans, Charles Kapar, the third USAID officer onboard, and John Costa, an American businessman, were tortured, severely beaten, and feared for their lives, before Iranian commandos boarded the airplane and captured the hijackers.

Charles Hegna, William Stanford, and Charles Kapar and their families were part of our small community of American expatriates living in Karachi.

"My god, this is horrible," Sue said, as the story unfolded. "You've met Charlie Kapar's wife, Na," she told me. "She's in my cooking class. It's got to be terrible for her. I don't know what I'd do if it was you."

"I'm probably safer than most," I said, not sure how true that really was. "I think the hijackers were looking for U.S. diplomats." I don't think my response was very reassuring, to Sue or to me.

I was gloomy and apprehensive, as were most of our American friends. One fellow said, "If they're targeting Americans, I'm not sure I want to carry an American passport." We heard from an acquaintance with the Consulate that the U.S. State Department was going to issue non-diplomatic passports to its officers to reduce their vulnerability.

David was especially upset. One of the Stanford children was his schoolmate. He didn't say much but the evening after he learned about the killing he asked, "Dad, will you be flying again soon?"

"No," I said, as I gave him a hug. "And when I do I'll be real careful." He looked doubtful. He was unusually quiet for several days.

The killing of two and the torture of a third from our own community jolted Sue and me out of our complacency and denial. We lived a posh life of privilege, but we were isolated from the realities of an increasingly troubled and dangerous world. Violence wasn't happening just among those on the other side of town or in other countries we barely knew. We were feeling vulnerable and at risk.

I no longer had any doubt that Americans were being targeted. Certainly the Iranian hostage crisis back in 1979 had been seminal, and then the kidnappings in Beirut. And there *had* been the burning of the American Embassy up in Islamabad.

Everyone in our community of expatriates in Karachi was fearful and befuddled and concerned for the Stanford, Hegna and Kapar families. Tony Horton said that Mrs. Stanford had received the bad news from her sister who had telephoned from the States when she saw the reports on television. "It had to be horrible," he said. "I pulled together school records for her. The family flew back to the States the next day."

The Stanfords were gone so quickly they couldn't have gotten much support from their Karachi friends. "The expatriate community is so transient," Sue mused. "It's always in flux; friends leave, new faces arrive. When you move from post to post, like they did, how deep do the ties go? Where do they call home? I hope they have friends and family somewhere who will love them and nurture them back to wholeness."

We guessed our own families back in Minnesota had better access to the news than we did. Their anxiety levels must have been very high, but our telephone wasn't working and it was several days before we could get through and give them assurance.

The new U.S. Counsel General met with leaders of the American community to answer questions and to help us decide how we should proceed during the holiday season. He recommended that we follow our routines and hold our usual Christmas parties and events so we didn't dwell too much on what had happened and become fearful and depressed.

As scheduled, the Annual Christmas Concert was held at the Holy Trinity Cathedral and the Holiday Ball was held at the Counsel General's residence. Sue and I got together several times with friends for dinner, although the conversation inevitably circled around to hijackings and bombings.

With some trepidation, we continued our plan to have Jennifer fly to Karachi for the holidays and to join us on a New Year's vacation trip. Even so, to lower our apprehension of traveling to Sri Lanka where Tamil Tiger insurgents were upsetting that country's tranquility, we made a last minute switch to Thailand where peace and quiet seemed more assured.

The Counsel General was partially right. We were able to fight off fear and anxiety by sticking to our plans, and maybe reinforcing our denial, but our disquiet didn't drop too far below the surface.

Our life in Karachi continued, but there was an edge to it that hadn't been there before. We were more aware of being *in* Pakistan but not *of* Pakistan. Our lives were separate and isolated from the bulk of Karachi's people. A Pakistani friend of Cheves Smythe put it sharply. "Cheves," he said, "you live in Karachi which is on the edge of Pakistan, and in KDA which is on the edge of Karachi, and work in a western derived institution which is on the edge of KDA. You are so far from the real Pakistan that you cannot even begin to sense what reality is." If he could say that to Cheves, who was far better connected to Pakistan than I was, then his admonition went double for me.

Our well-to-do Pakistani friends were at least as privileged as ourselves; some ranked among Pakistani's highest social strata and political elite. We hadn't realized how economically rare they were until we were invited by a couple to visit their rural estate not far outside Karachi. We picnicked under a tree next to their purposefully simple country home, the surrounding fields of sugarcane waving in the afternoon breeze. The place was run like a feudal estate, the owners controlling the lives and welfare of the families that lived under their domain.

When we returned to Karachi, Cheves said, "Those land-holder friends of yours carry a lot of political clout. They belong to one of the two dozen families that have controlled the government here for decades. They're losing control to the army, and they don't know what to do about it."

In February, to keep our nerves ragged, there was a bomb threat at the American School the morning the Karachi Olympics were to be held. The games were postponed indefinitely. We members of the Fun and Games Committee froze what food we could, dividing packages of frozen wieners among us and our friends. For a couple of weeks we all brought chili to every potluck and picnic we attended.

The day after the bomb threat at the school, Sue said, "I've had enough. I think we should leave in June like we planned. David's illness scared me, then John Cushing nearly died. Then that horrible hijacking before Christmas. Now this."

"I agree. It's been exciting living here, but it's getting to be scary. Bill Borton will be here soon. We'll overlap by several weeks. I'm not going to tell Shamsh I can stay on a few extra months."

"It will be a lot better for David to start the school year with his classmates. It would be hard on him to come in mid-term."

I took Sue's hand. "What next?" I asked, unsure what I meant by the question.

"Colorado, I guess," Sue said, answering for both of us.

"I can't wait."

# 43|

# |TRANSITION

My successor, Bill Borton, and his wife, Renee, arrived in Karachi late-winter. The weather was still sunny and cool and they quickly settled into a nice home not far from the University campus. I felt liberated.

The street scene in Karachi calmed enough by early March for the American School to reschedule the Karachi Olympics. Sue, as chair of the Fun and Games Committee, was determined that we hold the postponed event when we could do so safely. We did, a month late, but worth the second effort. After the event, both of us turned over our positions on the committee to others.

Sue's duties as an English teacher at KAS were finished but she continued teaching photography. She found a new editor for the American Women's Club newsletter. I stepped down as President of the school board. It was our swan song as volunteers. We were busy as ever but waddling like lame ducks.

In addition to helping the Bortons settle in suitable housing, Sue introduced Renee around the expatriate community. At work, I made sure Bill got a broad exposure to the international dimensions of the Aga Khan Health System. Unlike me, when Bill was interviewed by His Highness at Aiglemont, they talked at some length and Bill was given marching orders. I would have been delighted to get specific instructions from His Highness. All I got was a smile and a handshake. I soothed my bruised ego by rationalizing that HH now had a better idea of what he wanted in his new ping-pong partner.

Whatever HH and Shamsh told Bill, I wanted him to know how the University and the hospital fit into the whole, and what his role would be in the ongoing drama. The hospital he would manage was going to be the flagship for a large, international, and remarkably diverse health system. I wanted him to understand at his core that this grand and sophisticated institution also needed to serve the simplest of needs for the poorest of people in some of the most remote corners of the globe. In his first month he was sent to northern Pakistan, Bombay, and Nairobi to visit rural clinics and urban hospitals throughout the Aga Khan Health System and hobnob with patients and staff as well as managers.

It still wasn't clear when the buildings would be turned over to the hospital commissioning team, but I was hoping it would happen before I left. Even if all went well, though, we would not admit our first inpatient until sometime in the fall of 1985. I couldn't stretch my stay that long.

When Bill arrived back in Karachi, we met to review the final rendition of the Forecast. It had been accepted by ORD and His Highness with nary a comment. I wasn't sure if it was because the report was brilliant or because they'd given up the game.

"You're stuck with it," I said. "I hope it works. They will probably call it 'Taylor's Forecast' and hit you over the head with it every time you suggest an alternative or fall behind schedule."

"I can live with it. It's a good plan with enough contingencies to give me elbow room when something goes wrong. And I'm sure it will."

"You got that right," I said. "Last year I was up in Rawalpindi serving on a panel appointed by the Pakistani Army to help them select an architect/planner for a medical campus they're building. It was better than Vaudeville. We heard presentations from a half dozen prospective firms: prescreened, high profile outfits from the United States, Canada, and Europe—all very professional we were told. One firm showed their slides upside down, then backward. Another firm dropped their slides on the floor. Another tried hard but the electricity went out and they were flummoxed. Another made a presentation worthy of New York or Paris, but out-of-touch with Pakistan."

Bill laughed. "Sounds like a Chinese fire drill."

"Only one firm brought placards and a flashlight," I continued, "just in case the electricity failed, and it did, and they couldn't show their slides. Sometimes working here is a case study in Murphy's Law."

"I'm happy I don't have to come up with my own plan," Bill said.

I also briefed him on some of the differences I'd observed in the style and philosophy of American managers and our Pakistani counterparts.

"Shamsh and I have talked about it once or twice," I said. "We both believe in making our expectations clear. But I'm a great believer in delegation and encouragement, acknowledging good work when I see it. Shamsh believes more in providing specific direction and constantly monitoring performance. He uses praise sparingly. If you get some, relish it."

"You and I believe that we need to be realistic in our aspirations," I continued. "We need to move forward and make adjustments as required. Shamsh and Aziz and the members of ORB are romantically tied to ideals that need to be pursued regardless. Pragmatic considerations are dragged kicking and screaming into the dialogue. I think they overdo the ideals thing because they so want to meet His Highness's expectations. They may be right. In this country, where big talk and poor quality are rampant, maybe you do have to be uncompromising. It took me a while to come to terms with our differences. It's hard to argue with ideals and I had to learn to curb my impatience."

I also passed on the admonition I had gotten from Cheves. "Just keep reminding yourself, Bill, it's *their* project."

That spring we had a soft opening of the Filter Clinic, providing outpatient services to our own faculty, staff and students. The soft opening gave members of the commissioning team a chance to practice their skills and to work out the kinks in the building. Orville would have been proud. We also got a chance to tweak the procedures that would make the operation run smoothly. The Filter Clinic was located immediately inside the main entrance to the campus and directly across from the mosque; both well placed to handle the high volume of traffic we thought they would eventually attract. We expected the Clinic to serve a thousand patients a day once we were in full operation. I had no idea how many would use the mosque, but a lot I guessed, and five times a day to boot.

I was delighted to still be around for the Filter Clinic opening, soft or not, and I was really pleased with how the commissioning team performed. Neen Lillquist was happy as well. She had been successful in lining up a core of well qualified nurses, including several graduates of AKSON, the Aga Khan School of Nursing.

Neen was ecstatic with how Winnie Warkinton's nursing students were turning out. In 1982, out of the twelve students with first division scores on the national nursing examination, eleven were AKSON graduates. In 1983, seventy percent of those in the first and second division placements were Winnie's graduates.

More importantly, Neen was getting feedback that the graduates were performing very well working in maternity centers and clinics around the city. And they were gaining respect. Several months earlier, Neen had written a report on a conversation she had with a recent graduate who was taking midwifery at a nearby maternity home.[48] "She is a delightful, enthusiastic, sparkling young woman," Neen recorded. "She shows a great deal of maturity and has very clear perceptions of the events around her. I certainly consider her a potential nursing manager."

The young woman told Neen that her fellow AKSON grads stood out among the other midwifery students because of their maturity and skills. "At first," the young woman said, "we were resented. But then the Matron came to me to help her check her own blood pressure because she didn't trust the other staff. And then other faculty and other students started asking me and other AK graduates for advice."

The young woman also said her entire family, including her illiterate father, rallied to her support when a well-educated but conservative friend of the family criticized her for going into nursing. She said many of the people in her neighborhood were also supportive.

"I am just thrilled," Neen had said. "These young ladies are the future of this country."

"Damn, that's good to hear," I had told her. I think I had tears in my eyes.

# 44

# IN KARACHI, DREAMING OF VAIL

The first telephone call came at the end of April, and we missed it.

Sue was driving me to work when the phone at the house woke David. He was disoriented and the connection was bad. He didn't recognize either of the two female voices. He thought maybe my mother and sister had called. They asked if we'd call them back. It didn't seem urgent.

Sue was driving because, a few weeks before, Mohajir had fired our driver, Sohir, for having too many accidents. I talked with Mohajir about it and I couldn't disagree. The accidents were never serious and always occurred when Sohir was alone in the car, but I knew his eyesight was failing. A year before I was riding in the front seat while Sohir rapidly approached the rear end of a truck that he thought was moving but was actually stalled in our lane. He seemed not to understand my warnings and I finally had to grab the wheel so we wouldn't plow into the truck's rear fender. I had his eyes tested and bought him glasses. Even with his glasses though, I was increasingly apprehensive when he was driving Sue or David around town. After his most recent accident, when he smashed in the front grill, I couldn't continue arguing on his behalf.

"We'll need to hire someone else." I told Sue.

"I can be our driver for the next couple of months," Sue volunteered. "I know my way around town. And I can go the way I want and stop when I want." Our *chokidar* agreed to wash the car for a few rupees added to his pay, so Sue became our driver.

We waited until the next morning to call my mother back, but Mom said, "No, I didn't call, and I don't think it was Gail." Sue decided it was probably her mother but decided to wait to return the call until closer to her Dad's birthday, May 3, only a couple of days away.

We were in the final stages of packing our shipment back to the States, sending it all to Denver, Colorado, where it would clear customs. We would arrange to have it delivered as soon as we found a place to live in the Vail Valley.

We were near the end of the "Big Sort," a month long process deciding what to ship, what to sell, and what to give away or trash. It was a deja vu repeat of moving from Minnesota but with a few new wrinkles.

First on our list was finding homes for the puppies that Carrie had recently delivered. A few months earlier, a small, spotted and industrious dog, not at all like the common pi dogs that ran loose all over Karachi, had scaled our back wall and had a tryst with Carrie. Working through a veterinarian, we were lucky to place four of the puppies with a nearby farmer. The other two went to a woman who wanted a couple of watch dogs. Knowing Carrie's history, I could say with confidence they would suit her purpose.

We weren't so fortunate with Carrie. Her reputation was too well known. It hadn't been enhanced when she bit a neighbor boy who scaled our wall to retrieve a ball. Sue asked the boy's mother about his injuries, and apologized for Carrie's rude behavior. The boy's mother seemed easier with it than we were. "The dog had puppies," the woman had said. "My son wasn't hurt and he should have known better."

"We can't find anyone who will take her," I said to David. We were sitting on the steps leading out to the back yard. Carrie was at our feet, her nose on David's foot.

"I know," he said. "Will we have to put her down?"

"I'm afraid so," I said, and put my hand on his knee. Carrie looked up at us and whimpered, as if she understood.

Sue and I were there as David held Carrie's head and the vet administered a lethal injection. None of us will ever forget the look of betrayal in Carrie's mournful eyes.

Over four years in Pakistan we had accumulated some treasures: pieces of furniture, textiles, carpets and crafts—of no great monetary value, but each with a story. With some poking around Karachi's neighborhoods, we discovered that not all the furniture in Pakistan was huge and overdone like the pieces we'd rejected when we first arrived. We found a number of excellent woodworkers who made beautiful hand crafted trunks and desks, intricately inlaid with brass and adorned with hand wrought hardware. Tucked away in back alleys here and there we found furniture *wallahs* who collected antiques from the British Raj. We bought a campaign trunk in warm glowing woods with brass fittings, an intricately carved mirror frame, and a grand china chest that could be broken down in two pieces for easy transport.

In the Swat Valley we had found old wooden chests and beds, roughly carved pieces stained dark with shoe polish. From visits to numerous carpet *wallahs*, our rug collection had grown to where Nana Horton could be proud. Sue also found old camel bags and head scarves and linens adorned with silver trinkets by Bedouin nomads. She visited a small village outside Karachi where she watched men dunk colorful *ajark* fabrics in camel dung to fix the dye. She *had* to have a table cloth made that way, and a couple of extra as gifts. I just *had* to keep the seventy pound ship's telegraph I'd bought from a brass *wallah*. It was stripped off a Portuguese freighter that had been run up on Ghadani Beach.

Many of the belongings we had brought over from Minnesota we decided to sell: our artificial Christmas tree, David's boom box, the computer, kitchen utensils, and other items difficult to find in Karachi but easy to replace back in the States. We also left most of the furniture we'd made: our sofa, dining room table and chairs, bed frames, and coffee table. It had all been paid for by the Project and would eventually find its way to some other expatriate's home.

For weeks the house was a mess. Finally, a team of packers arrived and for a couple of days moved from room to room, hunkering on their heels as they wrapped each item, fragile or not, in a wad of newspaper before stuffing it into a cardboard box. They rolled up each carpet and wrapped it in oil cloth. They also built a wooden shipping crate to hold my precious ship's telegraph. Sue and I tried to make notes of what was going into each box but we finally gave up trying. "It will be an adventure when we unpack all this in Vail," she said.

The next day a steel shipping container, tied down to the flat-bed of a Bedford truck, pulled up in front of our house. By early afternoon everything from the house was packed into the container. "Come look," said our shipping agent, "before we close it up." Out in the street, Sue and I looked in at a terrace of boxes stepping back from the doors up to the container's seven foot ceiling. "We can stuff boxes with paper to fill the extra space," said our agent. "Or, if you have more things, we can put them in. It is up to you, isn't it."

Sue and I looked at each other. I shrugged my shoulders but Sue got a twinkle in her eye. "The wicker *wallah*," she said.

We jumped into the car and Sue drove us to the bazaar where the wicker *wallah* had a shop. We picked out a pair of wicker chairs with matching ottomans, a coffee table, and a six foot high book shelf. At first the shop owner gave us a price that seemed unusually high. "But we live here," said Sue, a pleading look of surprise on her face.

"Forgive me. I did not recognize you Memsahib," said the shop-keeper as he lowered the price by half. After we paid, he had our purchases loaded in a small Suzuki truck and told the driver to follow us home. We watched with satisfaction as our shipping agent puzzled the wicker pieces into the open space and then closed, locked and sealed the container's metal doors. "It will go straight away. It will not be opened until it comes to you in America," he said, as he handed me the keys.

Later that evening we got the second telephone call. Sue picked up the receiver. "Hi, Stuart," she said. It was my brother-in-law, Stuart Hanson. A second later her hand went to her mouth. "Oh no," she said and started to cry. She handed the telephone to me.

"I'm sorry," Stuart said. "Sue's father died last night. I'm sorry I couldn't get through sooner."

When I regained my composure, I said, "We'll make travel arrangements right away," I glanced at Sue and offered her the telephone.

"Stuart, thank you so much for calling," Sue said. "We'll be there soon." Tears were running down her cheeks as she placed the receiver back in its cradle.

Sue was sobbing as I gave her a hug. "I am *so* sorry," I said.

"I didn't expect this," she said. "I would have gone home earlier if I'd known."

Our friends with the airlines came through and got us flight connections leaving the next evening.

Before we left, Nana Horton told Sue, "You can't leave Karachi like this. You'll regret it if you don't come back to say a proper goodbye to all your friends."

We both thought Nana was right. Besides, David had three more weeks of school and I had more than a few loose ends to tie up at work. We booked our flights to Minneapolis round trip.

Nate's funeral was a blur, a jetlag haze of eulogies at a Jewish memorial service and gatherings of friends and relatives sitting Shiva in the evenings. After several days, David and I flew back to Karachi. Sue stayed on for another week to comfort her mother and mourn her dad.

When Sue got back to Pakistan she wrote her mother a letter reminding her that we'd be leaving Karachi in a couple of weeks and we'd be back in the States in just over a month. "Once we're settled in Colorado," she promised, "I'll come to visit often."

Our last two weeks in Karachi were a frenetic round of farewell parties. Good friends threw a party in honor of those of us who were moving on, including Tony and Nana Horton. "We're glad you came back," said Nana. "We're a lot alike. You were always up for our escapades. I know living here has been a great adventure for you both. Tony and I are going to miss you."

Tony said they were moving to Florida for a year. He was going to pursue a doctorate at the University of Gainesville. "My thesis is on the personal characteristics that teachers need to be successful working overseas," he told me. "I think at least one partner needs to be able to deal with ambiguity and the unknown. They've got to be flexible with good coping skills, open to change. If you have marital problems, they tend to be accentuated when you live abroad. I'm doing structured interviews of people who have been successful and those who haven't. I'm also going to do a Myers Briggs personality profile on everyone to see if there's any correlation."

"Sounds to me like you're on the right track," I said. "I'd like to know what you find out,"

"Wherever we're posted after Gainesville," Nana said, "You must come visit."

"We'll keep our bags packed and our passports up-to-date," Sue promised.

They also had a farewell party for me at work, an afternoon gathering of my associates from the Project and a number from the construction team I'd gotten to know. Mohajir made a few remarks, as did Aziz. Shamsh, in his most gracious manner, thanked me for my service and invited Sue, who was also there, and me to come back for the hospital opening ceremonies in the fall. I hoped his sense of being abandoned had eased a little.

I was given a beautiful leather briefcase. "Everyone chipped in," I was told.

The party ended with handshakes and hugs all around.

While Sue went for the car, I walked back to my office with Nazia to pick up a box of my personal things. "You made my work here a real pleasure, Nazia. Thank you for all you've done."

"You are a good boss, Mister Robert."

I wanted to give her a hug, but restrained myself.

I looked around my office one last time. The desk and credenza were bare, the pictures had been stripped from the walls. I glanced up at a gecko that crept from behind the chalkboard where I had printed "GOOD LUCK BILL" in bold letters. The gecko was fully formed with four legs and a long tail. It had shared my office for several months. I liked to think it was the progeny of the inspirational creature that had kept me company when I first arrived. "Goodbye friend," I said, before turning to leave.

Sue and I drove off campus and back to where Peter and Margaret were waiting in our empty shell of a house.

We thanked them and gave them chits Sue had composed and that Nazia had typed on University stationery. We were all crying when we said goodbye and they left the house.

Jennifer joined us for a long-planned, last hurrah vacation. We flew to Kenya and spent two weeks traveling by safari van through the Great Rift Valley and the game parks and then onward to the slopes of Kilimanjaro.

On June 14 we boarded a flight out of Nairobi headed to Turkey. When we changed planes in Athens, the airport was under tight security. They didn't allow us into the terminal while we waited for our next flight. They didn't tell us why. When the Kosals met us in Istanbul they were relieved to see us. "We were so worried," sighed Cholpan. "We thought you might be on the airplane that was hijacked in Athens."

"We knew nothing about it," I said.

Cholpan told us it was TWA flight 847, bound from Athens to Rome. Again, the hijackers demanded release of the Kuwait 17.

Over dinner that evening Ali said, "They're everywhere now, these hijackers, these extremists. We can't escape."

After an overnight at a hotel, the four of us joined the Kosals, including their two teenaged children, as we loaded onto a small bus and were driven down to Bodrum, a picturesque whitewashed village overlooking the Aegean. We spent the next week aboard a fifty foot broad-beamed motor sailor, hand hewn in a local shipyard, cruising from anchorage to anchorage while a crew of three managed the motor and sails and left us to our sloth and debauchery.

As we lay at anchor one balmy evening, a young crew member walked the shoreline collecting roe from black spiny urchins. We lounged on the back deck in our swimming suits as he served us dollops of the fresh caviar carefully allocated among eight salt crackers—one bite for each of us—along with olives and ice cold Raki.

Sue turned to me, "This is probably the end of our living large," she said, and lifted her glass. "But it sure has been an adventure."

"It's been hard work, but I think it's probably the most important thing I'll do in my career." I raised my glass to hers. "Here's to the Aga Khan, to the Project, to Pakistan, to us, and to the future."

On July 3, 1985, the four of us arrived back in the States. Jennifer would stay with us for the summer before returning to college in the fall. We disembarked at the Denver airport and took a taxi to a Jeep dealership. We bought a used four-wheel-drive Wagoneer, packed our luggage in the back, and drove up into the mountains with no job and no immediate ambitions—except to celebrate Independence Day in Vail with spontaneous unprecedented fervor.

# EPILOGUE:
# A CHANGED WORLD

The freshly painted curbs streaked by in the car's headlights as it drove me from the Karachi airport to the Bortons' home. Bill greeted me at the door in his pajamas, bleary eyed, with a welcoming laugh and hug, and directions to my room. "There's clean water in the pitcher by your bed. Sleep as best you can. See you at breakfast," he said, and went back to bed. I would be their guest for the next week. It was November, 1985, and I was back in Pakistan to celebrate the dedication of the Aga Khan University Hospital.

Shamsh had sent a formal invitation to Sue and me in the States. He enclosed a personal letter. "I have just returned to my office after my first walk through the hospital since the first inpatient was admitted on October 6. I cannot tell you how thrilled I was to see patients in their beds, nurses at their stations, and doctors doing their rounds. I wish you could have shared those exciting moments with me."

Shansh said he hoped both Sue and I would attend the dedication but that he could only pay travel costs for one of us. Sue elected not to go. "It's your big day," she said. "I'd mostly be an observer and in the way. I'll stay with David. When you get back I'll go visit my mom."

A full week of activity was planned for two thousand expected guests. There were tours of the campus, presentations in the auditorium, sightseeing tours of the city, shopping tours and day trips to nearby tourist sites.

The main event, the Inauguration Ceremony, was held Monday morning, November 11. I arrived in the early morning light and walked the campus. An extensive amount of landscaping had been done and the campus looked more complete, less tentative than when I'd left. Water fountains gurgled and flowed in all the courtyards.

A sprawling *shamiana*, designed and stitched for the occasion, had been erected out on the lawn, big enough to hold 2,500 people, with carpets covering the already well established grass. I was asked to sit in the "Red" section with other staff from AKU and Aiglemont, just behind members of ORB and other dignitaries.

I settled into a chair between John Cushing and Neen Lillquist, reaching out a hand to each. "Congratulations," I said. "You two have been key to making the opening go so smoothly."

Up on stage, Gulgee stood by a vertical wood disk, six feet in diameter, with the seal of the Aga Khan University printed at its center. As the opening prayer was recited, he slowly turned the disk and, in Arabic, scribed the quote from the Quran on its wide border, drawing the last stroke as the prayer ended.

Shamsh was the first to speak, outlining the history of the University and noting that eighteen professorships were already fully endowed. His Highness looked grand, dressed in the resplendent cap and gown of the University. He thanked Shamsh and all the staff who had made the Project a reality. He too emphasized the University's fund-raising success. He said their goal had already been surpassed, eight years ahead of schedule. He announced that a sizable fund to provide health services to the poor and a similar fund to support needy students had also been established.[49] His grandfather would have been proud.

President Zia was personable, warm and informal. He announced that the government was committed to funding two fully endowed post-graduate fellowships.

After the ceremonies, I spoke briefly with His Highness, offering my congratulations and best wishes for continuing success. "I am glad you are here," he said, as we shook hands. "Thank you for your hard work. I hope you will continue to be involved."

"I will be happy to serve in any way I can," I said.

When I got back home to Colorado, I wrote letters to His Highness and to Shamsh extending my congratulations on their remarkable accomplishment. I said I would always cherish the unique opportunity I was given to serve the Project.

The world changed in fundamental ways during those years we were in Pakistan, although it took awhile for the world to notice. I was more aware than most people I knew that Islamic extremism and global terrorism were on the rise.

In September, 1986, Bill Borton, my successor, spent several hours stranded in the back of an airplane parked at the Karachi airport while authorities dealt with another airplane, Pan Am Flight 73, which stood hijacked nearby. The Pan Am flight, en route from Bombay to Frankfurt, had been boarded in Karachi by hijackers dressed as airport security guards. The hijackers killed one American, pushed his body onto the tarmac, and ordered the flight attendants to collect the passports of the other passengers. One attendant, suspecting their intent, hid the passports of several Americans under a seat and dumped the others down a trash chute. Frustrated and angry, the airplane dark and running out of power, the hijackers opened fire on the passengers before they were overwhelmed by army commandos. Twenty two people were killed and 150 injured, several of whom were taken to the Aga Khan University Hospital.[50]

Bill said he and his fellow passengers were told to stay away from the windows. He had hunkered on the airplane floor for hours and had bad dreams for weeks.

The 1979 kidnapping of hostages from the U. S. Embassy in Tehran had moved the targeting of American's to center stage. Over the next two decades, kidnappings, hijackings, and bombings became the preferred methods of terrorism, escalating in frequency and destruction, and increasingly targeting Americans. Starting with David Dodge in 1982, ninety-six foreigners were kidnapped in Lebanon over the following decade, twenty-five were Americans.[51] In spite of increased airport security and passenger screening, there were thirty-four airplane hijackings in the 1980s and 1990s. The bombing of American targets that began with such force in Lebanon in the 1980s, extended over the next decade to Spain, Italy, Greece, Israel, Scotland, Turkey, and Egypt. For twenty years, the mayhem was focused overseas, until it all came home to America on September 11, 2001.

The growing friendship and cooperation between the United States and Pakistan cooled when the Soviet War in Afghanistan ended in early 1988. What remained in the region were a heavily armed hodgepodge of radicalized extremists, the Taliban and al-Qaeda being prominent examples, and an endemic mistrust of America.

The summer after the Soviet War ended, President Zia and thirty-one others were killed in a suspicious airplane crash. The American Ambassador, Arnold Raphal, and the head of the U.S. Military Aid Mission in Pakistan, General Herbert Wasson, were among those who died.[52]

Following Zia's death, Pakistan's government appeared to vacillate between military and civil control, although I don't think the military was ever far from the center of power. It hasn't made much difference what face was put on government. All have promised reform but continue to fail the people of Pakistan in terms of healthcare, education, and opportunities for economic development. The result is further tribal and religious fragmentation, widespread discontent, and a population ripe for further exploitation and radicalization. The country is so pathologically fractured and unsettled that it is close to ungovernable.

Still, there are embers of hope burning in Pakistan.

I've been back to visit Pakistan twice since the inauguration ceremonies in 1985. The first time was in 1996. Sue and I were on assignment with the International Finance Corporation, IFC, a branch of the World Bank that invests in private sector development. The Aga Khan University campus was a-bustle with medical and nursing students walking briskly with books in hand, or studying quietly in one of the courtyards or under the canopy of one of the then mature trees. We poked our heads into the medical college auditorium and, as I had envisioned a decade earlier, students were eagerly sitting forward in their chairs, actively engaged in learning. At the Filter Clinic, patients and their families milled about the courtyard. Faculty and staff filled every office and work space, and inpatients filled the hospital beds.

In 2004 I visited Islamabad and Lahore, again for the IFC, this time looking for a private hospital that might attract an IFC loan. Unsolicited, every hospital I visited said, "We want to be like the Aga Khan University Hospital in Karachi." The hospital had become the gold standard for acute health care in the region, *the* institution all others wanted to emulate.

Something else I learned on that trip in 2004. After September 11, 2001, many middle class Pakistanis who had been living and working in the United States returned to Pakistan, bringing their ambitions and financial resources with them. I talked to several who said they no longer felt so welcome in the States. They had always kept one foot in each country, historically to hedge against a deteriorating climate in Pakistan. Now they felt the need to shift more weight back to Pakistan as a hedge against an increasingly inhospitable environment in America. They built homes in Lahore, Islamabad, and Karachi; invested in new businesses; and expected better services from their hospitals. They also expected more from their government.

His Highness has more than fulfilled his promise to create a university and hospital of international standard. The Aga Khan University now has a billion dollar endowment and eleven teaching sites in eight countries: Afghanistan, Kenya, Pakistan, Tanzania, Uganda, Syria, Egypt and the United States.

His Highness has gone on to create the Aga Khan Development Network, a group of private, non-denominational development agencies that, according to their website, "seek to empower communities and individuals to improve living conditions and opportunities in sub-Saharan Africa, Central and South Asia, and the Middle East." The network focuses on health, education, culture, rural development, institution-building and the promotion of economic development.[53]

The Aga Khan Health Services is now an agency of the Aga Khan Development Network, and is one of the most comprehensive and far reaching private not-for-profit health care systems in the developing world. It provides primary and curative health services through 237 health centers, dispensaries, hospitals, diagnostic centers and community health outlets in five countries. The system serves one million beneficiaries and handles 1.2 million patient visits each year.[54]

That first year back in the States I was overwhelmed by how much the world had changed in the few years we'd been gone. Our local grocery store seemed extravagantly abundant, with a befuddling array of choices. Traffic on our local streets seemed so orderly. And the temperature in Colorado seemed unusually cold. Sue and I started wearing long underwear in July. Our knuckles ached for a year in the chilly climate.

America seemed so free and so affluent. News was so readily available. The choice of newspapers and magazines on the shelves was staggering. Television and radio stations were expanding, numbing in their numbers. I could get lost for hours in the wonders of our local bookstore.

I was also reminded of how our public and private sectors work together to make our American economy work. It's messy, but both are essential. I told a couple of my politically conservative friends, who complained of government intrusions, that they ought to spend a few years in a place like Pakistan where government is dysfunctional.

I was also more attuned to America's underside, to the plight of those in our country who were marginalized. It had always been that way, but I saw things with a fresh view, a beginner's mind. Television and radio programs seemed more interested in conflict and confrontation than in the objective reporting of news.

Computers were becoming ubiquitous. In 1983, *Time Magazine* declared the computer the machine of the year.[55] Still, no one could predict how they, and their progeny, would come to dominate so much of how we now live our lives.

As I feared, my career as a hospital administrator was ruined. Or, more accurately, I was ruined for going back to work as a hospital administrator in the States. The call to continue working in the developing world was too strong. There is a lot to do in the world to help improve healthcare and education. And if we Americans need a reason other than it's the right thing to do, it is increasingly evident that it is also in our best interests.

The international bug infected Sue as well. At age fifty she went back to graduate school to get a Masters in organizational development and we founded our own business, Taylor Associates International. Over the last twenty five years we have worked on health issues in over thirty developing countries.

We are always glad to come back to our home in the States, but after a few weeks, if we see the white contrail of a jet streaking across the blue sky, one of us will look up wistfully and say, "I wonder where they're going?" And after a few years living in one community, we seem to find a reason to move somewhere new. Like Pakistan itself, we too have become unsettled, much like some of our friends who continue the expatriate life, vagabonds living a life of privilege in one hardship post after another. Sue and I have concluded that we need to shake things up once in awhile, just to keep life interesting and our marriage fresh.

Jennifer graduated from Wesleyan and went on to study architecture at Yale. She is married and works as an architect in Portland, Oregon. David graduated from the University of Wisconsin. He is married and a construction contractor in Stevens Point. Jennifer and David have given us five grandsons.

Sue visited Adelle, her mom, frequently after we moved back to the States. We were both with her when she died peacefully at the age of eighty-four.

My mother lived to be a month short of ninety. Everybody who gave a eulogy at the celebration of her life said they knew Hildur had loved them best.

When Sue and I are at home, we can still be found many Saturday evenings listening to *A Prairie Home Companion*. And in August, 2012, Sue and I celebrated our fiftieth wedding anniversary.

# ACKNOWLEDGEMENTS

Living and working in Karachi was a life changing adventure, but it was thirty years ago and memory fades. This book could not have been written without all those letters that my wife, Sue, conscientiously wrote while we were living abroad. And bless her mother, Adelle, for keeping them.

I've tried to stay as close to the truth and sequence of events as I could, and the conversations are as close to true as I can make them. I may have inadvertently put somebody's words in somebody else's mouth, and I apologize if I didn't get it right.

In order not to confuse the reader with numerous names, I have not included many of the characters that made my experience in Pakistan so rich. Martha Anderson was the trusted friend who handled our mail and finances while I was off adventuring. I am sorry I couldn't mention Aslam Jindani, Mossadiq Umedaly, Almas Bana, Nadeem Khan, Abdul Pirbhoy, Nasir Pirani, Arif Altaf, and other major players at the Aga Khan University Hospital. I also left out Michael Curtis, Pat Cronin, Joel Montague, and George Purvis—all prime movers at Aiglemont.

In Karachi, Hazel and Ted Boyle lent us sheets and their telephone. Eunice and Deen Gupta were part of the expatriate community and kept us grounded by the warmth of their friendship. Mr. Bader was the heart and soul of the Karachi American School. He still sends us anniversary cards. And there were so many other friends and colleagues, way too many to include.

I apologize to our cook, John Peters. I changed his name to Peter Peters so you wouldn't confuse him with John Cushing.

My thanks to Cheves Smythe, John Cushing, and Neen Lillquist for helping to make the experience so rewarding but also for critiquing sections of this book.

I want to thank the members of my writing group at Edison State College, Punta Gorda, who were unfailingly supportive of my scratchings. Also James Abraham and Doug Houck for their guidance. I want to especially thank Debra Monroe, author and instructor, and my classmates in her masters' class at the Taos Writers' Conference, for their tough love in critiquing an early draft. "Yes, Robert, but how did you feel?"

I also want to thank the Florida Writers Association for awarding the manuscript of this book first place for unpublished memoir in the 2012 Royal Palm Literary Awards Competition.

And finally, I want to again thank my wife, Sue, for her steadfast support. She never complained of the endless hours I devoted to writing or to the accumulating list of neglected household projects. Also, she took the photo of me on the back cover, taken in a little Italian restaurant in Hanoi.

# NOTES

1   Mulligatawny is a peppery soup of Indian origin made with chicken, rice and curry.

2   As testimony to the population size of the Indian Subcontinent, before partition India was the second largest country in the world in terms of population, right behind China. After partition in 1947, India was still the second largest, with the new bifurcated Pakistan now in the top ten. When East Pakistan became Bangladesh in 1971, India was still second and both Pakistan and Bangladesh were in the top ten.

3   The burning of US Embassy in Islamabad was widely reported. Detailed accounts can be found at BBC, Wikipedia, and other sources.

4   Collins, Larry, and Dominique Lapierre, *Freedom at Midnight*, HarperCollins, 1976.

5   Hijacking of PIA Flight 326, March 2, 1981, as reported on www.historyofpia.com. According to Fatima Bhutto, in her book *Songs of Blood and Sword* (Perseus Books, New York, 2011) the hijacking was staged, with government complicity, to discredit the growing political popularity of her father, Murtaza Bhutto, the younger brother of Benazir Bhutto, and the eldest son of Prime Minister

Zulfikar Ali Bhutto who was hanged by Zia ul-Haq in 1979. The hijackers were captured but never prosecuted. Fatima infers that politically ambitious Benazir Bhutto was complicit in the 1996 assassination of her father, Murtaza. Benazir was assassinated in 2007.

[6]   Between 1915 and 1920, Muhammad Ali Jinnah worked to bring unity between Hindus and Muslims to jointly press for constitutional reforms and joint demands from India's British government. Jinnah's efforts were overshadowed by the success of the Hindu non-cooperation movement led by Mohandas K. Gandhi. In the 1940s, as the British withdrawal from the Indian Subcontinent drew near, the Muslim League, headed by Jinnah, briefly united the historically disparate Muslim forces behind the idea of a separate Muslim state. Source: www.biography.com and others.

[7]   Words and music for the National Anthem of Pakistan can be found on www.yespakistan.com.

[8]   The Pariah Kite Hawk is ubiquitous to the Indian Subcontinent and has adapted well to the urban landscape and the crush of humanity, foraging for food wherever it might be found. During the British Raj, the Brits warned newcomers that when they ate outdoors to cover their food with their hands. The kite-hawks were known to swoop down and snatch tidbits from their plates. Source: *Plain Tales From The Raj*, based on interviews of people who served in India before partition. The interviews were broadcast by the British Broadcasting Corporation, and edited by Charles Allen for publication. (Futura Publications, London, 1976).

[9]   Zulfikar Ali Bhutto served as Pakistan's elected President and then Prime Minister from 1971 to 1977, when he was deposed by Zia ul-Haq. Bhutto was a populist, calling for land reform, even though he was the head of one of Pakistan's elite land-holding families. At the peak of the cold war, he pushed for non-alignment, which made him suspect in America. His reforms won him support from the people of Pakistan but not with other land-holders, nor the

military. He was hung by Zia in 1979. Source: www.Wikipedia and others.

10 "Traffic Deaths: Karachi No 2 in the World," *Dawn Magazine*, Karachi, Pakistan, February 8, 1985.

11 Idi Amin became known as the "Butcher of Uganda" for his brutal, despotic rule while President during the 1970s. He drove out those of Indian descent—many of whom were Ismaili—who had been long time residents of the country and who had established themselves as successful merchants and business owners. Source: www.About.com

12 The exchange of business cards was a tradition established by the British during their long occupation of India. An army officer, newly arrived from Britain, would go from house to house dropping off calling cards to the officers already in residence. Source: Allen, Charles, Editor, *Plain Tales From The Raj*, Futura Publications, London, 1976.

13 The clever Bot fly of Central and South America, and the Tumba fly of Africa, lay their eggs in wet laundry among other moist habitat. The larva hatch several days later and can burrow into the skin, causing all sorts of discomforts.

14 Fraser, George McDonald, *Flashman*, Barrie & Jenkins, London, 1969. The first in a series of entertaining historical novels set in British India and Afghanistan between 1839 to 1842.

15 Taylor, Jennifer, *Shards*, Karachi American School, Karachi, Pakistan, 1983. Used with permission.

16 To over simplify, Shias or Shiits believe in divinely inspired leadership—similar to how Catholics view the pope—saying Mohammad ordained his cousin and son-in-law, Ali, to be the next Caliph. Sunni hold that Abu Bakr, Mohammad's father-in-law, companion, and first convert, was Mohammad's rightful successor. Their method of choosing or electing leaders is through a

Shura, the consensus of the Muslim community, and is more akin to how Protestants select their leaders.

[17] Ramazan (called Ramadan in most countries other than Pakistan) is the ninth month of the Islamic calendar. It is a time of daytime fasting, the practice of self control, and a reminder of the hunger suffered by the poor.

[18] Aga Khan, "Speech at the Opening Session of the AKF/WHO Conference on 'The Role of Hospitals in Primary Health Care,'" Islamabad, Pakistan, November 22, 1981. Source: www.ismaili.net.

[19] Henry Mahler's remarks at the AKF/WHO Conference, Islamabad, Pakistan, November 22, 1981. Source: Personal notes of the author.

[20] Aga Khan, "Speech at the Closing Session of the AKF/WHO Conference on 'The Role of Hospitals in Primary Health Care,'" Karachi, Pakistan, November 26, 1981. Source: www.ismaili.net.

[21] Taylor, Jennifer, *Shards*. Used with permission.

[22] David Dodge was abducted on July 19, 1982, from the campus of the American University of Beirut where he was serving as President. He was among the first of 96 foreigners, 25 of whom were Americans, who were kidnapped in Lebanon between 1982 and 1992. Sources: www.Wikipedia and others.

[23] Today there are more than one billion Muslims in the world, about one-fifth of the world population. Source: Prothero, Stephen, *God is Not One*, HarperCollins Books, New York, 2010. Other sources estimate the number of Muslims to be in excess of 1.5 billion worldwide, second only to Christianity in the number of adherents, but growing faster. About seventy percent are Sunni and fifteen percent Shia, with the balance a smattering of other groups. Source: www.Wikipedia.com and others.

24  Al Buraq, which means lightening, was a winged white horse with a beautiful face. Buraq is said to have flown Mohammad on his twelve year Night Journey up to heaven where he visited Allah and the earlier prophets. Mohammad is credited with negotiating the required number of daily prayers down to a practical five.

25  In the 1950s, the United States helped depose Iran's elected leader and elevate the regal and heavy-handed Mohammad Reza Shah to power. In 1979, the Shah was deposed in the Iranian Revolution and replaced by a theocracy headed by Ayatollah Khomeini. When the deposed Shah became ill, he was given shelter by President Carter, leading to the siege of the American Embassy in Tehran and the capture of the American hostages. Sources: www.iranchamber.com, www.Wikipedia, and others.

26  A provision to deduct Zakat (charity contributions) from various financial holdings was one of several reforms introduced by Zia in 1980, early in his reign, part of his effort to Islamize Pakistan's legal system and economy. The provision was widely unpopular. Sources: www.Wikipedia and others.

27  The pilgrimage to visit the Kaaba predates Mohammad and was incorporated into the Quran as Hajj, the fifth pillar of Islam. The prescribed dates for Hajj are from the eighth to twelfth days of DHU al-Hajjah, the twelfth month in the Islamic calendar. Mecca can be visited at other times of the year, but such visits are considered a lesser pilgrimage. Source: www.Wikipedia.com and others.

28  On another trip to France, the inn's chef served moules tangine, mussels in a rich tangine reduction. Tangine originated in Morocco but the French do it very well. There are several excellent recipes on the web.

[29] The Chandio are a major Baluch tribe, one of the largest and most powerful tribes in Pakistan. The Chandio currently number over six million people, distributed primarily throughout the Sindh province.

[30] As I write this, I'm the same age my mother was when she traveled with us in India. Her strength, resilience and good spirits don't seem so unusual from my current perspective.

[31] Mumtaz, Khawar, and Farida Shaheed, Editors, *Women of Pakistan: Two Steps Forward, One Step Back*, Zed Books Ltd, London, 1987, p. 106.

[32] One of the other honorees of the Yogi that night was Jim Klobuchar, a columnist with the *Minneapolis Star* newspaper. To my knowledge, he never learned to levitate either. His daughter, Amy Klobuchar, has had better luck. She was elected to the United State Senate in 2006, Minnesota's first woman senator.

[33] Karachi Air France office burning. Author's notes.

[34] The British Imperial system of weights and measures, established by King George IV in 1824, fixed the weight of one stone as equivalent to 14 pounds. It is still used in some areas as a measure of body weight, maybe because it allows considerable room to fudge.

[35] Speech at the Charter of the Aga Khan University, Karachi, Pakistan, March 16, 1983. Source: http://ismaili.net/speech/s830316b.html

[36] Source: http://en.wikipedia.org/wiki/Kashmir_conflict

[37] On April 18, 1983, a truck bomb exploded in front of the United States embassy in Beirut, Lebanon. Sixty-three employees were killed and 120 wounded. The attack was carried out by Hezbollah with backing from Iran. Source: www.jewishvirtuallibrary.org

[38] Gulgee completed several portraits in lapis lazuli, including one of Ronald Reagan which currently hangs in the office of the Speaker of the U.S. House of Representatives.

[39] *This Is My Song*, a poem by Lloyd Stone, frequently sung as a hymn to the melody of Finlandia. Text: 11 10 11 10 11 10; Vss 1,2 Lloyd Stone © 1964, Lorenz Corporation. All rights reserved. Used with permission.

[40] In 2007, the government of Pakistan allowed the Taliban to occupy the Swat Valley, that fertile and majestic area we visited in 1984. It was a colossal mistake, the most recent in a long line of misguided concessions to Islamic conservatives. When the Taliban threatened to impose their restrictive version of Sharia law, it was the local Swati population that rose up in protest and helped force the Army to drive the Taliban out.

[41] The Great Game is the name given to the struggle between the British and Russian Empires for dominance over Central Asia. Beginning in the early nineteenth century, with Russian advances into the Caucuses, the British feared Russia had its eye on British India. The British began an effort to explore and map, and build influence, in the inaccessible mountains and deserts that were seen as a potential barrier to Russia's ambitions. Serving in the Northwest Frontier Provinces—Peshawar and Gilget in what is now Pakistan—were viewed by British officers as the most exciting places to be stationed. The British made an unsuccessful bid to dominate Afghanistan in 1842 and concluded the Pathans were unbeatable. Russia tried it in 1979 and learned the same lesson. More recently, Peshawar was once again the center of battle, this time as a gateway in the American war in Afghanistan. The United States has learned that Pathans are still fierce fighters and resistant to government control. Sources: Hopkirk, Peter, *The Great Game*, Kodansha International, London, 1994, and current accounts.

42  United States Court of Appeals, Second Circuit, Lorraine Stanford, et al v. Kuwait Airways et al, July 16, 1996.

43  Hillenbrand, Barry; Johanna McGeary; and John Kohan, "The Gulf: Horror Abroad Flight 221," *Time Magazine*, December 17, 1984.

44  Ibid. Hillenbrand, et al.

45  Source: http://pfarrerstreccius.blogspot.com/2010/10/charles-hegna-and-william-stanford.html and other accounts.

46  Source: http://en.wikipedia.org/wiki/1983_Kuwait_bombings

47  Sources: U.S. Court of Appeals, *Time Magazine*, and others.

48  Lillquist, Neen, Paper on Aga Khan School of Nursing graduates, 1984. Source: Author's files.

49  His Highness the Aga Khan's Speech at the Inauguration Ceremony of Aga Khan University, November 11, 1985. Source: www.amaana.org/speeches/speechaku1985/htm

50  Pan Am Flight 73, September 3, 1986. Source: http://en.wikipedia.org/wiki/Pan_Am_Flight_73 and personal account.

51  Source: www.Wikipedia and other.

52  Source: www.nytimes.com/1988/08/18/world/zia-of-pakistan-killed-as-blast-downs-plane-us-envoy-28-others-die

53  According to its website, The Aga Khan Development Network (AKDN) is a group of development agencies with mandates that include the environment, health, education, architecture, culture, microfinance, rural development, disaster reduction, the promotion of private-sector enterprise, and the revitalization of historic cities. AKDN agencies conduct their programs without regard to faith, origin or gender. Source: www.akdn.org.

54   According to its website, The Aga Khan Health Services operates community health programs in large geographical areas in Central and South Asia, as well as East Africa, and 325 health facilities including nine hospitals. AKHS is one of the most comprehensive private not-for-profit health care systems in the developing world. Building on the Ismaili Community's health care efforts in the first half of the 20th century, AKHS now provides primary health care and curative medical care in Afghanistan, India, Kenya, Pakistan, and Tanzania, and provides technical assistance to government in health service delivery in Kenya, Syria and Tajikistan. Source: www.akdn/akhs.

55   "The Computer, Machine of the Year," *Time Magazine*, January 3, 1983.

CPSIA information can be obtained at www.ICGtesting.com
Printed in the USA
LVOW08s0835280713

344997LV00001B/203/P